THE EXTINCTION OF NATION-STATES

Developments in International Law

VOLUME 21

The titles published in this series are listed at the end of this volume.

L. ALI KHAN

The Extinction of Nation-States

A WORLD WITHOUT BORDERS

KLUWER LAW INTERNATIONAL
THE HAGUE / LONDON / BOSTON

A C.I.P. Catalogue record for this book is available from the Library of Congress

ISBN 90-411-0198-5

Published by Kluwer Law International,
P.O. Box 85889, 2508 CN The Hague, The Netherlands.

Sold and distributed in the U.S.A. and Canada
by Kluwer Law International,
675 Massachusetts Avenue, Cambridge, MA 02139, U.S.A.

In all other countries, sold and distributed
by Kluwer Law International,
P.O. Box 85889, 2508 CN The Hague, The Netherlands.

Printed on acid-free paper

Printed in the Netherlands

PREFACE

It is impossible to name all the individuals, both dead and alive, who have influenced my conception of international law. Among the dead, Hugo Grotius, Hans Kelsen, St. Augustine and Ibn Khaldun continue to shape and reshape my ideas. Among the living, I must mention a few teachers from New York University who had a deep impact on my ideas. David Richards, Ronald Dworkin and Graham Hughes taught me jurisprudence, Thomas Franck and Theodore Meron refined my understanding of international law and human rights. I am indebted to John Delaney in a special way as I continue to learn from him as a teacher and friend. He was kind enough to read a few chapters of this book. I thank Myrl Duncan (despite his sabbatical), Julie Gorenc (despite her pregnancy), and David Monicle (despite his surgery) for reading parts of the book. Rebecca Woodman, the *mater familia*, has been a constant source of inspiration and instruction. I am most grateful to Bryan Whitehead, class of 96, Washburn University School of Law, who provided useful assistance in the writing of this book. He has been a patient reader, incisive critic and excellent editor. While I remain indebted to many people, no one necessarily shares any or all of the views I present in this book.

Ali Khan, September, 1995
Topeka, Kansas

Table of Contents

Introduction

In his introduction to *The Law of War and Peace*, Hugo Grotius writes: "If any one thinks that I have had in view any controversies of our own times, either those that have arisen or those which can be foreseen as likely to arise, he will do me an injustice. With all truthfulness I aver that, just as mathematicians treat their figures as abstracted from bodies, so in treating law I have withdrawn my mind from every particular fact." Thus Grotius strives to sever his concept of law from the influence of history.

Not to do an injustice to Grotius but to appreciate his profound understanding of the controversies of his times, which most likely shaped his mind and soul, I begin this book with a historical narrative. I share a commonly-held belief of our times that legal concepts sprout, grow, dwindle and die in the realm of ordinary and extraordinary human stories. Based on this belief, I present an historical analysis of the classic struggle between the popes and the kings of the middle ages to explain the genesis of the sovereign state, a concept Grotius strives to articulate in the abstract realm of legal science. Relying on the still unfolding facts of our times, either those that have arisen or those which can be foreseen as likely to arise, I then present the concept of Free State and the attendant world without borders – a world that, if it ever comes into existence, would free the peoples of the world from historic notions of sovereign states and unaccountable ruling elites. While law, as a human artifact, is inseverable from history, I do not hold the additional view, as does the Marxist school of thought, that history itself has been predetermined. So if the future course of history takes a surprising new turn and the factual foundation I construct is eroded, the borderless world of Free States may never evolve. I believe, however, that the evolution of a world without borders currently seems unavoidable.

In presenting the concept of Free State, I rely primarily on the works of Grotius, most particularly *The Law of War and Peace*. This reliance demonstrates my belief that Grotius is the most influential expositor of classical international law. Grotius greatly benefitted from the works of Greek, Roman, Jewish, Spanish, German and French writers, whom he cites extensively both to seek support for his own ideas and to make counterpoints when he has a new or different idea. Nonetheless, the concept of the sovereign state that Grotius presents is a unique synthesis of what he calls "the testimony of philosophers, poets; finally also of orators." Grotius wished to establish a world in which states would behave in accordance with law rather than their narrow or lawless national interests. Most important, the Grotian concept of the sovereign state was essentially idealistic at the time. It was conceived in the era of empires, years before the Peace of Westphalia liberated Switzerland and the Netherlands from German and Spanish empires and centuries before the entire world would be divided into nearly two hundred states, many carved out of colonial empires.

The most important lesson that Grotius learned from the Thirty Years War (1618-48), in the midst of which he wrote *The Law of War and Peace*, was that no single superpower can or should rule the world. The idea of a single superpower, derived from the theological beliefs of the Roman Catholic Church, furnished a normative basis to unify the diverse tribes of Western Europe. Despite its profound moral influence over Western Europe and elsewhere, the single universal church was effectively undermined in the sixteenth century when Martin Luther launched a successful movement for the decentralization of faith. Despite the church's loss of universal sovereignty, the related concept of a single universal empire, maintained by conquest and colonization, continued to inspire the ruling elites of Western Europe to extend their power beyond the confines of their nations. This idea was also doomed to fail, however, since peoples throughout the world wished to live in intimate communities free of all forms of foreign domination.

Centuries before his ideas grew and blossomed in the real world, Grotius used the concept of the sovereign state to embody universal sentiments of freedom, diversity and self-government. In addition to providing independence to communities, sovereign states form an international legal system in which states are designed to be accountable to no external authority, whether that authority is a church or an empire. Accordingly, states may organize themselves in accordance with their own cultures, religions and legal traditions. In contrast to the single universal church that aspired to impose common values and the single universal empire that yearned for world domination by one king, the sovereign state as a legal construct offers diversity and flexibility by accommodating myriad forms of government, conceptions of justice and variations of faith.

Thus the concept of the sovereign state expedited the nationalization process by disassembling empires, just as the individuation process dismantles an unjust household in which the members of the family are forcibly united under the supreme authority of an almighty but oppressive patriarch. This dispersion of one human family into hundreds of independent communities was also a powerful reaction to the exploitative nature of the single household in which some family members dominate, exploit and abuse the others. So the notions of national sovereignty, political independence and state equality, enshrined in classical international law, became normative tools that nations used to dismantle the authority of the medieval legal order that sought to impose, without consultation, one set of values and one set of ruling elites on all communities, ignoring the communities' unique personalities, talents and developmental processes. After the brutal excesses of the two world wars, which witnessed the replay of medieval fantasies of domination and intolerance, the tenets of classical international law were incorporated in the United Nations Charter. Thus driven by painful historical memories, the one human family remains scattered and divided. Many communities are reluctant to compromise their individuation, fearing that they will be manipulated, subjugated or abused within the framework of a single household. This fear continues to impair mutual relations among nations.

Even though some people not conversant with history long to re-institute the idea of a single superpower, contemporary international law envisions a pluralist world in which communities may preserve their cultural and religious diversity. The norms of contemporary international law, informed by human rights concerns, outlaw world domination by any one people, nation, religion or civilization. If these norms of diversity, tolerance and mutual respect are once again undermined by a reincarnation of the failed medieval paradigm of a single superpower, the world will regress into the same old strife that has bred violence and cruelty over the centuries. Such an outcome would be a sad commentary on the moral intelligence of the human race, an outcome which deities will ridicule and say: "We swear by time, most surely this race is in loss."

While any effort to re-impose a single superpower over the entire world is doomed to fail, it does not follow that the human family cannot be reunited. Already the integration of national economies, the proliferation of information technology and an awareness of the environmental unity of One Earth have begun to unify the peoples of the world into regional and global networks. Hundreds of international organizations have arisen to solve common human problems, such as diseases and famine. They also serve to advance common human interests, such as the establishment of peaceful conditions and the pursuit of equitable development across the globe. This complex process of enmeshment is building a single household in which communities are invited to cooperate with each other without sacrificing their individual qualities. The construction of a global household, in which all members of the extended human family enjoy basic dignity, is the most formidable challenge of contemporary international law.

The concept of the nation-state itself is the most serious impediment to the creation of a global household. At points the process of individuation has tilted to the other extreme, prompting many nation-states, just like recalcitrant juveniles, to hold fast to their wild, wilful autonomy. Notions of national sovereignty and political independence have become shields for many nations to resist the emerging notions of cooperation and shared values. Affluent nation-states are reluctant to join the household because they believe their national interests are best served by confining their prosperity to their own populations. Some are even reluctant to share the methods and means of achieving prosperity with less advanced members of the extended family. Poor nation-states are also reluctant to join the household because they fear that they will be subjugated and exploited by the powerful members. Thus, self-interest and the fear of the other perpetuate the artificial borders of nation-states.

In fact, the concept of the nation-state has magnified the need for ethnic individuation. Some ethnic groups that for centuries lived together have severed their mutual ties and now live apart; others are determined to do so in the future. Some ethnic groups disentomb abuses from the remote past to seek severance from the same people with whom they lived in peace for decades. Some invoke linguistic concerns as bases for partition. Some wish to contain the ethnic purity of their nation-states. Some are determined to retain their religious homogeneity. The nations carved out of colonial empires add further confusion to the process of individuation, causing a proliferation of micro-identities. After decolonization, some ethnic groups succeeded in obtaining independence, some were forced into cohabitation with others, and some were partitioned into several separate states. The breakup of the former Yugoslavia and the consequent bloodshed in Bosnia have exposed the pathology inherent in the extreme versions of ethnic individuation.

Even less virulent versions of ethnic individuation can bolster group selfishness, intolerance and segregation. Ethnicity furnishes a natural basis for the establishment of micro-identities, satisfying a strong human need to form communities in which members share some unifying characteristics. An irrational attachment to micro-identities, however, disables individuals from relating to other groups. It can also lead to hostility and violence. To facilitate and even nurture such feelings, the nation-state provides a geopsychological box separating its people from others. To cement its internal solidarity and prepare its citizens to sacrifice their lives in war, the nation-state induces strong feelings of patriotism. Again, some attachment to one's nation is both natural and healthy. But excessive patriotism can be as dangerous as racism and fanaticism. Unexamined patriotism can force people to defend the interests of the nation-state, even when such interests breed unnecessary armed conflict, promote exploitation of other peoples or cause the citizens' own moral and spiritual unhappiness. When unexamined patriotism is coupled with irrational attachment to ethnicity, the nation-state can turn into a dangerous entity.

Contemporary international law does not outlaw patriotism or ethnicism. However, the law of human rights obligates nation-states to prohibit any propaganda for war. It also obligates them to make laws prohibiting any advocacy of national, racial or religious hatred that constitutes incitement to discrimination, hostility or violence. Some nation-states, including the United States, do not embrace the full scope of these prohibitions and outlaw hateful advocacy only when it may cause imminent violence. Despite varying interpretations of these prohibitions, a universal normative consensus is forming, suggesting that the pathological forms of national, racial or religious devotions impede the emergence of a gracious world in which people can develop healthy, peaceful and morally intelligent relationships not only with their own kind but also with peoples of other cultures, races and religions.

The norms of the gracious world also promote the ethic of sharing. Divided into rich and poor states, the present world maintains extremes of opulence and wretchedness. Although many rich nation-states are willing to share their wealth-producing means and technologies with poor nations, others are reluctant to do so. Derived from the dubious assumption that resources are scarce and therefore must be unequally distributed, the advocates of national interests deride the ethic of sharing as a utopian dream incompatible with human nature, which they presume is selfish. Even reputed scholars of international law embrace the doctrine of national interests as the prime engine of international relations. For them, the ethic of sharing is just an idealistic goal that sounds good on paper but has little relevance in the real world.

The advocates of national interests reinforce the geopsychological confinement of nation-states, pitting one against the other. Rich nation-states may then, without any moral anguish, close off their borders to the nationals of poor states, arguing that open borders will harm their peoples' high standards of living. The doctrine of scarce resources may also justify seizing resources by force. Thus, the combined doctrinal force of national interests and scarce resources turns the world into a predacious jungle in which the weak and the vulnerable have little protection. Such theories, when supported by legal scholars of international influence, impede rather than advance the emergence of a gracious world in which compassion and the ethic of sharing are the predominant values. Even if these scholars are truly describing what they see in the real world, they fail to understand that a description for one generation becomes a prescription for the next. The moral obligation of international legal scholars is not simply to describe things as they are but also to criticize and suggest possibilities for improvement, unless they morally believe no improvement is required.

Advocates of the scarce resource theory overstate the significance of national interests but underestimate the power of human will and intelligence to create new resources. They begin with a static view of the resources available, and then defend distributional inequities as an inescapable human condition. Of course, some resources are limited and some non-renewable. But history provides irrefutable evidence of the human ability to create new resources that preserve and enrich the joys of life. The creation of new resources has never been confined to any one class, caste, race, gender, people or nation. Even the untouchables in India, despite the stigma of inferiority, have made great contributions to Hindu society. The opportunity to create must be further extended to all the peoples of the world. The entire world would be better off if all classes, castes, sexes, races, peoples, and nations participate in the shared enterprise of creativity and expansion of resources. This, however, can be done only if the peoples of the world are first liberated from the threat of starvation, disease and armed conflict – a liberation that requires concerted effort and global cooperation.

In many ways, the era of international cooperation has begun to move nations toward an integrated world. The doctrine of national interests is losing ground as the need for cooperation is becoming more and more manifest. Thus, a process of enmeshment has begun in almost all parts of the world. Since no national economy is independent or self-sufficient and since no nation has all the resources needed to sustain let alone raise its standard of living, the exchange of both natural and manufactured resources has expanded the volume of international trade to unprecedented levels. A new understanding informs affluent nations that they benefit from the development of poor nations. It also informs businesses and corporations that they can sell more of their products if more people in the world have the ability to buy them. Thus the global expansion of prosperity increases wealth, not reduces it.

The example of the European Union demonstrates that when nations combine their resources, talents and political wills for mutual benefit, they all are better off. After fighting bloody wars for centuries, the nations of Western Europe appear to have reversed the painful historical process of mutual attrition. The continent that conceived the concept of the nation-state, impounding communities into separate national confinements, has now begun a process of dismantling the geopsychological borders of nation-states. The establishment of the European Union also demonstrates that diverse ethnic groups can be united into a single borderless entity. It remains to be seen, however, whether the Union will treat its non-European minorities with the same dignity that it promises to the nationals of its member states.

Following the example of the European Union, many other regions are beginning to establish similar economic communities. Although these regional communities, like the North American Free Trade Agreement, are still in their early formative periods, each such step renders the legal construct of the nation-state more and more dysfunctional. The borders that divide nations will have to be relaxed if vigorous regional communities are to thrive. Even though many nations actively seek to construct regional markets, they are nonetheless reluctant to open their borders for the free flow of workers and persons. Few are prepared to allow free immigration within the region. This reluctance is even more fervent when nations within the region have disparate standards of living or are populated by different racial and religious groups. Despite these impediments, however, the logic of economic integration asserts that once the people begin to reap benefits from regional enmeshment, they will intermingle and become more willing to relax their barriers.

A complete relaxation of national borders allowing free movement of peoples across the globe may not occur in the near future. The law of human rights recognizes that individuals should be free to leave any country, including their own. However, it does not obligate any state to allow foreign nationals, except refugees, to enter its territory. Thus nation-states have substantial discretion to control immigration. As a result, the nationals of rich states and even rich nationals of poor states enjoy the freedom to travel around the world. Even nations themselves promote tourism to raise revenues. But despite a thriving tourist industry, freedom of movement across the globe remains limited. In many cases, tourists are required to obtain visas from the countries they wish to visit. The nationals of poor states are often denied such visas, as many states fear that once they have escaped their impoverished homelands they will be reluctant to go home. Thus a majority of the world's people enjoy little freedom to see the planet we share, much less choose a new home for permanent residence. Even privileged individuals who otherwise freely travel cannot always choose to live wherever they wish. No nation-state has yet dismantled its borders for universal immigration.

Thus even though nation-states are willing to relax their borders for the free flows of goods and capital, they are reluctant to allow free movement of the peoples of the world. A commonly-held belief that poor people will migrate in droves to affluent states is exaggerated because most people, rich and poor, wish to live in their ancestral communities. Despite this longing for situatedness, migration is an equally deeply rooted human condition; it revives human spirits and interweaves communities. Many nations of the world came into existence as a result of migration. Even today, migration is a fact of global life. The European Union allows its citizens not only to reside in any member state, but also to work and vote there. Some states allow foreign nationals to invest capital in exchange for receiving permanent residence. Some states allow foreign labor to enter as guest-workers, some allowing these workers to even become citizens after a prescribed period. The borders of many states in Africa are almost completely open, in part because these states lack the enforcement resources to close them and in part because the notion of sovereign borders is an alien concept. Though not uniformly open to all peoples, the United States has nonetheless set a new precedent in accepting immigrants from all over the world, thus establishing a complex pluralist society. If the process of regional and global enmeshment is further intensified and the norms of pluralist association gain widespread acceptance, nation-states may have to relax their geopsychological borders.

Even contemporary legal and economic imperatives are positioned to further weaken the construct of the nation-state. For example, if the law of human rights is implemented in good faith, the unaccountable ruling elites may have little choice but to embrace forms of government derived from the will of the people. If economic and social interests are joined in more intricate regional and global networks, warfare may become unaffordable. If the rights of women are universally accepted, the exclusive domination of men over the affairs of the world may be unsustainable. If the European Union and other regional communities can successfully counter ethnic obsessions, the pluralist concept of society may weaken the paradigm of the ethnic state. As these changes occur, the nation-state will evolve into Free State.

Free State is not a revolutionary or ideological entity. No military might is needed to establish Free State, nor is an authoritarian legal order necessary to preserve it. As an evolutionary entity, Free State emerges only if suitable legal and moral conditions are established. For example, Free State cannot evolve if nations are at war or if economic disparities continue to divide nations and regions. However, Free State is not simply a product of fortuitous circumstances. It is a dynamic entity that strives to establish legal and moral conditions most conducive to its own evolution. As a dynamic entity, Free State seeks to construct a stable and fair global household in which the principle of exclusion is replaced with the principle of inclusion, self-interest with compassion, singular domination with shared consultation, warfare with peaceful conditions, and selective prosperity with social justice. In establishing such a global household, Free State encourages artists, poets, teachers, scholars and other members of epistemic communities to play an active role in reducing the cynicism and negativism associated with human nature, law, power, economic principles, human intelligence, and distributional inequities. Arguing that certain fundamental principles are in themselves manifest, Grotius quotes the following verses from Euripides's *Phoenician Maidens*:

Mother, these words, that I have uttered, are not
Inwrapped with indirection, but, firmly based
On rules of justice and of good, are plain
Alike to simple and to wise.

If nation-states mutate into Free States, the norms of international law that support nation-states will undergo gradual transformation in the same way as the norms that sustained the era of empires and consequent colonialism did. The present division of One Earth into almost two hundred nation-states, each claiming sovereignty within its borders, may linger for a while but it will gradually concede the day to freedom of movement, freeing the planet for the peoples of the world to enjoy and preserving its seamless nature and beauty. It seems unlikely that Free State would institute a single world government, because such a concept seems both imprudent and impractical: it is imprudent because the human will to live in small, diversified communities appears to be indomitable, and it is impractical because no one authority can control all the peoples of the world. If such a single government is imposed many communities will rebel, and human civilization will suffer a momentous setback as it did in the last two world wars. Free State supports the purposes of the United Nations Charter, striving "to save succeeding generations from the scourge of war, and to establish conditions under which justice and respect for law can be maintained, and to promote social progress and better standards of life in larger freedom, and for these ends to practice tolerance and live together in peace with one another as good neighbors."

A global community of Free States will come into existence when sovereign borders evolve into open borders, allowing the free flow of goods, services, capital, labor and persons. When Free State establishes open borders, the nation-state loses its identity as a distinct legal entity. Driven by historical inertia and the forces of ethnicity and culture, some nation-states may continue to resist this structural change and refuse to relax their borders. Others may more willingly adapt to the changing conditions of regional or global life. The adaptive attitude of the nation-state toward the forces of integration may vary from region to region. Regions, such as the European Union, in which economic prosperity is more or less evenly distributed among member states may provide a less threatening environment for regional states to dissolve their sovereign borders. Other regions such as North America, in which the standard of living among various states is markedly uneven, may impede the dissolution of sovereign borders. Other factors, including actual or potential armed conflict, may similarly obstruct the evolution of sovereign borders into open borders.

The dissolution of sovereign borders does not imply that all government would become extinct. In fact, each Free State must have a separate government. In accordance with the principle of subsidiarity, however, Free State establishes an intimate government closer to the people. No such intimacy can exist if the government is non-democratic or otherwise remote from the people. Therefore, Free State establishes a representative government so that the people may be actively involved in the creation of state policy. An intimate, representative government does not necessitate that Free State have a small territory. As a result, Free State comes in no one territorial size. Some existing nation-states may evolve into Free States without territorial changes. Others, however, may undergo territorial readjustments.

Thus Free State performs two seemingly opposite functions: on one end it facilitates the people's participation in global life, while on the other end it preserves their aspiration to institute a meaningful, intimate self-rule. At the global level, Free State is interlinked with world-wide networks; it contributes to, and benefits from, international organizations involved in diverse aspects of global life. At the local level, Free State organizes communities through self-rule and active involvement of the people. No Free State is independent or sovereign in the performance of these complex tasks. Instead, each is an interdependent entity that maximizes human freedom at both local and global levels.

This book explores an idea I first presented in an article published in the 1992 American University Journal of International Law and Policy. In that article, I cautioned the reader: "The concept of Free State presented here is rudimentary... Furthermore, I am not proposing any revolutionary theory similar to the Marxist idea that the state is destined to wither away... the idea of Free State appears premature, because many nation-states are powerful and many people do not envision beyond their national boundaries. Widespread patriotism and psychologically charged phrases such as 'my country,' 'the fatherland' and the 'motherland' reveal that many peoples of the world maintain an attachment to the idea of the nation-state. To men and women willing to die for their country, the proposed concept of Free State may seem merely poetic, if not offensive." These cautions are relevant here as well. Finally, I must borrow a few more words from Grotius, from whom I have borrowed throughout this book: "And now if anything has here been said by me inconsistent with piety, with good morals, with Holy Writ, with the concord of the Christian Church, or with any aspect of truth, let it be as if unsaid."

Part I:

Advent of the Nation-State

Chapter One

Historical Formation of the Sovereign State

The sovereign state is a human construct shaped by the forces of history. It is a mode of sociopolitical organization that satisfies a deep-seated human longing to forge a sense of identity in communion with others, preferably with those who share the same characteristics such as ethnicity, language and religion. The idea of a community in which individuals live in families, families in tribes and tribes with each other is universal in character, found in all parts of the world, stretching back to ancient Sumerian, Egyptian, Chinese, Hindu, Greek and Roman civilizations. Equally universal is the idea of an empire in which diverse communities living in remote areas and having no mutual contact are held together under a single ruler, real or symbolic, a prince or a god. The concept of the sovereign state, however, is distinguishable from both communities and empires. An innovative construct that emerged in the seventeenth century Europe, the sovereign state is a halfway house between communities and empires, joining the former and dismantling the latter. In addition to providing sociopolitical organization, the sovereign state furnishes a legal order in which the authority to govern flows from within. Accordingly, the sovereign state accepts no external law-giver.

The historical events that furnished the essential ingredients for the formation of the sovereign state involve the era of empires when imperialism clashed with the universal church, a fierce struggle leading to their mutual attrition. The eventual triumph of the sovereign state over mighty empires and universal religions is a story of the human will to resist the authority of a single superpower, striving to rule all communities in every corner of the world, sometimes in the name of One Emperor and sometimes in the name of One God. It reminds us that no single people or church can control the destiny of the world. Nor can the social, moral and spiritual development of humanity ever be uniform. Diversity, not uniformity, is the driving motif of the human story. Thus the rise of the sovereign state reveals a simple historical secret: any attempt to impede the flowering of diversity is doomed to fail. Even when sovereign states seek to mutate into Free States – a central theme of this book – the human desire to create and preserve culturally divergent communities will continue to thrive. A single world government is, therefore, not a new vision of future society; it is a failed medieval dream to be avoided.

The history of Western Europe in the middle ages illuminates a protracted effort to establish one superpower over diverse communities. The idea had some conceptual charm, since one superpower could in theory institute a global system using its might to maintain order and its prestige to mediate disputes between kingdoms. In reality, however, the idea generated territorial and ideological conflicts. Entombed in the splendor of the ancient Roman empire, the idea of a single superpower was resurrected in the teachings of Roman Catholicism. Most clerics and princes shared the view that there ought to be only one *Imperium Christianum*. But a dispute arose over who should head the empire. Two claimants vied for power: the pope and the emperor. Each derived his superior claim from the same source, One God.

The grand contest between pope and emperor was a recurrent medieval phenomenon, part of a complex interplay of forces originating in the ninth century when the so-called Holy Roman Empire was established in Western Europe. The contest took place at many different levels. Politically, it was a contest between German emperors and Roman popes, between two separate geographical regions and legal traditions, between North and South. Normatively, it was a contest between competing conceptions of law, one derived from the power of material resources, including weapons, and the other from the authority of theology including morals. Sometimes the contest was clear and robust as each side attempted to dominate the other. At other times, it was confusing and subdued as each side needed the other: the holy chiefs in Rome needed the power of distant German emperors to pretend that the defunct Roman empire had been resurrected in a new form while the emperors in Germany needed the glorious past of Rome and the theological majesty of the popes to deepen and legitimize the claimed universality of an otherwise modest empire.

To further complicate the contest between emperors and popes, other actors entered the dialectical struggle for supremacy. While scholars continued to advocate the virtue of one empire, some of the empire's principalities yearned for political and religious freedom. All along, the French nursed their own ambition to lead the empire, defying both German emperors and Roman popes. Thus early on, territorial and dynastic rivalries between French rulers and German emperors began to sow the seeds of the modern sovereign state. In later centuries, Muslim Turks entered the scene, challenging the physical boundaries of the empire. The rise of a formidable Ottoman empire revealed that no single empire was destined to rule the world. The idea of theocratic-secular imperialism was mortally wounded when a German priest, Martin Luther, questioned the theological omnipotence of the Roman church and prompted German princes to even more strongly question the authority of the emperor. This conceptual deconstruction of the empire from within underscored the point that neither theology nor imperialism was a sustainable basis for an international legal order. At this critical juncture, the idea of the sovereign state promised to release distinct communities of Western Europe from papal supremacy as well as German imperialism.

In due course, the French, the English and the Dutch established their own separate kingdoms, denying Germans the wherewithal to entrench a continental imperial order. While Germany, with its imperial ambition, remained locked in Europe, other nations of Western Europe took a new turn. The French, the English, the Dutch and the Spaniards diverted their power and ambition to dominate other parts of the world. The Americas, Asia, Africa and the Middle East were colonized, imparting a new meaning to the medieval concept of empire. Imperialism assumed the form of colonialism, allowing the era of empires to linger well into the twentieth century. Ironically, colonialism in its deepest recesses contained and even nurtured the idea of the sovereign state, in part because many of the new imperialists in the guise of colonizers had opposed imperial authority over their own people in their own homelands.

Thus colonialism carried the seeds of the sovereign state to other parts of the world. The establishment of the United States in 1776 anticipated the future course of colonial history, demonstrating that the human will to live free of external control is irrepressible – even when the imperialists speak the same language and share the same ethnicity. The sovereign state, as an embodiment of freedom, was an even more powerful construct for those peoples of the world who shared little in culture or legal tradition with the imperialists. Ancient countries, such as China, India and Egypt, would later emulate the example of the United States, demanding freedom on the one hand but showing little reluctance on the other to embrace the legal structures the colonizer had instituted in their own homelands. Even territorial pieces of lesser known lands would demand to be converted into new sovereign states. All over the world, the sovereign state would become the ideal political construct and a symbol of self-government and independence from foreign control.

The secret of the sovereign state, however, does not lie in the struggle against colonialism. Nor does it originate from the superb formulation of the American Declaration of Independence. Rather, it rests in the tumultuous developmental history of Western Europe where both internal and external challenges to the concept of a single empire paved the way for the emergence of the territorial state as an inviolable international entity. The process of dismantling the pyramidical structure of imperialism was by no means easy or peaceful. The struggle for territorial independence even in Western Europe was piecemeal, spread over many centuries. Slowly and steadily, the sovereign state emerged as dysfunctional attributes of church and empire brought conflict and sorrow. If there is a single moment in history when the concept of the sovereign state first fledged into reality, it was the 1648 Peace of Westphalia, which ended the Thirty Years War. The creative genius of the Peace of Westphalia restructured the genetic composition of the Holy Roman Empire, vesting its principalities with a degree of autonomy and legally freeing them from both papal and imperial institutions. The sovereign state was thus no philosophical apparition leaping out of nothingness. It was a natural, evolutionary development in the bosom of history, a creature more adaptive to the realties of a changing world. It gained strength as church and empire declined, stripped of power, glory and utility.

1. Decline of Papal Supremacy

The Roman papacy laid the theoretical foundation of a global order in which diverse states would be subject to the authority of a universal institution. The theory of papal supremacy asserts that the pope, as God's vice regent, is the head of both spiritual and temporal realms. Accordingly, clergy and princes alike serve on behalf of the papacy to which they remain accountable. Papal supremacy creates a supranational order in which earthly lords wielding power over cities, nations and empires are subject to the pope's morally impeccable authority. Vested with complete sovereignty over both spiritual and temporal domains, the pope is not only the head of the church but the king of kings. Even mighty emperors are obligated to swear allegiance to the pope. When the emperor receives imperial authority, the pope retains the right to oversee his temporal domain. The temporal power delegated to kings and emperors is conditional; if the ruler abdicates or dies, his power reverts to the pope. Furthermore, the pope has the exclusive authority to judge and punish despots and neglectful rulers, protect nations from their oppression, and when appropriate release their subjects from the oath of fealty.[1]

This kingship over kings suggested an institutional framework in which national rulers would be accountable for their deeds. It provided a code of universal law, the canon law, binding on all believers, a code based not only on the formal authority of law but also rooted in a functional moral sense of right and wrong – indeed a theology-based natural law applicable to all nations and all peoples of the world. According to this code, the papacy oversees the conduct of governments in order to secure their compliance with norms of universal behavior and mediate intergovernmental disputes. The proposed global code is not confined to kings. Even ordinary people must conduct their lives according to law and morality. Moreover, the people may seek papal redress against unjust rulers. This direct complaint procedure to a supranational entity, though elementary in scope, was a remarkable remedy – a norm recently restored in contemporary international law.[2]

For those who anchor the authority of law in the fear of sanctions, the papal order derived from the hermeneutics of a metaphysical theology appears abstract in origin and legitimacy, since the papacy lacks enforcement mechanisms to implement the awesome power it claims over individuals, kings and emperors. But the papal order functions in a shared realm of law and morality, a realm in which law is enforced through the efficacy of morality. That is why the papacy, in order to obtain widespread obedience, creates a shared conscience of virtues that propels individuals, including kings, to obey the code. The papal order, however, is not without its own system of sanctions. It institutes a sustainable consciousness of fear – an intersubjective world in

1. The absolute power of the papacy is expressed in aphorisms such as *Papa judex ordinarius est omnium* (the Pope is judge of the world) and *Omnia de jure potest, ut Deus* (the Pope can lawfully do everything like God).
2. Individuals may, for example, complain about human rights violations to the Human Rights Committee, provided their state has accepted the Committee's jurisdiction. This procedure is fundamentally no different from the one under the papal order, because the complaint was available only against rulers who had accepted papal jurisdiction.

which the kings, the clergy and the laity fear the wrath of God, here or in the life hereafter, if they defy the code, papal decisions or orders.

Social and spiritual engineering through fear of a suprahuman deity has been typical of almost every religion; and therefore, the papacy should not be singled out for criticism. It is true that in the middle ages, the papacy, particularly through the doctrines of purgatory and judgment day, skillfully created a religious consciousness that valued and feared the church. In the early thirteenth century, the papacy also introduced the inquisition as an additional tool to punish heretics and witches. The critics of the papacy, however, ignore its tremendous influence in the early stages of West European civilization. The papacy, informed by the ancient Roman law, introduced a refined concept of law, a humane sense of right and wrong, compassion for the weak and the vulnerable, the norms of social justice and an overall view of human ties with time and space in a mysterious and obscure universe. It fused notions of law and morality, emphasizing that law without moral conviction is empty and even ineffective. Despite this contribution, however, the church could cast only a thin veil of obedience over the Faustian spirit of Western nations determined to exalt matter over mind, law over morality.[3]

The idea of a universal papal order originated in the eleventh century in the teachings of a Roman bishop known as Hilderbrand, who later became Pope Gregory VII (1073-85). Pope Gregory waged a theological and armed revolution to assert papal supremacy. "The glory of the Church was the all-controlling passion of his life." In *Dictatus Papae*, a document of twenty-seven brief propositions, Gregory presented a revolutionary agenda intended not only to free the church from its feudal masters but also to establish papal supremacy over kings and emperors. At the heart of these proposals lay the assertion, "the Roman church is founded by the Lord alone." Arguing for the freedom of the church, Gregory challenged the feudal system under which secular lords made ecclesiastical appointments. He asserted that the power to appoint and remove bishops is vested exclusively in the papacy. Gregory knew, however, that in the real world no genuine freedom of the church could be maintained unless the papacy itself was liberated from imperial domination. He therefore advocated taking the power to elect the pope away from the emperor and vesting it in the college of cardinals.[4] Turning the table on imperial supremacy, Gregory argued that all princes must "kiss the feet of the pope," since it was within papal jurisdiction to depose temporal rulers and release the people from allegiance to them.

---

3. "The final key to the Middles Ages is the Faustian spirit – the insatiable, inextinguishable willfulness that distinguished Western civilization from all others." Herbert J. Muller, The Uses of the Past, Oxford Univ. press 1952
4. In 1059, the council of Rome fixed the mode of papal election. At that time, Gregory was the chancellor of the Roman church and had the pontificate under his full control.

Gregory's idea of papal supremacy was a significant landmark in the history of supranational ideas. It represented the triumph of the church over the empire. In addition to establishing the glory of the church, papal supremacists wished to create a universal institution that would monitor the conduct of mighty rulers, disciplining them if and when they acted in violation of the higher law. But unless a theory is put into practice it remains doubtful, even fictional. Thus a serious clash between the pope and the emperor occurred during the pontificate of Gregory VII. When the Holy Roman Emperor Henry IV refused to submit his authority and clergy to the papacy, he was excommunicated. The princes of the empire side with the pope.[5] After losing critical wars to Gregory's allies, the besieged emperor and his wife were forced to stand for three days in snow and ice before the gates of Canossa, until the victorious pope agreed to forgive the humbled German king – an event that continues to stir German passion.

Thus Gregory introduced a powerful theory of a global order in which the institution of the papacy would oversee the conduct of nations and their rulers. From that point on, each subsequent Roman pope would reassert the doctrine of papal supremacy. More than a century later, Pope Innocent III (1198-1216) reinforced Gregory's concept of papal supremacy, arguing that "the pope judges all and is judged by none." He for the first time added the title of "the Vicar of God" to the titles of the pope. To defend papal supremacy over kings and emperors, Innocent invoked an ancient episode showing how the papacy elevated a German warrior to the office of Roman emperor. On Christmas Day in the year 800, Pope Leo placed a crown on the forehead of Charles Augustus, later known as Charlemagne, declaring him the new Roman emperor. This coronation in its historical context was a theoretically dramatic but practically unimportant coup d'etat against the Greeks, who had established a rival church in Constantinople and claimed to be the "original custodians of the Christian faith." However, Innocent interpreted this episode as a defining moment for the power of the papacy. He maintained that Leo acted as God's representative in taking away the empire from the Greeks and bestowing it on the Germans. He further asserted that Leo's act shifted the center of Christianity from the East to the West. This was the famous doctrine of the *translatio imperii*, or translation of the empire. On the basis of this doctrine, Innocent insisted that Germans should acknowledge that the "right and authority to examine the person elected as king, who is to be promoted to the imperial dignity, belong to us who anoint, consecrate, and crown him."

---

5. "They were anxious to narrow the prerogative of their head, were the natural allies of his enemy, whose spiritual thunders, (were) more terrible than their own lances..." James Bryce, The Holy Roman Empire (New York, 1907), pp. 163.

On the basis of this historical logic, he further insisted that the papacy has the right to recall a king who is "a sacrilegious man or excommunicate, a tyrant, a fool or a heretic."[6]

Critics of the papacy argue that the doctrine of *translatio imperii* was a convenient, self-serving interpretation of a distant past, allowing the Roman papacy to assert the triumph of Roman Catholicism over Greek Christianity and to establish the authority of the Roman pope over that of the German emperor. Of course, history can be manipulated to advance a specific viewpoint and often stands revised when the new version is widely accepted. Innocent's exaltation of Charlemagne resonated well in the early thirteenth century. The idea that the Roman pope had the authority to transfer the kingdom created a mystical alliance between Rome and Germany, providing German rulers with a religious basis to assert power over the peoples and resources of Western Europe. It boosted the self-image of German emperors, who could invoke the glorious past of the ancient Roman empire to embellish their otherwise modest kingdoms. It also supplied an oppositional identity to the Greek Church and the Byzantine empire.

Despite Innocent's advocacy, papal supremacy remained in doubt. The champions of the separation of church and empire were determined to challenge the universal legal order the papacy wished to institute under the guidance of the Roman pope. They invoked "the concept of two swords" to drive a wedge between Caesar and God, emperor and pope. Initially, long before the idea of papal supremacy was put forth, the church itself had advocated the separation of temporal and spiritual domains, a theory under which the pope headed the church, the emperor ruled the empire, and neither interfered with the other. The "two swords" theory was created to release the church from the control of kings. But when the church began to assert papal supremacy over both spiritual and temporal matters, opposition forces including the imperialists embraced the separation doctrine. Thus the opposing sides swapped philosophical positions.

Papal scholars and popes of the thirteenth century, however, were determined to repudiate the theory of separation. The prince-laureate of the Church, Thomas Aquinas (1225-1274), rejected any absolute separation of church and state. Prompted by his own theological feud with the Greeks, Aquinas defended the concept of papal supremacy, though sometimes in careful words.

---

6. As a German emperor challenged the authority of Pope Gregory VII, an English king tested the will of Pope Innocent III. In 1208, King John of England refused to accept the pope's nominee for Archbishop of Canterbury, Innocent excommunicated him. Perhaps unable to bear the weight of conscience and public disapproval, John yielded to the papacy and swore an oath of submission. Furthermore, John instituted the concept of the "free English church" in the first article of Magna Carta. In its contemporary sense this "meant, of course, free under the papacy from control by kings or barons." Harold Berman, Law and Revolution (Harvard, 1983), pp. 262-63.

Conceding that "in those things that pertain to civil good, the secular power is to be obeyed rather than the spiritual," Aquinas nonetheless states that "the pope holds the apex of both authorities, the spiritual and secular." At several places in his writings, he tends toward the ideal of papal supremacy. It was beyond dispute that "The Vicar of Christ has universal jurisdiction over the entire Church of Christ." However, Aquinas further argues that the pope is both king and priest, and the temporal realm gets its authority from Peter and his successors: "To no one else but Peter and to him alone Christ gave what is his fully."[7] *Reges sunt ergo vassalles ecclesiae* (kings are vassals of the church).

The most vivid rejection of the separation theory may be found in the teachings of Pope Boniface VIII (1293-1303). In his famous bull, known as *Unam Sanctum*, Boniface proclaims that "it is the law of divinity... that the lowest are ordered by the intermediate and inferiors by superiors. But that the spiritual power excels any earthly one in dignity and nobility we ought the more openly to confess..." He derides the two swords concept, under which the pope and the emperor were equal in their respective realms, as *duo capita quasi monstrum* (a two-headed monster). "Therefore we declare, state, define and pronounce that it is altogether necessary to salvation for every human creature to be subject to the Roman pontiff."

Thus in the thirteenth century the theory of papal supremacy was fully established in the letter of canon law. A theoretical international legal system was put in place under the guidance of the papacy. There was even some compliance. Submission to the papacy was perhaps an article of faith for most German emperors, who by and large were willing to maintain some sort of papal tie – if for no other reason than to legitimize the mystical nature of the Holy Roman Empire.[8] For Catholic rulers outside the German empire, however, papal supremacy was a theological-imperial doctrine that allocated theological power to Italy and imperial power to Germany. In retrospect, one might even argue that the doctrine of papal supremacy forged in the form of the Holy Roman Empire was little more than a powerful alliance between Germany and Italy. Whatever its character, papal supremacy was nonetheless often

---

7. To further cement the authority of the Church over the faithful, Aquinas taught that heresy must be punished with death. Although Aquinas argued that there ought to be no compulsion in matters of faith, this principle applied only to non-believers such as Jews and Muslims. However, heresy is more than unbelief: the heretic disbelieves after having once believed. Thus there is a clear distinction between a non-believer and a disbeliever. The non-believer never accepts the faith, the disbelieves rejects it after having first accepted it. Soon after Aquinas' death, the University of Paris, where Aquinas obtained his doctoral degree and taught for a while, condemned some of the extreme views he had preached.
8. Pope Boniface VIII experienced the ultimate power and glory of his high office when Albert I of Habsburg, the new ruler of the empire, accepted the *translatio* doctrine and the concomitant concept of papal supremacy.

incompatible with the national and personal interests of other rulers in Western Europe.

The French were not the first to defy the papal order, but their defiance was the first to be motivated in part by an emerging sense of the sovereign state. They viewed the Roman papacy as no more than a legitimizing force for German imperialism. French intellectuals, some groomed at the University of Paris, began to prepare a theoretical foundation for asserting French nationalism against the self-serving omnipotence of the papacy. French jurists argued that their king was accountable to God alone. Consistent with the prevailing mood among his French subjects, King Philip the Fair (1285-1314) claimed the authority to tax the clergy, thus asserting financial and legal sovereignty over the church and attacking the sacred rights of the papacy. Boniface VIII demanded complete submission. When Philip refused, the pope pronounced the French throne vacant and offered it to the German emperor, who declined to accept such a dangerous gift.[9]

From this point on, the French adopted a course of action destined to weaken the papacy. Jean Bodin (1530-1596), an eminent French jurist, recalled the French attitude toward the papacy: "For these the popes interdictions, or excommunications, were wont with other nations, to draw the subjects from the obedience and reverence of their prince: but such had always been the love of our kings toward their people (and so I hope shall be forever) and the loyalty of the people towards their kings" that the French nation would protect its sovereignty against the power of the pope.[10]

In 1305, during the reign of King Philip the Fair, the seat of the papacy was moved from Rome to Avignon in the south of France. This *translatio ecclesiae* from Rome to Avignon, five hundred years after the coronation of Charlemagne, was in some way a replay of history, this time to reorient the association of the papacy from the German empire to the French kingdom. The geographical shift from Rome to Avignon exposed the French ambition to appropriate the papacy to their own use. As the Roman papacy was tied to Germans, the Avignon papacy was tied to the French. Thus the former ran afoul of French nationalism, the latter collided with German nationalism.

---

9. The controversial life of Boniface VIII came to a tragic end in his own small hometown. In a surprise attack, engineered by a close adviser of Philip the Fair, Boniface was captured, assaulted and detained for three days. Disgraced in the eyes of his own community and perhaps unable to endure the humiliation, a few weeks later, the king of kings, *unum caput,* died. This death was a sure sign for the victory of jealous nationalism over the Vicar of God.

10. Jean Bodin, The Six Books of a Commonweale (trans. Richard Knolles, 1606) Bk 1, chap. 9. This English edition is based on both Bodin's French and Latin versions, published ten years apart, differing substantially one from the other. The French version was published in 1576, the Latin version in 1586.

The Avignon papacy met its gravest crisis when it attempted to assign the empire to the French king. Following the death of Emperor Henry VII, the electors of the German empire failed to produce a replacement. Frederick of Austria and Ludwig of Bavaria, both of whom received electoral votes, claimed the empire. Pope John XXII (1316-64), a French nationalist at heart, saw this dynastic conflict as a golden opportunity to bring the German empire under French control. Accordingly, his choice for emperor was the French king, Charles IV. When Ludwig (Louis IV) finally defeated Frederick and seized the throne, he rejected papal supremacy. The Avignon pope promptly excommunicated the new German emperor, releasing all laymen and clergy from allegiance to the unlawful ruler. The defiant German emperor went to Rome to receive the crown from lay hands. Romans resentful of the Avignon papacy shared the jubilation. To further assert his temporal power, the excommunicated emperor deposed the Avignon pope – the two denounced each other as heretics – and installed a rival pope in Rome. This was a low point for the doctrine of *unum caput* but a high point for competing national interests.

The failure of the Avignon papacy to command respect across Western Europe exposed the inherent weakness of the idea of papal supremacy. It appeared as if papal supremacy was a symbolic authority which could not transcend the city of Rome. The Avignon papacy had neither the historical mystique nor the spiritual magic of the Roman papacy. It lacked the pretense of universality. Rome was universal; Avignon was just a place in the south of France. Consequently, the Avignon papacy remained a French pageant that the English, Italians, Germans, and many others refused to join or respect. But even when the seat of the papacy was restored to Rome, the Avignon papacy was a constant historical reminder, particularly to those who wished to create an international system, that powerful nations would manipulate the papacy to augment their power and prestige, and if necessary would subject the papacy to their national interests. In a bitter war of national interests, papal supremacy failed to unite Western Europe into a supranational system.

At the global level, papal supremacy was even more problematic. Vast kingdoms of China, India and other Eastern nations existed outside the actual and theoretical reach of the papacy. So the claim of the papacy as a universal institution was a misplaced exaggeration even in the middle ages. Nonetheless, the papacy continued to claim sovereignty over the entire world. In 1493, for example, Pope Alexander VI issued bulls of donation to grant to Spain the lands that Christopher Columbus (1446-1506) had discovered in the Americas a year earlier. One bull reads: "Now therefore, We, out of our own motion, certain knowledge and the plenitude of our Apostolic power, have given, granted and assigned unto you for ever all lands in general and in particular and far remote and unknown lands, situate westward towards the Ocean, discovered or to be discovered in the future by you or your messengers sent for that purpose..."

Such papal claims and grants of distant lands of the globe supported the colonialism that Spain began to undertake in the fifteenth century. The rise of Spain in the fifteenth century also established a new dynamic in the geopolitics of Western Europe, to the dismay of the French and even the Germans. Above all, the expanding influence of Spain was the victory of a nation that had successfully ousted the Muslims from its southern province of Andalusia. The Muslims had occupied most of Spain for seven centuries and still controlled massive areas around the Mediterranean. The clash between West Europeans and Mediterranean Muslims, prompted by their related but differing faiths, nurtured by geographical proximity and sustained by their contentious wills to dominate the world, would underscore the point that no global order could be built around any one religion since it would require the untenable subordination of all other religions and sects.

Few would dispute that over the centuries, the papacy has taught peace and compassion as well as law and morality to its followers. However the papacy was willing when necessary to crush all opponents by force whether they were local heretics, the Greek church, the dissenters within the Roman church or the Muslims of the Mediterranean. Prominent among Gregory and Innocent's revolutionary teachings was the idea of the crusade, the medieval foreign policy of the Latin Church aimed at the recovery of Jerusalem and Constantinople. For the Gregorian concept of a spiritual global order to make sense, these two cities were deemed essential for the completion and unity of *Imperium Christianum Romanum*. The crusade for Jerusalem required defeating Muslims who had occupied the city in 638, six years after the Prophet's death. The crusade for Constantinople was a campaign against the Greek patriarchs who had established the rival church. Pope Urban II (1088-99), a Frenchman, led Europe into the first crusade, which massacred thousands on its way through Mainz and other cities along the Rhine.[11] Jerusalem was conquered, only to be reconquered by the Muslims about a century later.[12] Unable to stem Islamic expansion, the crusades also failed to heal the schism between the Greek and Latin churches. The crusades were a setback to the authority of the papacy as European kings and monarchs became reluctant to devote their national resources to fight distant, fruitless wars.

No idea fails as badly as the one eroded from within. Even though Christian rulers used every means to enhance their power at the expense of the Roman church and even though Muslims refused to accept the papacy as a universal institution, the greatest adversity to papal supremacy came from within the ecclesiastical domain. Heretical movements, which began as early as the eleventh century, defied papal doctrines and domination. They gathered even more momentum when Gregory VII and Innocent III pressed papal supremacy over both spiritual and temporal domains. Communities of dissenters,

---

11. "The scenes of carnage which followed belong to the dark pages of Jerusalem's history..."David Schaff, History of the Christian Church, at 239.
12. Almost from the beginning holy Jerusalem has been an unfortunate city, a victim of love by those who wish to control it even if they must spill blood in its streets. Today, the city is a source of fierce acrimony between Israelis and Palestinians.

often common people, arose in many different parts of Europe. But medieval Europe belonged to princes, not to the people. So the challenge to papal supremacy was more effective when it came from elite classes of Western Europe.

Eminent professors at the universities of Bologna, Paris, Oxford and Bohemia played a critical role in weakening the power of the papacy. Even here, however, scholars followed national interests. The Italian jurists weakened the Avignon papacy while the French and the English jurists weakened the Roman papacy. Jurists at the University of Bologna, for example, issued a legal opinion favoring the defiant German emperor (Louis IV) in his conflict with the Avignon papacy. At the University of Paris, Marsilius of Padua, author of *Defensor Pacis*, argued that the church was a state institution and thus the state could lawfully regulate the functions of the priesthood and watch over the church to see that it was strictly confined to spiritual affairs. At Oxford, John Wyclif argued for a church without property, altogether rejecting the concept of papal supremacy. Czech students who studied at Oxford brought the heretical message back to Bohemia, where Jan Hus launched a nationalistic movement to liberate "the faithful Czechs" from the tyranny of both the Roman church and the German empire. The scholarly opposition to the papacy was not confined to theology; it also exposed corruption within the church, breeding disillusionment among common believers.

At the Council of Constance (1414-18), Hus was burnt for heresy. But the professorial invective issued from various national seats of learning had inflicted irreversible damage on the theoretical supremacy of the pope. The very idea of convening the Council of Constance under the auspices of the emperor was a severe blow to papal prestige, as was the fact that the Council was called to remove three rival popes who had become puppets of their earthly lords. The Council deposed two of them and forced the third to resign.[13] The Council also issued two decrees: *Sacrosancta*, which established the supremacy of the council over the papacy; and *Frequens*, which required the pope to summon a general council every five years. Having already lost his supremacy over the temporal domain, the pope now would be subordinate even in the spiritual realm. If a council composed of national bishops and powerful laity was supreme, it could override even doctrinal and administrative decisions of the papacy. Since these decrees were never confirmed by the papacy, the idea of a supreme council remained controversial.

To dismantle the concept of papal supremacy, the leading Spanish jurists of the sixteenth and seventeenth centuries resurrected the old debate of two swords and argued for the separation of temporal and spiritual domains. Francisco Vitoria (1485-1546), a legal scholar at the University of Salamanca, argued that the pope could not lawfully interfere in temporal matters to over

---

13. Perhaps as a symbolic reversal of magnificence that Boniface VIII achieved over the empire, a member of the Collona clan which had opposed Boniface VIII was made the Pope.

rule the decisions of princes. Arguing against the universal sovereignty claimed by both pope and emperor, Francisco Suarez (1548-1617) said that the emperor never possessed such dominion over the whole Church; nor did the pope have such an authority since "it is incredible that Christ the Lord should have united these two supreme and universal forms of power in one supreme pontiff of the Church." Under the impact of the separation doctrine, the division between church and state, religion and law, would assume a permanent character in Western political theories as secular forces battled to limit first the political then the moral influence of the church over states' affairs.

As the papacy was losing its hold on secular authority, Western Europe began to come in contact with pre-Christian Greek and Roman art and literature that offered an alternative way of thinking about life, law, God and society – a phenomenon known as the Renaissance. The dignity of the individual, long disparaged by political and religious doctrines of the middle ages, arose again in the study of ancient literature. To Renaissance men and women, the historic feud between the imperial and papal parties seemed too narrowly focused. The time was ripe to involve the lesser children of God into the great divide between church and empire.

Still, neither Spanish jurists nor the forces of the Renaissance could deal a mortal blow to the lingering supremacy of the papacy. The movement to sever Germany from the Roman church began at the University of Wittenberg. As a lecturer on the arts faculty, Martin Luther (1483-1546) was required to teach the Hellenic conception of justice, vividly articulated in the *Nichomachean Ethics* of Aristotle. The Aristotelian concept of the subjective self, the ultimate repository of right and wrong, coincided with Luther's developing theology repudiating the need for a ritualistic, external medium in order to reach God. Although he advocated a ban on the study of Aristotle, Luther nevertheless offered an introspective concept of Christianity, in essence a personal faith derived directly from the Holy Scripture without assistance from the pope, his clergy, his doctrines or his rituals. Lutheranism was the triumph of the ordinary *Christenmenschen* over the dysfunctional, scholastic establishment of the thousand-year-old church. Excommunicated, Luther refused to recant his beliefs before the Imperial Diet at Worms (1521) and was declared a heretic. The German princes sided with Luther and formed a party, called the Protestant League, which would eventually defeat the Catholic emperor tied to the Roman papacy. Thus the stage was set for a prolonged confrontation between Protestants and Catholics.[14] Universities, regional churches and principalities joined the battle with books, sermons, edicts and intrigues.

Protestantism, despite its universal message, had a strong nationalistic appeal for territorial sovereigns. Whereas Roman Catholicism aspired to build a universal legal and moral order under a single leader, Protestantism encoura-

14. Erasmus of Rotterdam (1466-1536) sought to reunite the shattered faith by taking a studied moderate course, but was denounced both by Luther and the papal party.

ged small-scale nationalism. While Catholicism was more suited to the era of empires, the success of Protestantism paved the way for the rise of the sovereign state. In *An den christlichen Adel deutscher Nation*, Luther mixed religion with nationalism, making a case for secular intervention to amend the grievances of the German people against the papacy. Lutheranism, despite its bid to free the individual from the church, was more popular among German princes who wanted to get rich by appropriating church property. It was particularly popular in the Teutonic lands, where rulers saw Luther as one of their own. Containing the elements of a universal message, Lutheranism was nevertheless a simple, easy to understand faith derived from long-brewing German mysticism. It was a home-grown, German alternative to the religion which Italian and French popes had used to accumulate wealth, land and influence over other nations. Thus, Luther Germanized a global religion.

John Calvin (1509-1564), in his work *The Institutes of the Christian Religion*, which was dedicated to the French king, offered an international version of Protestantism no longer confined to the Germanic lands. But even Calvin could not resist the tide of nationalism. Headquartered in Geneva, he spent the last years of his life masterminding an underground ecclesiastical network to "unlawfully" spread Protestantism in his native France.

The English had no native rebel matching the stature of Luther or Calvin. But they had a Catholic king who did more than any theologian could do. Henry VIII (1491-1547), who had written in Latin a refutation of Luther and received the title "Defender of the Faith" from the pope, turned against the papacy when the pope refused to grant him a divorce. The angry king gradually assumed sovereignty over the English clergy. In 1534, one year after having his marriage annulled by the Archbishop of Canterbury, Henry had Parliament pass the Act of Supremacy under which the king, not the pope, headed the Anglican Church. Moved by patriotism and loyalty to the king, most Englishmen accepted the break.

Having nationalized a global religion, nations were poised to seek their own linguistic identity. Hence next to go was Latin, the universal language of the middle ages. Any language associated with divine or secular superpower gathers an awesomeness that few dare to question. Papal supremacy was inextricably bound to Latin, which was, ironically, the language of pre-Christian Rome. In the fourth century, St. Jerome translated the Bible into Latin. His text, called the Vulgate, remains the ultimate source of authenticity for the Roman Catholic Church. The schism between Greek and Latin churches occurred partly because of the languages they used in worship. The mutual aversion of the churches severed the East Roman Empire centered around Constantinople from the Holy Roman Empire instituted in Germany.

Under the domination of Italian popes for many centuries, Latin became the language of sacred writings and of worship in all of Western Europe. In medieval churches and royal houses alike Latin was the predominant language of the educated and the powerful, providing a common medium for the elites of diverse lands to communicate with each other. The mystical power of Latin lay in its sustained imperial heritage, first derived from ancient Caesars and then from Holy Roman Emperors. As a result, Latin relegated national languages to a perpetual status of subordination.

Protestantism liberated national languages from the supremacy of Latin, allowing the common people to worship God in the language they knew and felt. As Martin Luther put it: "Why should not we Germans say mass in our own language, when the Latins, Greeks and many others observe mass in their language?" Soon after Henry VIII's death, England took a momentous step by making English the language of religious services. It was a bold act of state sovereignty. The fall of Latin as a preferred church language made it possible for local communities to associate religion with their own languages. The common people no longer felt excluded by their inability to speak the spiritual language of the papacy. Once the use of a national language was established, any continuation of services in Latin sounded archaic and foreign, creating linguistic and psychological barriers between the clergy and the congregation.

Even though the Anglican Church broke off from Rome in 1534, setting an example of the power of a nation to choose its own religion, the power of the papacy was not dealt a mortal blow until German princes obtained the power to determine the religion of their territory. In principle, such a power is offensive to the modern concept of freedom of religion under which individuals practice their religion without state intervention. But politically the power to dictate religion struck deep into the heart of the Roman papacy, which for centuries had claimed the exclusive authority over religion for all Christians.

Ironically, German princes obtained the political power to determine the religion of their territory in the midst of the counter-reformation. To stem the tide of Protestantism and appease the faithful Catholics who had for decades demanded reforms of the financial practices of the church, the counter-reformation sought to recapture the church's hold over the faithful if not the princes. A call for the unity of Christendom still had some emotional value, but the logistics of summoning a council, which would reform both doctrine and clerical conduct, were prohibitive in a divided Europe. Choosing a place and participants proved problematic. Moreover, the idea of a council was a potential disaster for many constituencies: an independent council over which the pope had no control was a threat to the papacy. And a council under the domination of the pope was unlikely to bring reforms satisfactory to both Catholic and Protestant rulers, who were more interested in augmenting their power than they were in the niceties of disputed doctrines.

Interrupted by political strife, military events and papal opposition, the Council of Trent (1545-1563) was nonetheless a triumph for the papacy.[15]

---

15. There were days when in the streets of Trent the supranational papal order was under attack. Retainers of bishops of different nationalities drew their swords and railed at each other with the cries of "Italia" and "Espana." But the fathers of Trent were determined to reach a compromise.

Under the clever leadership of Pope Pius IV and Cardinal Morone, both experienced diplomats, the council completed its arduous eighteen-year-old enterprise. The council fixed the canon, brought sweeping reforms of head and members, recognized the authenticity of the Vulgate, and reinvigorated the old faith. Trent however was by no means a council of reunion. Opposed to Protestantism, it was a council of counter-reformation. It strengthened the papacy but alienated the followers of Luther and Calvin, sowing the seeds of future religious wars.

But the greatest setback to counter-reformation came from the German Empire. In 1555, "to protect the German nation, our beloved fatherland, against ultimate division and collapse," the emperor and the German princes acknowledged Roman Catholicism and Lutheranism as the two public religions of the empire. Furthermore, the secular princes were granted the right to determine and change the religion of their territories. Under *cuius regio ejus et religio*, the people had to follow the religion of their territorial ruler; however, those who did not follow the official religion were permitted to leave the territory. Thus Protestant principalities were released from the jurisdiction of Catholic bishops. This was the famous 1555 Augsburg Compromise.

Thus the supremacy of the Roman papacy in temporal affairs crumbled brick by brick, creating an environment for a historical change in the way communities would organize their legal and moral systems. Nationalism was already on the rise in Western Europe. The French, the English and the Muslims weakened the papacy from without while Protestantism undermined it from within. Foes of the papacy who prepared the groundwork for the emergence of the sovereign state would no longer be accountable to any external religious authority. The German empire was still Catholic in name, but the Augsburg Compromise detached the Roman church from its Protestant territories. This bifurcation would later reaffirm the medieval principle of separation of church and state, once propounded by the church but now advocated by secularists, creating a defining attribute of the Western sovereign state – with some appeal even to non-Christian communities. By allowing the people to worship in their own language, Protestantism championed the identity of linguistic communities that previously lay dormant in the divine universality of Latin. The Augsburg Compromise conferred on territorial princes the power to embrace a religion over which the papacy had no control. Piece by piece, the ingredients for formation of the sovereign state were falling in place. And yet, the lingering ideal of a single superpower still impeded the emergence of the sovereign state.

2. Decline of Imperial Supremacy

In contrast to the metaphysical nature of the universal papacy, a universal empire built upon force and finance had a more tangible basis in reality. A supranational entity held together by the muscle of a fighting army as well as by dynastic inter-relationships had more substance in a continent ravaged by mutual invasions and occupations. Driven chiefly by the secular wish to accumulate land and other material resources, the Germanic tribes of the eighth century began to invade and conquer the lands of Western Europe. In its initial stages the empire was known as the Empire of the Franks. Yet for those who viewed the empire as a spiritual ideal and for those who saw the emperor as *vicarius Dei*, the supranational imperial order that came to be known as the Holy Roman Empire was born in St Peter's basilica in Rome on Christmas Day in 800, when Pope Leo III crowned Charlemagne while the king knelt in prayer. The empire Charlemagne built was centered around Aachen, located near Cologne.[16] Although the physical empire of Charlemagne, christened in Rome and ruled from Aachen, fell apart soon after his death, its mystique nonetheless survived. In the thirteenth century, to highlight its theocratic authority and connection with Rome, the empire began to be called *Sacrum Imperium Romanum* (the Holy Roman Empire). Two centuries later, in deference to German nationalism, the empire was renamed the Holy Roman Empire of the German Nation.[17]

The concept of an all-powerful emperor, the protector of body and soul, peace and faith, the vicar of God, was intriguing. It provided an antithesis to an all-powerful pope. In the middle ages, when Western Europe was poor and undeveloped, the empire was more powerful as an idea than it was in reality. As an idea it was a supranational order including all present and future Christian fiefs, territories, cities, estates, kingdoms and monarchies in the North, South, East and West. In reality, the empire was modest both in size and influence. At its high point, the empire included most of what is now Germany, Austria, the Czech Republic, Slovakia, parts of France and the Lombard cities of northern Italy. Most parts of Western Europe, such as France, Spain, Portugal, Sweden and England, were not part of the empire. Thus despite containing within its boundaries a complex mix of ethnic groups, which guarded their identity more in medieval times than they do now, the imperial order was universal in theory but predominantly German in reality, holding its fragments together with a tangle of strings. An ambiguous partnership between the German emperor and the Roman pope, suitable to their respective interests and camouflaging the niceties of hierarchy between the two, became the foundation of the Holy Roman Empire. When the relationship worked, the empire acted as a German-Italian alliance.

In spite of its strong Italian connection, the Holy Roman Empire was a German empire wrapped in the mystique of a universal religion. Association

---

16. Never as popular as St.Peter's, Aachen has been a place of coronation and pilgrimage, luring many Christian emperors and kings eager to identify with the mythical power of Charlemagne, the first father of the mystical empire. To the consternation of the French who claimed Charlemagne as their own, the center of the empire over the centuries continually shifted eastward, from Aachen to Prague to Vienna.
17. In August of 1806, the empire was dissolved by Napoleon.

with the Roman pope accentuated the symbolism of the empire, fostering the fascinating myth that the empire was the continuation of the ancient Roman empire – a myth that Dante advanced in his poetry. This association assumed a further air of universality when the Roman papacy claimed jurisdiction over the entire Christian world. Even when the church and empire were at odds with each other, the fact remained that both still claimed to be the supreme institution of the world.

The supranational character of the empire was further boosted by the process under which the emperor was chosen. The imperial order began as an ancestral system governed by hereditary rules of succession. But gradually the elective principle emerged as the dominant mode of succession. The precise origin of the elective principle remains controversial, but as early as 1077 the princes of the empire passed a resolution asserting the right to elect the emperor. Pope Gregory VII, who had championed the idea of establishing a body of cardinals to choose the pope, approved the resolution. In 1125, the elective principle was applied for the first time when influential princes rejected the heir apparent and instead elected a duke as the emperor. By the end of the twelfth century, emperors were elected by a group of ecclesiastical and secular princes, of which the archbishops of Mainz, Cologne, and Trier and the count palatine of the Rhienland were the most influential.[18]

The elective mode of succession distinguished the empire from hereditary kingships such as France and England. An imperial order founded upon the elective process had an air of universality, since in theory it tied the office of the emperor to no one nation, principality or royal family. This universality of the imperial office further advanced the myth of a single universal empire that represented all Christians whoever they were and wherever they lived. While the theory was universal, the reality remained national. The elective process in the hands of German princes assured that the imperial office would be occupied by no distant foreigner such as a French or English king. This duality served neither the idea of a single empire nor the development of a German nation. While hereditary rules of succession preserved a relatively healthy nationalism in England and France, the elective process of choosing the emperor produced a schizophrenic and confused Germany – a nation attempting to be both global and local, open to all and yet closed to non-Germans.

---

18. Since 1257, a group of seven princes claimed the exclusive right to be the imperial electors: the archbishops of Mainz, Cologne and Trier, the duke of Saxony, the margrave of Brandenburg, the king of Bohemia and the count palatine of the Rhine. (Why seven? Revered in medieval mysticism, the number seven might have had some superstitious meaning.) In the Golden Bull of 1356, the emperor conceded the right of election to these seven princes, to the exclusion of the powerful dukes of Bavaria and Austria. The bull further stated that the emperor would assume office as soon as he was elected, undermining the pope's authority to grant approval before the emperor could lawfully assume the office.

Due in part to this confusion, the empire was destined to regress into a dynastic order held together by intermarriage. Instead of subjecting the imperial office to the rule of primogeniture, the dynastic mode kept the elective process intact but made sure the emperor would be elected from within the same royal family. The elective process determined by dynastic ties was still somewhat broader in scope than primogeniture. It was also unpredictable, since the succession to the imperial office was not automatic but determined by the internal politics of royal houses. Gradually, however, the elective process and the presumed universality of the empire became an obvious sham, particularly when in the fifteenth century the House of Hapsburg expropriated the imperial office to the exclusion of all others. The empire was Germanized, but still without producing a Germany.

The Hapsburgs had no universal vision of what the empire ought to achieve, particularly when the religious basis of the empire lost credibility. They failed to produce universal law or institutions. Nor could they cure the simmering tension between the emperor and the hundreds of German princes who ruled small and large territories. By the time Charles V (1519-56), a Habsburg, was elected emperor after paying large sums of borrowed money to the electors, the degenerative character of the empire was no longer a secret.[19] In fact, the Habsburgs turned the empire into a disoriented giant without a cause, corrupting the elective process, tarnishing the image of the emperor as God's deputy, and sowing still more confusion in the relationship between the supposedly universal emperor and local German princes.

The empire was not only losing its pretended universality from within, its external enemies, the French and the Turks, were also determined to weaken its real power and glory. The idea of a single universal empire suffered a great setback when France began to challenge what it perceived to be a German-Italian alliance codified in the sacred title of the Holy Roman Empire. Inspired by their own national ethos, the French seemed determined to own or, if ownership was not possible, to at least weaken the authority of the empire. Some French kings aspired to become emperors themselves, conniving with popes and princes to have the empire transferred to them.

All along, the French attitude toward the empire was aroused by a spirited mix of ambition and fear. Ambition was imperial in its driving force: infused with the memories of the Carolinian empire and Frankish kings, the French claimed a superior right over the "barbaric" Germans to be the most deserving recipients of the ancient empire. Fear was real, particularly during the reign of the Habsburgs, who had encircled the French territories by occupying the Low Countries (the Netherlands, Belgium and Luxembourg) in the northeast and Spain in the south. So to resist and undermine German imperialism, the Catholic French did not hesitate to make "unholy alliances" with Muslim

19. Recall that Charles V's coronation as emperor joined the empire with Spain and its European and South American possessions, forging a grand empire.

Turks or Protestant princes. Thus the grand medieval concept of building one empire for all Christians of the world lost its vigor on the battleground of national politics. German emperors and French kings seemed far less qualified, let alone willing, than Roman popes to submit their power and ambition to the ideals of a universal religion.

The contest between French kings and German emperors was driven by rival territorial ambitions and royal jealousies. The most intriguing dispute involved the duchy of Burgundy. Situated between France and the empire, the duchy had been a stable buffer and its duke a useful vassal of both the French king and the German emperor. Duke Charles the Bold (1467-1477) wished to change both the role and the fate of the duchy. Promising to send ten thousand men to fight the Turks, the duke began to lean toward the German empire. Furthermore, he aspired to enlarge the duchy's territory. These ambitions did not play well with the French king, Louis XI, who had his own imperial designs. But enterprises of great pitch and moment often take bizarre turns. In battle against the Swiss, who were financed by the French king, the duke was killed. Since he left no male heir, the duchy was divided according to feudal custom. Most of its possessions reverted to the French throne; other parts, including the Low Countries, passed to the empire as the duke's daughter was married to the son of the reigning emperor.

The extinction of Burgundy as a separate entity was perhaps a minor historical event at the time. But it would prove to be a great milestone in the emergence of the sovereign state. The division of Burgundy between France and Germany was a personal wound for Emperor Charles V. Raised in Burgundy, Charles's chief aim was to regain his ancestral homeland. But the emperor's dream, driven primarily by his boyhood memories, was too narrow in its scope and motivation. The emperor needed a political vision matching the might of his large empire. Coached by his mentor, Mercurino Gattinara, an Italian, the emperor began to see the Burgundian problem in its wider European context.[20] The French must be expelled not only from Burgundy but also from Italy, where they had established a dominion to the exclusion of the empire. Moreover, the emperor needed Italy to bring the papacy physically within the realm of the empire.

This grand enterprise recalled the holy idea of one universal empire which had been languishing in the theories of medieval universalism. To Charles the boy, an empire without Burgundy was emotionally deficient; to Charles the emperor, an empire without Rome was spiritually flawed. But restoration of Burgundy and the conquest of Italy would require a direct conflict with the French king, Francis I, a dynastic and imperial rival and the emperor's brother-in-law.

---

20. Charles V's assumption of the holy empire was a high point for the power and glory of the Habsburg, who now controlled both Spain and the empire. This was certainly bad news for the French king, Francis I, whose imperial ambitions were now mixed with fear and resentment.

War broke out in 1522. The French army was defeated at the battle of Pavia in Italy. The empire's victory expanded its geographical boundaries, tightening the noose around France. It also inflicted extreme personal indignity on Francis, who was captured and held in a Spanish prison until he renounced his claims in Italy, Burgundy and the Netherlands. This national disgrace for France provoked Francis and his successors to continue to fight the empire. Due to heavy financial and territorial losses, however, the French finally gave up their dream of a French empire in Europe until it was revived by Napoleon Bonaparte. Looking away from the European continent, the French turned their energies to the colonization of distant lands.

The Hapsburg victory over France further exposed the earthly character of German imperialism. No longer was the German empire the grand kingdom of God that other Christian nations were obligated to hold in respect.[21] It was a vast fortune of the Habsburg dynasty, obsessed with expanding its territories and influence. Nations outside the empire began to question the sacred authority of Habsburg imperialism, an order maintained by gold and silver extracted from South America and money siphoned from the Low Countries. In the midst of war, carnage, religious intolerance and rival imperial ambitions, many in Western Europe began to see the virtue of the sovereign state, a relatively small political entity, hoping that it would protect cultural and religious identities of many ethnic groups that had been forced in the past to live under a mystical imperialism.

Thus, the sacred ideal of one universal empire failed to counter rising nationalism in France and other West European territories. The collision between France and Germany revealed how Western Europe, let alone the entire world, could not be brought under the hegemony of any one superpower. But this lesson remained fuzzy in the midst of rival imperial ambitions of French kings and German emperors. In 1527, for example, the unpaid German and Spanish soldiers of the empire descended on Rome, the holy city, murdering and plundering at will. This was not the first *sacco di Roma*, but this time it was perpetrated by soldiers of the Holy Roman Empire itself. Such episodes expose moral emptiness of the universal ideology – any ideology driven by empire, religion or economics – which in its zeal to create a new order unleashes heartless mercenaries with no respect for ancient cities, temples, books and paintings. Steered by unexamined fervor, they obliterate what previous generations have meticulously built and preserved. Renewal often comes slowly, gently and thoughtfully. But sudden and deliberate annihilation of unfamiliar peoples, towns, cultures, temples and languages has been the most wicked flaw of the so-called universal ideologies. This was even more clear when the Ottomans reached close to the boundaries of the German empire.

21. During the Thirty Years War (1618-48), the Swedish and French kings had no spiritual scruples in sending their soldiers to attack the sacred borders of the empire and to appropriate its lands.

Despite the power and glory of German empire under Charles V, the most powerful empire of the world belonged to the Turks under the command of Sulayman the Magnificient (1520-66).[22] The age-old ideological conflict between West Europeans and Mediterranean Muslims was an ominous signal that an armed clash of empires would bring further disorder rather than divine unity among the peoples of the world. In the late thirteenth century, the rise of the Ottomans began to pose a direct threat to German imperialism. Armed with deadly weapons and a vigorous Islamic faith, the Turks began to advance on Europe like an avalanche. Having already occupied northern Greece, Macedonia and Bulgaria, the Ottomans seized the western Balkans by their victory at the battle of Kosova in 1389. But the Turkish eye was on Constantinople, the heart and soul of the Eastern Roman Empire, which the Arabs had failed to capture in the seventh century. Stopped in 1402 on the eastern front by the rival Islamic forces of Tamerlane, the Turkish forces rested and then regrouped to occupy Serbia. Constantinople fell in 1453, allowing the Turks to absorb the Balkans (including Bosnia, Herzegovina and Albania) and to reach as far as the Danube and the Aegean. In the fourteenth and fifteenth centuries, the Ottoman conquest of Slavic territories planted Islam into the heart of eastern Europe, not far from the borders of German empire.[23] The crusade of 1444, launched by the papacy and a coalition of Slavic and Italian powers, failed at the battle of Varna. Turks captured Constantinople but the Moors lost most of Spain occupied since the eighth century. In 1492 Spain reconquered Grenada, the last Islamic foothold in Iberia, forcing Muslims to convert to Christianity or leave the country. But at the same time the Christian populations in the Balkans fell under Islamic rule. In 1529 the Ottomans advanced on Vienna, endangering the might of the Habsburg dynasty.

Religious advocates saw Islam in Europe as an encounter between *Imperium Christianum* and *Dar-ul-Islam* (the world of the Muslims), a holy war between rival ideologies adoring the same Middle Eastern God. In more mundane terms, two supranational empires derived from different but related religions, two parallel ideas with opposing armies, stood face-to-face, each convinced of its own superior right to rule the world.

History had no permanent place for any single superpower, however. There ensued a collision of two earthly empires, each aspiring to create a global order based on conquest and subjugation. But in the sixteenth century the rhetoric was religious and imperial. Charles, who in his war against the Turks called himself "God's standard bearer," repulsed the attacks on Vienna but could not save Hungary from falling to the Ottomans. Claiming to be the sole heir of the Caesars and the master of the East Roman Empire, Sultan

---

22. In a historic reversal of fortunes, a prosperous Germany currently has a considerable population of Turkish guest workers. Many Germans resent the presence of Turks and what was once a religious conflict has now become ethnic in character.
23. More than fifty million people of different nationalities were thus brought under the sway of the Ottoman empire.

Sulayman the Magnificent assumed the name of Emperor, denying the title to Charles V – the only Emperor who would ever control Spain, South America and the German empire at once. In 1571 Spain and Venice, at the urging of the papacy, attacked and defeated the Turks in a decisive battle at Lepanto in the Gulf of Corinth, ending the threat of Turkish domination of the Mediterranean as well as the aura of Turkish invincibility. Despite the Lepanto setback, the Turks continued to pressure the southeastern front of the Holy Roman Empire until the late seventeenth century, when they were expelled from Hungary and Transylvania.[24]

The way in which we recall history makes a difference. If the conflict between the Hapsburgs and the Ottomans was a feud between two empires driven by desire for land and glory, each failed to institute a sustainable supranational order – losing in the struggle its own existence. If the conflict is remembered as a grand contest between Christianity and Islam, which at the rhetorical level perhaps it was, its tremors continue to undermine a mutual understanding between followers of the two religions, particularly in the Balkans.

The Balkan fault line presented the potential cracks in the idea of the sovereign state. If and when the era of empires would come to an end, would it be possible for a sovereign state to accommodate rival religions, ideologies and ethnic groups within its boundaries? Does the concept of the sovereign state presuppose a homogeneous population? In the Balkans, sovereign states would later emerge as pathological entities, containing disparate peoples who carried in their genetic memory the bitterness of past centuries when rival royal houses wished to establish but one empire in the name of one God.

Like the papacy, the Holy Roman Empire was destined to fail from within. The greatest challenge to the empire came not from the Turks but from Protestant princes, who shook its centuries-old mystical foundation. The conversion of German princes to Protestantism introduced an irreconcilable conflict into the meaning of the empire. The dilemma was cruel: if the empire accommodated the new faith within its domain, it would have suffered within its jurisdiction those who denied the truth of Roman Catholicism. Such a concession would tear down the special spiritual link between the empire and the Roman church. For the logical mind there was an additional agony: Protestantism was incompatible with the very name of the Holy Roman Empire. If the empire was to retain its historical identity and conceptual purity, it had to suppress the new faith.

Driven by nationalism, the 1555 Augsburg compromise legitimized the new faith within the empire. Yet this compromise was a superficial solution to a much deeper conflict. To accept Protestantism without changing the name and concept of the empire was a logical oddity – an unresolved contradiction bound to plague the "Holy Roman Empire of the German Nation" in the years to come.

24. The Ottoman empire was dismembered at the end of World War I.

To resolve this contradiction, the fall of the Holy Roman Empire became an inevitable prerequisite to the rise of the German nation. England and France had established separate national identities and were for all practical purposes sovereign states. Yet the presence of the empire confused the notions of nationalism and sovereignty. Even the de facto separation of Swiss Cantons and Dutch provinces into distinct entities did not advance the concept of the sovereign state, since their legal link with the empire was still intact. Most important, there lurked in the shadows of history the grand possibility, though remote, that the idea of a single superpower would survive and finally succeed in forging a supranational power to which all nations at least in Europe would willingly submit.

However, the concept of the sovereign state and the ideal of a single universal empire could not coexist. The empire would have to be dismantled so that the sovereign state could be erected in its place. Thus the internal collapse of the empire was much more significant than its containment from the outside by the French and the Turks.[25] For those who cherished the fall of the empire, weakening the relationship between German princes and the so-called universal emperor was a constant effort. This was so because the princes, not the emperor, were the true custodians of German nationalism. The emperor still represented universal imperialism. Therefore even a small triumph of the territorial prince over the emperor was a step away from the empire and toward the sovereign state. Even if German princes would not establish separate sovereign states by breaking up the empire, their increased authority over the territories they ruled diminished the psychological, historical and legal existence of the empire. The challenge was to reduce the Holy Roman Empire of the German Nation to a sovereign German state.

The process by which German princes dismantled the empire from within was tedious. The new religion helped princes set up a faith counter to that of the emperor. But the Thirty Years War, the religious war that began in 1618 and engulfed all of Western Europe, carried in its fury an important assertion: the German princes would fail to muster full sovereignty unless they won the legal freedom to enter into defense treaties with foreign nations. German princes already had territory, people and their own local governments. But territorial sovereignty would be incomplete without the power to conduct foreign relations, the fourth defining element of the emerging sovereign state.[26] This the princes would at last obtain through the Peace of Westphalia.

---

25. This is also true about the former Soviet Union, which ultimately fell from within.
26. According to international law, no nation can claim statehood unless it satisfies four criteria: it must have (1) a defined territory, (2) a permanent population, (3) an effective government and (4) the capacity to conduct an independent foreign policy.

3. THE PEACE OF WESTPHALIA

In 1648, after a brutal war spanning over thirty years, the monarchs of Europe held a multinational conference to establish religious peace and abolish both papal and imperial orders that, over the centuries, confused and tormented Western nations in general and princely states in particular.[27] The conference produced the Peace of Westphalia, consisting of two treaties signed on the same day, October 24, 1648. The treaty between the empire and Sweden, which had played a decisive military role in defeating the imperial forces, was concluded at Osnabrug. The treaty of Munster was signed between France and the empire. The Peace of Westphalia sought "a Christian, universal and perpetual peace, and a true and sincere friendship and amity between" the warring parties so that "there be on both sides a perpetual oblivion and amnesty of all that has been done since the beginning of these troubles..." For a long time thereafter, these lofty intentions failed to institute a durable peace. The treaties of Westphalia nonetheless fostered three significant goals: they dismantled the supranational papal order by recognizing Protestantism as a religion coequal to Roman Catholicism; they reduced the imperial order into a form without substance by elevating the German princes to the rank of territorial sovereigns; and they affirmed the legal existence of two independent entities, Switzerland and the Netherlands, created from within the empire.

To dismantle the supranational papal order the Osnabruck treaty confirmed the 1555 Augsburg Peace of Religion, preserving "exact and reciprocal equality" between princes and states of both religions. Recognizing that the grievances of one or the other religion had in part caused the preceding war, the treaty stated "what is just of one side shall be so of the other, all violence and force between the two parties being forever prohibited." The Augsburg Peace had recognized only Roman Catholicism and Lutheranism as the two protected religions of the empire. Article VII of the treaty of Osnabruck, by the unanimous consent of his imperial majesty and all the estates of the empire, extended the same right and advantage "to those who call themselves the Reformed," meaning the Calvinists. However, if Protestant princes changed their faith from Lutheranism to Calvinism or vice versa, they could not lawfully change the public religion of their territories, nor could they appropriate churches, schools, hospitals and the like belonging to owners espousing the

27. The population of Germany and Austria fell from 21 million to 13 million. In Bohemia, the population was reduced from 2 million to 700 thousand. Commenting on the atrocities of religious wars, Grotius wrote: "Throughout the Christian world I observed a lack of restraint in relation to war, such as even barbarous races should be ashamed of; I observed that men rush to arms for slight causes, or no causes at all, and that when arms have once been taken up there is no longer any respect for law, divine or human; it is as if, in accordance with a general decree, frenzy had openly been let loose for the committing of all crimes."

other faith. To prevent any further fragmentation of religion, the treaty provided that no other sects "shall be received or tolerated in the Sacred Roman Empire."

The Westphalia treaties repudiated the letter and spirit of the Council of Trent, which had fixed the canon in opposition to major Lutheran doctrines, and thus recognized Protestantism as a religion equal to Roman Catholicism. This political resolution of religious controversies seems odd if one regards politicians just as unfit to judge matters of faith as they are to settle questions of science. But the history of the Western church had for centuries been inseparable from the history of Western kingdoms. The Peace of Westphalia belonged to this same tradition; it was a triumph of political pragmatism over doctrinal dogmatism.

To offer any other faith as coequal to Roman Catholicism previously had been a heresy, an attack on the premise of papal supremacy. For centuries, Roman Catholicism had rejected the Greek church in order to assert its exclusive monopoly over Christian truth. The treaty discarded the historical assumption of Catholic supremacy, not with respect to the Greek church but rather with respect to Protestantism, a faith born in Germany. The political legitimacy of the new faith, approved with the active connivance of the Catholic emperor and the Catholic French king, demonstrated how far the temporal domain had displaced the authority of the church.

To weaken the papal hold over Christianity, the treaty instituted territorial sovereignty and religious tolerance. It reaffirmed the right of secular princes to determine and reform the religion of their territories. The ecclesiastic reservation was extended to Protestant bishoprics, which meant that Protestant territories would remain Protestant even if their prince changed his religion. Individual liberty of conscience was also expanded, allowing whoever "shall profess and embrace a religion different from that of the lord of the territory shall... be patiently suffered and tolerated, without any hindrance and impediment to attend their devotions in their houses and in private..." Even though private liberty of conscience was granted, the territorial lord still determined the public religion of his state. Public exercise of state religion, as opposed to private worship, had tremendous influence as it generated nationalistic pressure on the people to convert to the religion of their land.

The political power vested in princes to determine and reform religion within their territories stood opposed to the supranational papal order under which disobedient kings could be excommunicated, deposed, and their subjects released from oaths of allegiance. Thus the Peace of Westphalia separated the territorial state from the church but not from religion. In fact, it subordinated religion to the will of the territorial sovereign. More important, public religion in Protestant territories was declared free from the jurisdiction of the papacy or any other Catholic institution. "Thus the last link which bound Germany as a whole to Rome was snapped, the last of the principles by virtue of which the Empire had existed was abandoned." Pope Innocent X denounced the treaty as "null, void, invalid, iniquitous, unjust, damnable, reprobate, inane, empty of meaning and effect for all time." This papal response confirmed that the authority of the church over nations of Western Europe had significantly tapered off.

In addition, the Peace of Westphalia weakened German imperialism in two distinct ways. First, it released the territories of the empire from central authority. The electors, princes and states were established in their ancient rights, prerogatives, liberties and privileges in both spiritual and temporal domains to the extent that "they may not be molested at any time in any manner, under any pretext whatsoever." This right of territorial autonomy was extended even to the free cities of the empire, thus recognizing and in some ways entrenching states within states. The free cities were granted their regalian rights, annual revenues and the liberties and privileges of confiscation and of imposing duties – "an entire jurisdiction within the inclosure of their walls and territories." Thus the empire became labyrinthine riddle of near-independent duchies, principalities and cities, in which laws, religions and loyalties changed from border to border and within borders. This atomization of Germany into over three hundred self-regulated Catholic and Protestant territories seemed incongruous with the ideal of universal unity underlying the concept of *Sacrum Imperium Romanum* – a phrase frequently used in the text of the treaties of Westphalia.

Moreover, the estates of the empire (i.e. the electors, princes and states) were "freely and forever" granted the right to make alliances among themselves or with foreigners. The authority of estates was not limited to building commercial alliances across Europe so that "commerce and trade should flourish again every where" – a declared objective of the treaty. They were also vested with unprecedented authority to enter into defense pacts with foreign powers for their own preservation and security. Although the treaty prohibited alliances against the emperor or the empire, an estate could still make a defense pact with a foreign country against another estate within the empire. The pieces of the empire could not rebel against the whole, but they could freely conspire against each other. Such was the metaphysics of a decaying imperial order, retained in form but not in substance. From another perspective, the right to make defense pacts with foreign nations added a new and potent element to the concept of territorial sovereignty.

Regarding the independence of their territories against imperial encroachment, both Protestant and Catholic princes were equally unbending. The revolt against the papacy was thus different from the rebellion against the imperial order. With respect to undoing the church, the princes were divided; with respect to defying imperial supremacy, they were not.

The second way in which the treaty lessened imperial supremacy was to subject it to the collective power of the electors, princes, states and cities. The treaty mandated the formation of a free assembly of all the states, referred to as a diet, for conducting the affairs of the empire. The emperor was obligated to seek the advice and consent of the diet before interpreting laws, declaring war, imposing taxes, ordering levies, quarting soldiers, building fortresses, making alliances, or any other such affairs. The diet was authorized to regulate the election of the emperor and to determine the terms of imperial capitulation. Furthermore, the diet determined the taxes of the empire and the renewal of the *matricula*, the quota of each state to the imperial army. The Imperial Chamber, a central judicial body instituted in 1495, was redesigned to include Protestant judges, and the treaty empowered the diet to supply and amend the procedures necessary for the reformation of justice. Thus the imperial order was reduced to a useless federation under which its separate parts were made almost independent, subjecting whatever authority was left at the top to the collective will of independent estates.

The Peace of Westphalia crystallized the German nation's identity crisis. It recognized, even bolstered, the schizophrenic nature of the empire, which was historically intended to create a united Christendom but which in reality failed to weld together even the atomistic territories located in the land now called Germany. In retrospect, it appears that German imperialism was an embodiment of contradictions. German emperors failed to create a strong German nation because in their deep memory they continued to cherish the romantic idea of creating a vast, supranational empire in which Germans would be the masters of the world. German princes, the real custodians of power, opposed the *Roman* empire because its goals and historical orientation were supranational and not German. Any nation wishing to be supranational and national at the same time risks developing a character flaw serving few but tormenting many. Germany, therefore, was not yet prepared to become a sovereign state. Switzerland and the Netherlands, however, were prepared to take the crucial step.

The birth of Switzerland and the Netherlands as independent entities was a significant reversal of the historical process by which the German empire had been built and enlarged. Their independence sirened the extinction of the mythical empire that sought to unite all nations into a single geographical and spiritual union. The Swiss and the Dutch conversion to Protestantism was only one factor in the complex motif of their individuation. More important, their *de facto* independence achieved long before the Westphalia deliberations had exposed structural weakness of an empire maintained through a complex interweaving of religion, dynastic rule and claims to universality – a set of ties now in conflict with national and local interests of autonomous Swiss cantons or fiercely free Dutch provinces.

Swiss nationalism had been on the rise since 1477, when Charles the Bold unsuccessfully attempted to conquer the Swiss cantons. In 1499, the Swiss defeated the imperial army in a furious battle and declared their independence. Since then the Swiss cantons had been practically free. Yet their legal status as an independent confederation remained unclear until the treaty of Osnabruck explicitly exempted them from the empire. The treaty of Osnabruck reaffirmed the decree that had declared "Swiss cantons to be in possession of a quasi full liberty and exemption from the empire." Furthermore, the treaty recognized the decree "shall remain firm and lasting" and therefore all procedures and orders issued from the Imperial Chamber in any form whatsoever "ought to be of no validity or effect." Thus, Switzerland was carved out from the corpus of the empire.

The story of the Netherlands was one of constant transfer from one royal house to another. Located in the north of the region called the Low Countries, the Netherlands had been part of the duchy of Burgundy. In 1477, the Low Countries were severed from the duchy and delivered, as a wedding gift, to the House of Habsburg.[28] In 1566, the Low Countries experienced a turning point in their history when they were turned over to the Spanish king. Within a few years, the Low Countries began a united armed struggle against Spanish rule. But soon religious suspicions between the Protestant north and the Catholic south divided the Low Countries into two distinct ideological camps. In 1581, the seven northern provinces, called the United Provinces, declared independence from Spain. Mainly an act of unilateral valor, the declaration failed to win concessions from Spain, which claimed dominion over all seventeen provinces, north and south. Under the skillful guidance of Maurice of Nassau and Jan van Oldenbarneveldt, the Dutch rebels continued to fight against Spain until a truce was arranged in 1609. This truce meant for all practical purposes the end of Spanish supremacy over the United Provinces. The United Provinces (the Netherlands) obtained legal independence from Spain in a separate treaty signed at Munster on January 30, 1648, the first treaty composed at the Westphalia peace conferences. The ten southern provinces (Belgium) remained under Spanish rule.

The legal separation of Switzerland and the Netherlands from the imperial houses of Germany and Spain was in a sense the triumph of local sovereignty over universal empire. It would be a mistake to insist, however, that the Peace of Westphalia produced in the guise of Switzerland and the Netherlands two independent "sovereign states." This is so because individual Swiss cantons and the seven northern provinces of the Low Countries were more inclined to preserve their local independence against any central authority located outside the canton or the province itself. For each canton or province, the very idea of independence implied the absence of control exercised from a remote center; each cherished a distinctive sense of the self. In the United Provinces, for example, Holland maintained an identifiable national and psychological reality. In contrast, the entity called the United Provinces was strictly conceptual, lacking the emotional content essential to forge a nation. Thus both Switzerland and the United Provinces at the time of their legal independence were much less cohesive than the sovereign states they would later become.

The struggle for provincial autonomy in the Netherlands demonstrates how the idea of the sovereign state as an entity, which could hold several distinct territorial units within its fold, was problematic in the early seventeenth century. It is therefore important to further pursue the story of the Netherlands to examine how the idea of a composite state triumphed over a more intimate concept of sovereignty.

---

28. The Low Countries experienced a period of pride and prosperity during the reign of Charles V (1519-1556), who had a nostalgic affinity for the defunct duchy of Burgundy.

Soon after winning their de facto independence from Spain, Maurice of Nassau and Jan van Oldenbarneveldt turned against each other on the issue of provincial autonomy. The two men stood for two different ideas. Maurice, the head of the States General, wished to create a strong central authority – a unified entity better able to compete with maritime rivals such as England, Spain and France. But this could be done only by subordinating the provinces, particularly powerful Holland, to the States General. Oldenbarneveldt, the advocate of Holland who had cultivated extraordinary personal power well beyond the capacity of his office, resisted the idea. In fact, he and his lieutenant, Hugo Grotius, the pensionary of Rotterdam, advocated the sovereign rights of Holland.[29]

Oldenbarneveldt and Grotius worked together to fight the domination of the States General. To resist invasion, small armed forces were raised in the towns of Holland, including Rotterdam. Even the idea of declaring Holland completely independent from the States General had some following. The idea of provincial autonomy gave way to the authority of the States General, however. To assert the authority of the States General over Holland, Maurice moved his troops into the province; there was no resistance. Those who stood for the sovereign rights of Holland were defeated, without a fight. This quiet victory over a passive Holland was a significant event in the evolution of the Dutch republic, and the evolution of the sovereign state as well. [30]

Whether the empire can repudiate papal supremacy to accommodate a rival faith, whether a portion of the empire can separate to establish a sovereign territory, and whether a people can choose their own government were difficult questions introduced into the realm of law and sovereignty. And, more important, the question of which conception of sovereignty would furnish the sturdiest foundation for international law was even more tangled. In the seventeenth century, these questions were equivocal because the answers were rooted on the one side in the old norms of medieval universalism and on the other in the new aspirations of popular sovereignty and territorial independence. In the midst of the Thirty Years War and years before the Peace of Westphalia was concluded, Grotius undertakes to answer these questions.

---

29. In line with the temper of the time fueled by the initiation of religious wars, called the Thirty Years War, the conflict between Maurice and Oldenbarneveldt was shaped by theological controversies raging between the Calvinists and the Armenians over the doctrine of predestination. Maurice sided with the Calvinists who advocated predestination, whereas Oldenbarneveldt inclined towards the Armenians who believed in free will. "Among strict Calvinists Grotius was hated with an intense odium theologicum."
30. Oldenbarneveldt and Grotius were arrested, tried in a special court and found guilty of high treason. Oldenbarneveldt was executed in 1619, Grotius was sentenced to life imprisonment. On March 22, 1621, however, Grotius escaped from the prison to begin his scholarly journey toward his greatest work, De Jure Belli ac Pacis.

Chapter Two

Competing Conceptions of Sovereignty

The concept of sovereignty has been the traditional basis of law. That is why any discussion of law must reckon with this difficult and elusive notion. Sovereignty in a raw form is simply another name for power exercised over people and their resources. Thus one who exercises this power is the sovereign. This power may be exercised justly or unjustly, arbitrarily or in accordance with rules. Regardless of outcome or method, difficulty arises when sovereignty seeks a source of legitimacy. The proposition that the most powerful man, family, tribe or nation has an automatic claim to sovereignty is easy to comprehend but fails to satisfy the human quest to find a more intelligent basis for law. Consequently, many conceptions of sovereignty compete with each other. Each specific conception of sovereignty is unique. For example, theocratic systems lodge sovereignty in the will of God while secular systems may invest sovereignty in the office of the emperor or the will of the people.

The concept of sovereignty is even more elusive in the realm of international law, a system that proposes to institute order and justice among diverse nations of the world. Even today, the competing conceptions of sovereignty continue to muddle relations between nations. The search for an appropriate and functional conception of sovereignty, an approach acceptable to diverse nations, was the single most important step in the process of laying the foundation of classical international law. Legal scholars of the sixteenth and seventeenth centuries wrestled with an era when national liberation movements began to collide with the still-looming claims of papal and imperial supremacy. Sentiments, both for and against territorial and religious independence, ran rampant in the excesses of the Thirty Years War, which was by all means a war about competing conceptions of sovereignty.

More than twenty years before the conclusion of the war and before Switzerland and the Netherlands gained their legal independence by the Peace of Westphalia, Grotius presented his visionary theory. Imagining a future world, Grotius builds the theoretical edifice of international law on the foundation of territorial or state sovereignty, a concept that divides the earth into distinct portions and vests each such subdivision with equal sovereignty. Although state sovereignty is a commonplace concept in contemporary consciousness, it was far less prominent in the seventeenth century; then it competed with two other powerful conceptions: universal sovereignty and popular sovereignty. Universal sovereignty supports the establishment of a single world government over all the peoples of the world. In contrast, popular sovereignty argues for a form of government under which rulers derive the right to rule from the people. Grotius rejects both. In their stead, he establishes the theoretical superiority of state sovereignty, the dominant conception in the development of classical international law.

1. UNIVERSAL SOVEREIGNTY

Simple and elegant, the theory of one superpower has fascinated generations of theologians, poets and philosophers. It offers to construct a universal system in which princes and kings ruling different parts of the world are placed in a hierarchical order in accordance with their status and power. At the peak sits the One King, the chief law-giver. Princes conduct the external affairs of their lands through the medium of the One King, who provides rules and mechanisms to facilitate cooperation, resolve disputes and punish unjust and disobedient princes. This vertical chain of authority promises an orderly world in which One King has universal sovereignty.

The idea of one superpower is closely related to the Middle Eastern notion of One God – a root belief shared, followed and promoted by Judaism, Christianity and Islam. The biblical command, "Hear, O Israel, the Lord thy God is One" is in harmony with the Quranic injunction, "there is no god but He, the Mighty, the Wise." According to this view, sovereignty over the entire universe belongs to One God. Man, being God's most supreme creation, is the trustee of His sovereignty and exercises the authority God has delegated to him. Man, therefore, acts as the agent of One God and remains bound by His dictates.

The concept of One God serves as counterpoint to ancient Greek and Hindu mythologies, which feature many gods, some more powerful than others, each vested with a specific jurisdiction or power. Whereas the Greek and Hindu gods wage wars against each other to assert and increase their influence, One God is above all conflict and combat. One God simplifies the understanding of the cosmos: He is the source of all and ultimate authority. All forces, things, creatures and natural phenomena obey the sovereignty of one and the same God, who commands each and every one, who is beyond doubt, and whose authority cannot be usurped or defied.

The constitutive principle of polytheism is pluralistic: many and different gods of unequal strengths and different natures live and operate without any set hierarchy. In their mutual quarrels and intrigues, many and different gods mimic human life as it is, highlighting how princes all over the world engage in an unending struggle to conquer and subjugate one another. Universal order in such a system depends on the collective will of the many gods to cease battle and agree to a peaceful cosmos. Since any one god could generate mischief and no one god is powerful enough to dictate a normative order for all, the values underlying a peaceful and orderly world are derived by balancing the interests, values and visions of many gods.

In contrast, the constitutive principle of monotheism is unity. "God, the absolutely one, is before and above all the world's plurality, and is the one source and one goal of every being." Monotheism offers a vision of human life as it should be. All earthly rulers must submit their ambition, power and, more importantly, their laws to the universal sovereignty of one and the same God. Since monotheism imposes an inherently consistent normative order, all interests, values and visions must be adjusted to reflect the will of One God. The monotheistic order demands submission to one set of universal values.

To reflect the oneness of God in their statecraft, the monarchs of the middle ages imagined a universal empire, a single, all-inclusive entity in which diverse communities would be subordinated to the authority of One King whose power was derivative, held and exercised on behalf of One God. The idea of One King therefore mirrors the divine likeness. If there is One God, there must be One King.

In *De Monarchia*, Dante Alighieri (1265-1321) asserts: "(M)ankind's condition is most perfect when it reproduces the perfections of the heavens, so far as human nature allows. And just as the heavens are governed and directed in every movement by a single mover, which is God...so...mankind is at its best when all its movements and intentions are governed by one Prince as its sole mover and with one law for its direction." One King institutes a single moral commonwealth, a global network of nations and peoples, bound together in virtue and justice under the wisdom of One God.

Dante sees the world in its plurality but wishes to transform it into a harmonious unity. "The component parts of mankind," Dante argues, "are brought into harmony by a single principle ... the one Prince." Without an ultimate authority over and above all princes, Dante contends, there would be no mechanism to resolve disputes between princes, none of whom is subject to the others. Thus the world needs "a first and supreme judge whose judgment will either directly or indirectly solve all disputes: he will be the Monarch, or Emperor."

The theory of One King under One God trumps questions of national identity, diversity and plurality. First, it stands in opposition to the sovereign state. If all territorial rulers are accountable to One King, no ruler can be sovereign even within the territory he controls. Second, it mandates uniformity, even subjugation. Historically, for example, those who believed in One King under One God had no doubt that their religious, cultural and social values were superior to those of other nations, particularly the ones that professed a polytheistic mythology. Monotheistic imperialism painted peoples with different belief systems as infidels, pagans and savages, justifying their physical and spiritual suppression. This ideology was later invoked to carry out and defend colonialism.

The idea of One King was problematic even among peoples who believed in One God; the perfect office of One King is easy to create but difficult to fill. Problems inevitably arise not only in selecting a particular monarch to fulfil the role but also in defining the fundamental nature of the role itself. Among Western Christian nations, two claimants sought the office: the pope and the emperor. Presenting himself as God's vice-regent and chief spokesman, the pope claimed the divine right to hold universal sovereignty. The logic was simple. The pope commands the highest authority to interpret the scriptures, to tell good from bad and right from wrong. In close communication with the wisdom of God, the pope possesses a superior spiritual ability to settle difficult moral questions regarding how individual and collective life ought to be lived.

On this theory, therefore, it is asserted that all Christians, including prelates, bishops, knights, kings, queens, and even the emperor must obey the laws of God as interpreted by the pope. Bartolus of Sassoferrato (1314-1357), an Italian jurist, contends that secular princes derive their power from the pope. Asserting that canon law is superior to civil law not only in spiritual matters but in temporal matters as well, Bartolus upholds the universal jurisdiction of the papacy. The pope is thus the one and only head of all mankind.

Not all agreed with this logic of papal supremacy. Dante, for example, argues that the emperor, not the pope, ought to be the One King. Dante asserts that the papacy could not claim a superior right over the empire, since the papacy did not even exist when the empire first flourished in power and glory as the pre-Christian Roman empire. So for Dante the universal empire does not originate with Christianity, as does the papacy and its claims to universal sovereignty.

Dante also questions the sources from which the papacy attempts to derive its supremacy. Nothing in the Old or New Testament commands the papacy to take care of temporal affairs. Nor could the papacy rely upon the universal consent of men to assert its power, since "not only everyone in Africa and Asia but even most inhabitants of Europe revolt at the suggestion." Dante concludes that the emperor derives his authority directly from "the One who is the supreme source of all being, God."

Of course, Dante's logic is as faulty as pro-papal reasoning he criticizes. Tied to material possessions, conquest and political power, the emperor could claim no universal moral authority derived from the scriptures. And even if the emperor could claim divine authority he lacked the aura the pope enjoyed as the vicar of Christ. The emperor could invoke the imperial tradition of the Caesars to assert his superior claim over the One Throne, but the pagan glory of the Caesars would not be as effective as Christianity to unite medieval nations. Moreover, as Suarez points out, "at no time, whether through election or through a just war, has a single emperor subjected to his sway the whole world, or the whole church."

Dante creates the unity of mankind through the medium of one superpower, an idea in harmony with the monotheistic view of the cosmos. The Dantean global order superimposes a just and mighty superpower over all the peoples of the world. This concept however is flawed. If the Dantean superpower is a divine entity, it faces the same criticism that Dante himself levelled at the papacy. A religiously diverse world will not submit to the moral code of any one superpower, regardless of who heads it. If the Dantean empire is a militarily superior entity, there is no guarantee that such a superpower will institute a stable or fair global system. If one superpower uses the global system primarily to advance its own interests, other nations will refuse to obey, raising the risk of global strife and consequent cost of law enforcement.

Even if the power struggle between pope and emperor had yielded a single king, the unity of the Christian world would still have been incomplete. The schism between the Greek and Roman churches seemed beyond repair, as there was little chance the Greek church and its temporal counterpart, the

Byzantine empire, would ever submit to Rome. Moreover, the rulers of Western Europe, despite their ties to the Catholic church, were reluctant to relinquish their sovereignty to the pope. Neither of these impediments were theoretically fatal, however. So when the Roman papacy emerged as a powerful institution in the eleventh century proposing to unite churches and kingdoms under its authority, the concept of universal sovereignty seized hold of the medieval mind.

This concept, however, was not unique to Christianity. More than a century before the coronation of Charlemagne in the holy city of Rome, the rapidly expanding Islamic empire of the seventh century had already instituted the office of One Caliph. Many nations and populations, ranging from Mesopotamians in the east to Egyptians in the west, fell under the rule of One Caliph, supporting the theory that human institutions ought to mirror the monotheistic divine order just as the advocates of One King had sought to do in Western Europe.

The idea of One Caliph had its own problems. Even if the idea was politically sound and consonant with the teachings of Islam, practical difficulties still remained. The procedural question of who should be the One Caliph became a source of friction among Muslims soon after prophet Mohammad's death. As a result, three of the first four caliphs were slain in political warfare. The Muslim community, the *Umma*, was later divided between Shias and Sunnis, each group arguing for a different method of succession to the all-inclusive office the prophet held during his life.[1] Thus the idea of One Caliph, intended to tie the entire Muslim community together into one politico-spiritual entity, suffered a serious setback early in Islamic history. In addition to the feud over the method of succession, the *Umma*, divided into tribes and nations ignored the teachings of One God commanding unity beyond tribal and geographical boundaries.

To counter the imperial ambition of successive caliphates and to contain the spread of Islamic faith and dominion, the idea of one unified Western empire encouraged the pooling of resources to establish a strong, common defense. But power politics in the West could not transcend the grand contest between pope and emperor. The papacy enjoyed times of glory when kings and emperors, to legitimize their rule and save their souls, submitted to the supreme father. At other times the earthly lords resisted, defied and even humiliated the pope. The conflict between pope and emperor on the one hand, and between Christians and Muslims on the other, exposed the difficulties and dangers of atempting to institute universal sovereignty. Dante's vision of mirroring divine likeness in temporal affairs carried poetic power but in real life bred war and contorted values of diversity, tolerance and local government

Some ideas, universal sovereignty among them, live well beyond their practical usefulness. Despite persistent failure, the idea of One Empire under

---

1. The Shias sought to keep the caliphate in the prophet's family, whereas the Sunnis adopted a method of succession that included a mix of democracy and appointment.

One King under One God continued to stir imagination in parts of the world influenced by Judaism, Christianity and Islam. In contrast to Hindu and Chinese kingdoms, which remained confined to their historic boundaries, Islamic and Christian empires aspired to dominate the world.

Historical developments, seemingly unleashed by the forces of political polytheism, shattered the dream of universal sovereignty. While Muslims failed to create a new political theory to replace the dying institution of the caliphate, the Protestant movement transformed Western Europe by repudiating the historic notions of one church or one empire. Faith was privatized, eliminating the need for any central, interpretive bureaucracy between the believer and God and perhaps planting the seed of individual entrepreneurship. The ages-old bond between temporal rulers and the Roman papacy snapped, dissociating the prince from the pope. Political power was territorialized, weakening the institution of the mighty emperor. As a result, most of Western Europe under the influence of Protestantism was prepared to banish the idea of One King under One God from its political theories, paving the way for the advent of the sovereign state.

At this critical juncture in Western European history, Grotius provides a powerful critique of universal sovereignty associated with the idea of One King under One God. Without discarding the concept of One God, Grotius rejects unity as the constitutive principle of a world imbued with religious and national diversity. For Grotius, who witnessed the Thirty Years War, the concept of universal sovereignty in all forms was anachronistic, futile and destructive, unable to unite Western Europe, let alone the world. Therefore, his theory of international law embraces a pluralistic vision of the community of nations, each different in ethnicity, culture and religion. To him a more realistic world would be composed of sovereign states in the image of a polytheistic order under which many and different gods contend with each other to settle the issues of war and peace. Grotius works with the world as it is, without forcing it to conform to a theological belief in constitutive unity.

But to construct such a pluralistic world, Grotius must first conceptually dismantle the notion of universal sovereignty. Arguing for the separation of church and empire, Grotius seeks to confine the church to the spiritual realm. Bishops, he points out, have no right to use force to expand the power of the church. Since rule by compulsion is derived from human powers, it is the right of kings, not bishops. For the truth of its teachings to be accepted, the church must persuade rather than coerce; no religious empire can lawfully be imposed on unwilling subjects. This criticism was directed at the involvement of the papacy in religious wars raging in Europe. But the idea itself was not new; the principle of persuasion that Grotius advocates was also consonant with the 1555 Augsburg Compromise that housed both Catholic and Lutheran faiths within the German empire.

Grotius, however, does not confine his analysis of universal sovereignty to the rather narrow gap between Protestants and Catholics. He also addresses the position taken by some that the church has universal sovereignty not merely over Christians of all denominations but "over the peoples of the hitherto unknown parts of the earth."[2] Invoking the authority of St. Paul, Grotius demonstrates that even the apostle did not claim "the right to judge those who are outside the bounds of Christendom." Even if the church lawfully undertakes missionary work to spread the word of God to the peoples of the world, it cannot do so by "the sword and the scourge" without violating the basic teachings of Christianity.[3] Men of wisdom, Grotius points out, condemned Justinian's conversion of the Samaritans to Christianity by force and threat. In short, Grotius provides a powerful indictment of the use of religious compulsion as a method of subjugating non-believers and promoting universal sovereignty.

Grotius further questions the subjugation of those who deny monotheism and God's exclusive sovereignty over all the universe. To spell out his position, Grotius makes a distinction between the theological tenets of Christianity and what he calls "crimes against God." He unequivocally asserts that the church has no authority to use force to impose its doctrines on dissidents. With respect to crimes against God, however, Grotius makes an exception. In almost all ages and among all known peoples, he states, two ideas have been universally accepted: There is a deity (but not necessarily only one), and the deity cares for the affairs of men. Since these religious ideas are fundamental to all human communities, those who subvert them may be restrained in the name of human society. In the name of crimes against God, Grotius thus articulates a fundamental principle now known as *jus cogens*. This principle recognizes that certain rules of behavior are so universal in nature that no community should be allowed to violate them.[4]

Having identified the principle of *jus cogens*, however, Grotius is reluctant to actually apply it to punish crimes against God. The specific crimes against God Grotius proposes to prohibit by force are so abstract in concept and weak in content that he practically eliminates the jurisdiction of the church to wage any religious war. He admits that the idea that "God is, and is One, and is the creator of all things" constitutes true religion common to all ages. But he denies the right to wage war against those who repudiate strict monotheism. The church, Grotius believes, cannot lawfully invoke universal sovereignty over those who worship the powers of the sun (e.g. American Indians), or over those who make gods out of images and animals (e.g. Hindus), or over those who worship the souls of their beloved ancestors (e.g. the Japanese).

By excluding vast populations of diverse faiths from the jurisdiction of the Roman church, Grotius sees the world in its full complexity. Citing the Greek

---

2. This was a reference to the Iberian conquests in the Americas which resulted in the forcible conversion of the American Indians to the Catholic faith.
3. Many religions formally prohibit force in matters of belief. The Quran, for example, clearly states: "There is no compulsion in religion."
4. Under contemporary international law, crimes against humanity constitute the rules of *jus cogens*. For example, no state may lawfully commit genocide or practice slavery.

philosopher Philo and the Roman rhetorician Cicero, Grotius makes a simple observation: to each man his religion seems the best. This implies that each faith, ranging from monotheism to polytheism, has dedicated followers who wish to practice their faith without interference and who will bear arms for the right to do so. A principle of universal tolerance of all religions is therefore conducive to peace, whereas universal sovereignty asserted by any religion leads to war.

These views were essential for the recognition of sovereign states in non-Christian lands, without which international law would be confined to Western Europe. Non-Christian nations would not submit to the authority of the Roman pope or the German emperor. Nor would they abandon their religions in favor of Roman Catholicism. To accommodate diverse religions within the fold of international law, Grotius offers a system in which peoples may practice different faiths without fear of external interference or aggression. A peaceful discourse among the religions of the world could still take place, advancing mutual understanding and laying the foundation for a common human civilization. But no nation ought to be coerced to alter or abandon its belief system. Nor should any religion place itself above all others, directing its followers to fight infidels, pagans or savages.[5]

In equally strong terms, Grotius disputes the secular notion of one superpower. The very title "universal empire," Grotius states, is absurd. The proposition that the Roman emperor is the lord of the world presupposes that he has "the right of ruling over even the most distant and hitherto unknown peoples." Associated with the Dutch East India company, an enterprise engaged in exploring the distant lands of Asia, Grotius knew that the real world was much larger and more complicated than the world medieval men had in mind when they conceived the "sacred" idea of One King under One God. Universal empire, Grotius argues, is not a real entity containing all of the parts and peoples of the world. It is merely an expression "in hyperbole, or in high praise." Similar expressions have been used, Grotius further explains, to describe Judaea (the area now known as the West Bank) as the world and Jerusalem as the center of the earth.

Exposing the earthly nature of the German empire, Grotius demonstrates that the emperor's right to his possessions is not sacrosanct. Many events may cause the empire to shrink in size. The emperor may lose a war, as many did, conceding to the victor conquered lands that formerly belonged to the empire. The emperor may simply relinquish control over possessions within his imperial jurisdiction. Likewise, the emperor may transfer territories by treaties to other nations or kings. Portions of the empire, once subject to the central authority, may obtain *de facto* autonomy or declare independence. Grotius uses these

5. In the seventeenth century, these ideas did not sit well with the Roman church, which insisted that its faith was the only true one. Accordingly, *De Jure Belli ac Pacis* was placed on the papal index of blasphemous books.

examples not only to show the inherent frailty of the German empire but also to demonstrate, at a more conceptual level, how even a single superpower with aspirations to universal dominion is not exempt from political realities.[6]

Furthermore, Grotius opposes Dante's argument that one emperor ought to rule the entire world. To demonstrate the defect of a single world government, Grotius makes a practical argument: "For as a ship may attain to such a size that it cannot be steered, so also the number of inhabitants and the distance between places may be so great as not to tolerate a single government." This pragmatic approach counters the mystical idea of universal sovereignty, exposing the difficulty one superpower would face in controlling all the peoples and places of the world. It also highlights the usefulness of intimate local governments as more appropriate entities to regulate the affairs of their communities.[7] This simple truth was obvious to Grotius, who lived in a century in which German princes within the empire had become even more determined to amplify their independence from the emperor.

In rejecting the Dantean concept of one superpower, Grotius makes a fundamentally different assumption: the world must still achieve harmony, but it should do so by creating a system of international law. Since no stable global order can rest on the might of one superpower or the divine code of one specific religion, stability must flow from the rule of law, emerging from the shared wisdom of the peoples of the world and the mutual consent of sovereign states that, through a deliberative process, recognize and construct rules of international behavior.

Grotius's own life experiences contributed to his thinking. As a Protestant, he was disinclined to accept a vision of global order under the leadership of the Roman pope. As a Dutchman, he was unwilling to concede to the German empire even vague sovereignty over his beloved Holland. But it would be a mistake to make too much of these existential factors in evaluating his theory of international law. Any vision that withstands the test of time cannot be reduced to the personal circumstances of its author. Ideas that live, as Grotius's have, must be larger than their creator.

Closely related to the idea of universal sovereignty is the notion of a chosen people, a notion that also has done tremendous harm to human harmony. Many religious communities assert a sense of inherent superiority, believing God has chosen them to be the exclusive rulers and inheritors of the earth. Sometimes even within a single religion, a certain theological group claims a superior, God-given authority to be the exclusive custodian of the faith, destined to lead the faithful toward the right course. This sense of superiority inspires these religious groups to assert their moral, legal, even military authority over others.

---

6. The recent disintegration of the Soviet empire demonstrates the point.
7. Recall that Grotius advocated the sovereign rights of Holland against the central authority of the United Provinces.

Nor is the notion of the chosen people confined to religious communities. Some secular communities claim a similar superior right to rule the world.[8] They assert this right on the basis of wealth, military power, ancient glory or race. Dante, for example, maintains "that it was by right, not by usurpation, that the Roman people acquired that monarchical office over other men which is called the empire." This is so, Dante insists, because the Roman people are "the noblest beneath the heavens." This is indeed an ironic assertion, since the rulers of the Holy Roman Empire, whom Dante defends in his treatise as the masters of the world, were mostly Frankish rather than Roman in origin.

The idea of the "chosen people" becomes deadly when the asserted power flows from the barrel of a gun. Force is used to serve supremacy and supremacy justifies the use of force. Although the imperial enterprise in Europe drew its power from a mystical mix of religion and materialism, the Iberian conquests in the Americas set a new precedent for mixing religious conviction with deadly force. The Spanish *conquistadors* came to the Americas equipped with superior military technology and strength. But they were motivated as much by religion as by imperial ambition to subdue, even massacre, the native, pagan populations whom they called the *Indios*. Their zeal caused a direct clash between a religious imperial army conquering in the name of universal sovereignty and native peoples whose first loyalty was to their tribal chiefs and beloved land.

The concept of universal empire, for ages confined to Europe, was now employed to subjugate distant lands and peoples. Driven partly by the logic of universal sovereignty, Western kings and queens sought to reign over everything in the world. The constitutive principle of unity was thus extended to all the peoples of the world. The emperor or the pope must not only resist the advance of the Ottomans, he must also bless the invasion of hitherto unknown parts of the world to spread the word of One God and expand the empire. Moreover, the presentation of faith to the pagans of foreign lands must be resolute; force must be used to overcome any resistance from the savages. Such was the reasoning of sixteenth century slavery and colonialism.

Colonialism was thus an extension of the medieval concept of universal sovereignty. Of course, gold and silver found in the Americas added a commercial dimension to the quest for spiritual-temporal empire. Although arbitrary killings of native Americans, even in the name of One God, occasionally generated criticism and pangs of conscience, the idea of universal empire was too powerful to be modified in the name of compassion. Coming at a time when the empire was beginning to dissolve in Europe, the conquest of the Americas was the desperate attempt of a dying world view to evolve rather than face extinction.

---

8. "We're the only country complicated enough, sophisticated enough, big enough to lead the human race." Newt Gingrich, Speaker of the United States House of Representative (June 8, 1995).

This extention of the concept of universality was not without its critics. Francisco de Vitoria condemned the murder, expropriation and exploitation of the *Indios* in the name of Christianity. He further concluded that neither the pope nor the emperor had any inherent right to universal sovereignty, much less dominion over the non-Christian populations of the New World. Vitoria's lectures on the subject attracted over a thousand students, causing unprecedented commotion and condemnation. He was denounced "for doing damage to the papacy, the emperor and to Spain."

Relying in part upon the teachings of Vitoria, Grotius disputes all claims of universal sovereignty over the peoples of the world. "Not less iniquitous is it to desire by arms to subdue other men, as if they deserved to be enslaved." The notion that some people are slaves by nature is invoked not only to rationalize slavery but to unjustly deprive such "inferior" people of their lands and possessions. "For the exercise of ownership," Grotius argues, "neither moral nor religious virtue, nor intellectual excellence is a requirement." Any magnification of the empire by subjugation of men and women allegedly lacking faith, virtue or reason, is wrong. "Equally shameless is it to claim for oneself by right of discovery what is held by another, even though the occupant may be wicked, may hold wrong views about God, or may be dull of wit." Likewise, the paternalistic theory that inferior people, were they enlightened, would willingly surrender themselves for their own benefit does not confer an automatic right on every conqueror to subjugate such people. Even slaves by nature, Grotius insists, must have a 'free choice' to determine what is best for them. Thus Grotius rejects colonialism as a lawful means to expand the boundaries of any empire.[9]

This criticism of colonialism imagined a future in which the colonized peoples of the world would be able to assert the right of self-determination, demanding independent sovereign statehood. In theory, Grotius perfected the concept of the sovereign state in the seventeenth century. In practice, sovereign states first emerged after the peace of Westphalia was concluded. But a fully fledged world of free and independent sovereign states on all continents of the world, embracing even the rights of the colonized to independence, would not come into being until three centuries later, after the Second World War. The benefits seventeenth century Europe derived from slavery, colonialism and dispossession of native populations were too substantial to relinquish for the sake of a moral view of the world that demanded respect for all peoples. Moreover, the European monarchs were preoccupied with territorial possessions rather than people. Accordingly at the time, the question of whether all peoples everywhere have the right to institute a popular form of government was somewhat premature if not hypothetical.

---

9. Grotius vigorously argued for free trade and free oceans, supporting legal and commercial claims of the Dutch East India Company, called VOC. Even though the Dutch and the British commercial enterprises later turned into colonialism, one need not argue that Grotius, by his support for the VOC, condoned any form of colonialism.

2. POPULAR SOVEREIGNTY

Medieval philosophies extolled the virtues of the monarchical form of government. Derived from the concept of One God as the arbiter of the cosmos, One King as the head of the world made sense in an age when human institutions were considered best when they resembled the divine order. Thus the theocratic belief that the monarch in power had God's approval was entrenched in medieval political theories. However, a difficult question remained: what procedure is most consistent with God's design to find a replacement if the monarch dies, abdicates or becomes unable to rule? Several options are available: the monarch could be selected by the powerful princes in the community, chosen in accordance with primogeniture or some other hereditary principle, or elected by the community as a whole.

Regardless of the method by which the next ruler was chosen, faith in divine right could still be maintained. For example, it could be said that God blessed a certain family with the authority to lead the community, thus legitimizing hereditary monarchy. It could similarly be maintained that God inspired the electoral college in its choice of a ruler, thus legitimizing the elective process. The theocratic belief that no ruler could obtain or retain the office without God's consent could even be considered consistent with popular sovereignty. This is so because no community could act against God's will to elect the ruler. If no event could occur without God's will, even a successful rebellion or deposition could be justified as an act of God. Thus, in an odd way, the notion of popular sovereignty can be derived from divine law by the simple assertion that nothing occurs without the will of God.

Whatever its source, divine or secular, popular sovereignty had many legal implications. One implication involves the contract of subjection, the idea that the legal relationship between ruler and community is contractual in nature. By the force of such a contract, the community may lawfully retain the exclusive right to elect, recall or remove the ruler. Furthermore, the community may require the ruler to act and legislate in accordance with the wishes of the community, forcing the elected ruler to remain accountable to the community during his tenure in office. These attributes of popular sovereignty were known and discussed in the political literature of the middle ages. But even as late as the seventeenth century, the idea of popular sovereignty had few followers. Even Grotius was skeptical of its efficacy.

Grotius rejects the notion that the people are always the ultimate custodians of sovereignty. Care must be taken, however, to understand the precise reach of his position. Grotius is not opposed to popular sovereignty. Nor does he claim that popular sovereignty is inherently evil, never to be the basis of government. Rather, he contests the overly-demanding notion "that everywhere and without exception sovereignty resides in the people." In fact, Grotius derives several arguments from the notion of popular sovereignty itself to demonstrate that non-democratic forms of government can be equally legitimate. Even if the people are sovereign, Grotius argues, they can still renounce their sovereignty in favor of some powerful individual, particularly in cases of necessity or emergency such as famine or foreign aggression. This derogation of the exercise of popular sovereignty could be conditional, temporary or permanent. Thus popular sovereignty, or self-rule, is a much a larger concept than democracy.

A limited concept of self-rule establishes a democratic form of government under which elected officials seek reconfirmation of their authority through periodic elections. Under a more flexible concept of self-rule, the people are free to institute democracy but are not required to do so. They are also free to establish even non-democratic forms of government, such as hereditary monarchies, under which they relinquish their right to choose future rulers. "Just as, in fact, there are many ways of living, one being better than another, and out of so many ways of living each is free to select that which he prefers," Grotius advises, "so also a people can select the form of government which it wishes."

Of course, different forms of self-rule might be compared, exposing their relative merits and demerits. One might claim that one form of self-rule is better than another. There might even be a consensus that a particular form of self-rule is the best in the world. But the legitimacy of self-rule, Grotius argues, "is not to be measured by the superior excellence of this or that form of government, but by its free choice." Under the Grotian calculus, the broader construction of self-rule is a higher principle than democracy. If a nation freely repudiates democracy and chooses a monarchical form of government, it has legitimately exercised popular sovereignty. It appears that Grotius uses the concept of self-rule in a more fundamental sense, equating it with the principle of political independence – a norm now shrined in the United Nations Charter.

The Grotian principle of self-rule is a great contribution to international legal theory. In an era in which the monarchy was still considered the best form of government due to its correspondence to the divine order under One God, self-rule or political independence introduced a measure of philosophical tolerance for many and different forms of government. This was a grand shift from political monotheism to political polytheism, accepting the simple fact that not all nations, when given a free choice, institute one and the same form of government. This accommodation of diversty in the forms of government was in direct opposition to the self-righteousness underlying "One Empire under One King under One God."

Grotius, however, does not adhere even to the principle of self-rule. Providing a comprehensive critique of popular sovereignty, Grotius concludes that in the real world not all forms of government are derived from popular sovereignty. First, Grotius quarrels with the very notion of popular sovereignty, stating that there is no such thing as pure democracy, a true and complete reflection of popular sovereignty. This is so, he argues, since "no republic has ever been found to be so democratic that in it there are not some persons, either very poor people or foreigners, also women and youths, who are excluded from (the political process.)" Grotius points to these practices of exclusion in concluding that popular sovereignty, in its full reach and effect, would dictate the inclusion of many groups into the democratic process, groups that power elites are unwilling to embrace. Thus democracy cannot realistically be universally required.

Second, Grotius argues that a logical extension of popular sovereignty would further require that no territorial transfer be made without the approval of its inhabitants, a mandate he wishes to avoid. Even in Grotius's own time, many territories had been shuttled back and forth between kings, nations and empires without the consent of the people who lived in them. Grotius's own homeland had been so transferred; upon the death of Charles the Bold, the duchy of Burgundy, including Holland, was given to the German empire. Holland and other Dutch provinces then came under Spanish rule, against which there was a prolonged Dutch resistance, a struggle with which Grotius was closely associated. This constant shifting of Holland from one dominion to another took place without the consent of its people. Drawing on the experience of his own country, Grotius realized that a strict devotion to self-rule implied that "all these territorial adjustments must be set aside as null and void." Such an application of popular sovereignty, he concluded, was a recipe for war, not peace.

Third, Grotius argues that if the people are free to choose a form of government, they are then equally free to renounce self-rule. Accordingly, the people may accept domestic dictatorships, alien domination, even slavery. Just as some people are suited to slavery, Grotius declares, "so there are some peoples so constituted that they understand better how to be ruled than to rule." In view of their slavish nature, some people prefer a form of government in which they have no voice. This is a logical deduction from the questionable assumption that some people are indeed slaves by nature. To any keen mind, the concept of slavery by consent is no more than a contradiction in terms, a tool of oppression often used by those who seek to clothe naked acts of subjugation with philosophical legitimacy. And Grotius had a keen mind. Still he used every available argument, even yielding to logical extremism, to rebut popular sovereignty. In other parts of his treatise, however, Grotius disparages dubious generalizations about human nature, asserting that "No one is born free, no one a slave; it is after birth that fortune has imposed these distinctions upon individuals."

Fourth, Grotius draws an analogy between private property and public authority, arguing that just like private property, public authority can be obtained by lawful use of force. A broad reading of this concept could lead one to defend many oppressive forms of government imposed on conquered nations. Difficult questions then arise, such as whether the occupied nation automatically loses all right to self-government, whether the occupied nation may lawfully resist a form of government imposed by the occupier, and whether the occupier may lawfully dictate a constitution denying the occupied nation the right to repeal it in the future, even after the occupation ends.

These questions had a different legal and moral context in the early seventeenth century than they do today. Grotius seems to concede in theory that the victor has some lawful authority to impose foreign rule on the occupied nation, particularly if the occupied nation started an unlawful war and lost. But caution must be used in understanding the precise limits of the theoretical argument Grotius makes to refute the universal application of popular sovereignty.

At other places in his treatise, Grotius is much more skeptical of extending such unlimited rights to conquerors. For example, Grotius disapproves of the extension of national borders by armed force. Only a lawful war, which must satisfy strict criteria, provides a legal basis to conquer and subdue other nations. A war to make peace by putting down an ongoing criminal mischief could be lawful. But even in such wars, Grotius warns, moderation in the acquisition of sovereignty is preferable. A greater good is achieved if the conquerors mingle with the vanquished rather than segregating themselves; similarly, it is better if the defeated enemies are made citizens rather than serfs or slaves. It is an act of humanity as well as prudence, Grotius argues, if the victor allows conquered kings or peoples to retain their sovereign power. Even when all sovereignty is denied to the occupied nation, "it is still possible to leave to them their own laws, customs, and officials." And the conquered may never be coerced to give up their faith or worship. By imposing these restrictions even on lawful conquest, Grotius weakens the moral foundation of the medieval inclination to automatically deny self-rule, citizenship and liberty to a subjugated nation.[10]

From this discussion, one may conclude that Grotius was confused, or at least inconsistent, as he straddled the fence, approving and disapproving popular sovereignty. However, his ideas may be reconciled by drawing a distinction between domestic rule and foreign rule. If popular sovereignty is denied in one's own state, it poses no inherent danger to survival of that state. But when self-rule is denied to a foreign people, the foreign state faces the risk of absorption by the occupier. Alien domination thus poses a direct threat to the very existence of the subjugated state. Furthermore, domination in the form of colonialism or conquest increases international disorder and instability. Both alien domination and domestic dictatorship deny popular sovereignty, but the risks to global order are measurably different. As an international law theoretician, therefore, Grotius is less willing to deny all forms of popular sovereignty with respect to foreign nations.

Even a superficial reading of the works of Grotius reveals that the ideas of popular sovereignty and self-rule were close to his heart.[11] Yet he realized no

---

10. Recall that the Spanish conquerors in the Americas used the right of conquest to its most oppressive limits. This might be contrasted with the British rule in India under which considerable liberty was left intact for both Hindu and Muslim populations, including a measure of sovereignty for more than three hundred local princes.
11. After all, he lived in a country which was still striving to seek independence from Spanish rule.

peaceful international order could be built on the strict requirement of popular sovereignty. Scarcely any government in the seventeenth century could have been described as democratic in the modern sense of the word. Even in nations where monarchy had broad social approval, not all monarchs were fully accountable directly to the people or even to an electoral college. In a world in which the princes and not the people were the social engineers, any advocacy of popular sovereignty would have been idle if not dangerous talk.

Related to the question of popular sovereignty is the concept of benevolent government. If rulers derive their authority from the will of the people, it is easier to insist that all government be constituted for the benefit of the governed. Grotius concedes that in most cases the benefit of the governed is indeed the primary purpose of the ruler.

But just as Grotius is unwilling to accept popular sovereignty as the sole basis of all government, so is he reluctant to recognize that the ruler must always act for the good of the people. Again Grotius invokes pragmatic logic, analyzing the world as it was to demonstrate that not all governments are constituted for the well-being of the people. Some governments exist only for the benefit of those who govern while others are instituted for the mutual advantage of both the ruler and the ruled. Thus no universal practice compels the ruler to be benevolent under each and every form of government.

Furthermore, Grotius denies the people the right to disobey rulers who govern badly. Quoting Tacitus, Grotius preaches an almost fatalistic attitude toward government: "Endure, endure the luxury or avarice of those who govern, just as you put up with unfruitlessness or too heavy rains, and other scourges of nature. There will be faults so long as there shall be men." Quoting Euripides, Grotius advises the people: "Crass blundering of them who rule must be endured." When there is a difference of opinion between the ruler and the ruled over what is right and what is wrong, anarchy will ensue if each side asserts the power to defend what is right or correct what is wrong. Valuing law and order over justice, Grotius concludes that in matters relating to the state, the moral goodness or badness of an action should be left to the judgment of the ruler.

In cases, however, where the people have conferred only a limited sovereignty upon the ruler, they can lawfully demand that the ruler not exceed the scope of his constitutional authority. Consistent with the manner of his time, Grotius further concedes, at least in theory, that any command of the ruler contrary to the law of nature or to the commandments of God should not be carried out. Even here, however, Grotius prefers that the people endure the unjust ruler rather than resist him by force. Quoting Augustine and Homer, Grotius points out that the right of rebellion is limited in civil society. If the right of resistance is boundless, the state cannot exist.

The idea that the ruler is under no obligation to institute a benevolent government accountable to the people has had a significant impact on the development of international law. Accordingly, the activity of sovereign states is divided into two distinct realms, one containing matters of foreign concern, the other involving domestic matters. Matters of foreign policy, such as when and how war ought to be waged, are subject to the law of nations. But issues such as whether a ruler treats his subjects well or whether the people approve the form of government are regarded as domestic matters, concerns outside the scope of international law.

This exclusion of the people from the domain of global law was, in some ways, a new historical development. Under the concept of universal sovereignty founded upon religion, the princes and the people alike were proper subjects of the universal order, since the church had direct jurisdiction to make rules governing both individual and collective conduct. How individuals should behave in their homes and communities was the concern of the church. Similarly, whether the princes were just to their subjects and worked for their welfare were also matters over which the church could exercise its supreme authority. If the ruler was unjust or tyrannical, he could be excommunicated and his people released from allegiance to him. Of course, this theory was flawed to the extent that not all peoples of the world shared the values of the Roman church. Nonetheless, it imagined a world in which peoples, not just princes, would be integrated into a comprehensive order of shared values and in which no ruler would be free to impose his or her arbitrary will on the people.

The seventeenth century world, however, was too diverse, too fragmented, too self-righteous to forge common values for the protection of the people against their rulers. So to accommodate diverse cultures and concepts of justice, Grotius proposes a global order limited in scope to relations between states. Each state is set free to practice within its boundaries whatever system best reflects its values and aspirations. No state is allowed to dictate another's domestic policy. On the basis of this logic, domestic matters are placed outside the domain of international law. This bifurcation of foreign and domestic matters deprives the people of direct rights under international law. As a result, how the rulers treat their people is a matter relegated to the domestic jurisdiction of the sovereign state.

One might argue that Grotius's theory of international law leads to tyranny, subjugation and injustice, since it obligates no government to protect the basic rights of its people. This accusation has some merit. It must be remembered, however, that the mission Grotius set for himself was to develop an international legal order in which all nations of the world could participate without adhering to any single theory of government or justice. Grotius was no revolutionary who wished to tear the world loose from its roots. He was a pragmatic man who hoped to create an international system without disturbing too many kings and nations.

To achieve maximum participation of nations in the global order, Grotius thus repudiates democracy as a central value of international law. The principle of self-rule is introduced but not fully integrated into the concept of state sovereignty. Instead, a different norm surfaces from his theory: If a government is effectively in control of the people, no further inquiry is permitted to determine whether the government is democratic or benevolent. This norm clarifies the point that in order for a sovereign state to exist it must have an effective government. But whether that government is just or benevolent is a domestic matter, outside the domain of international law. Thus effective rather than just government emerged as a key element in the structural definition of the sovereign state.

3. State Sovereignty

The State, not universal empire or the people, "is the common subject of sovereignty." Thus Grotius proposes a global order in which states recognize, create and observe the rules of international behavior – a paradigm in opposition to both universal and popular sovereignty. This formulation of state sovereignty is designed to disassemble the era of empires in which the desire to conquer more land and subdue more people was defended in the name of the universal empire, an empire many believed God had already conferred upon the emperor. Moreover, the notion of sovereignty is detached not only from the people but also from the person of the ruler. Accordingly, neither the people nor the ruler is sovereign. In their stead, sovereignty is vested in the state. What, then, is a state?

Before examining this question, a key conceptual difference between universal and state sovereignty may be noted. Universal sovereignty presupposes its own validity. It exists *a priori*, even before the actual empire is built or enlarged. It neither depends upon nor derive itself from any specific territory. The logic of state sovereignty, on the other hand, is simple: state sovereignty cannot exist without actual control of a territory. This logic was detrimental to the claims of universal empire that asserted sovereignty over the entire earth without ever actually controling more than a limited territory.

Notwithstanding its future viability, the Grotian blueprint for an international legal system comprised of sovereign states was originally only speculative; it surfaced at a time when the idea of a single superpower was still theoretically tenable. Neither the emperor nor the pope had yet abandoned the medieval desire for a universal empire consisting of vast kingdoms and territories. Therefore, the success of the Grotian theory, presented in the midst of the Thirty Years War, depended on whether the claimants to universal sovereignty failed.

History sides with Grotius. By recognizing Protestantism as coequal to Roman Catholicism, the treaties of Westphalia dismantled papal supremacy. And by granting German princes the right to conduct foreign affairs without prior imperial approval, the treaties more or less established a key element of the sovereign state, that is, the state must have the competence to conduct independent foreign relations.

The power of Grotian theory resides in its bold vision of a horizontal order in which no one nation is superior to any other. State sovereignty challenges political monotheism, which wishes to construct one universal empire under one prince. It derives its vigor from political polytheism, under which the diverse princes and peoples of the world conduct their communal lives within the confines of their sovereign territories without external interference.

At the outset it must be noted that state sovereignty is no prescription for the atomization of the human community. Nonetheless, it offers a powerful conceptual and practical medium to conduct interstate affairs and maintain global peace. From their respective bases of equality, dignity and independence, states willingly pool their sovereignties to create a global order in accordance with the principles of natural law rooted in the common intelligence of the human race. This order is called international law.

According to classical international law, a sovereign state must possess four elements: a territory, a people, an effective government and the competence to conduct independent foreign relations. These elements are essential to distinguish sovereign states from uninhabited and dependent territories. An uninhabited territory is not a state since no entity without people can have the legal status of a state. Likewise, a people without a territory can institute no sovereign state. Even if a people occupy a territory, they must have an effective government to enjoy statehood. Finally, no dependent territory having a people and an effective government is a sovereign state until it musters the wherewithal to freely conduct foreign relations. The four elements must be simultaneously present to create a sovereign state. An entity that lacks any one of the four essential characteristics fails to acquire sovereignty under classical international law.

The four elements constituting the sovereign state were introduced into customary international law long after Grotius died. Nonetheless, all four elements are present in his theory. To perfect the concept of the sovereign state, Grotius relied upon the works of many philosophers, legal scholars, theologians and poets. No one scholar, not even Grotius, can be credited with inventing the idea of the sovereign state. Each of the four elements of the sovereign state emerged from an unknown mix of historical events and theoretical speculations. Nonetheless, the synthesis of otherwise scattered ideas Grotius provides is unique. Historically, Grotius wished to dismantle the era of empires that claimed authority over otherwise independent nations and territories. Theoretically, he imagined an international legal order in which states are independent of each other. It is therefore important to examine how Grotius constructs the four elements of the sovereign state.

In presenting the first two elements, Grotius explains that state sovereignty is customarily extended over two kinds of subject matter: the territory and the people. Thus the existence of both the territory and the people is a *sine qua non* of state sovereignty.

To clarify the concept of territory as an essential element of the sovereign state, Grotius invokes Seneca and others to distinguish between ownership and sovereignty. Ownership is tied to the estate; sovereignty is tied to the territory. The land an individual owns constitutes a private estate. Public estates are the land the state owns. All private and public estates within a state's borders jointly make up the territory of the state. With respect to public lands, the state possesses both ownership and sovereignty while over private property the state has sovereignty without ownership. Thus even if every inch of land is privately owned, the *territory* remains subject to state sovereignty. This is so because the same land can be both an estate and a piece of the state's territory, simultaneously containing the rights of both the owner and the state. The ownership of an estate may be transferred from one person to another, even from the individual to the state or vice versa. But changes in ownership do not affect state sovereignty over the territory.

The concept of territorial sovereignty might be derived from the feudal principle that the king is the ultimate owner of all land, a principle that served a useful purpose in supplying services and funds for many kings. Grotius's concept of territorial sovereignty, however, is not inextricably bound to the feudal concept of land. By separating sovereignty from ownership, Grotius provides a cogent basis for the state to assert its authority without claiming to own the land. Territorial sovereignty is an overlay on the concept of ownership. Its universal appeal as an organizing principle lies in the simple assertion that "the state is the sovereign over its territory."

Just as the owner of an estate may lawfully mark out and fence his property, so a state may delineate and guard its territory. Just as an owner may exclude trespassers from the estate, so a state may exclude foreigners from its territory. Even though private ownership and state sovereignty coexist in law, they may or may not be in harmony.[12] Invoking the concept of ownership, one may cultivate one's land, lease it or sell it. Yet the estate's owner is not free to do whatever he pleases on the land he owns. In fact, the owner's rights over the estate are in some measure subject to the state's territorial sovereignty. The state may lawfully forbid the owner from committing any crime on the estate. Ordinarily, an estate's owner is free to invite any person to his property, without interference from the state. Yet one whose estate is located on the border of a territory may be prevented from allowing foreigners to enter his property. This is so because in this case the state's right derived from territorial sovereignty is superior to the owner's right derived from estate ownership.

The inclusion of people into the definition of the sovereign state was conceptually easier. Henry Maine (1822-1888) explains "that during a large part of what we usually term modern history no such conception was entertained as that of *territorial sovereignty.* Sovereignty was not associated with dominion over a portion or subdivision of the earth." Before the era of empires, sovereignty was most often derived from the people – a common sense and pragmatic notion tying the tribe to the chief, the people to the ruler. The king was

---

12. For example, the state may appropriate private estate for public use. It may also regulate the use of private property, severely limiting traditional rights and privileges of ownership. Whether the state can take private property without adequate, prompt and effective compensation has been a controversy in both municipal and international law.

king of his people, not of his people's lands. In simpler communities, the chief exercised sovereignty derived from a complex mix of personal charisma and popular will. In more institutionalized communities, such as elective and hereditary monarchies, sovereignty was formally derived from the prevailing formula for succession.

Even when determined by complex succession rules, however, the authority to rule was people-oriented. That is why ancient tribes that migrated from place to place in search of sustenance associated sovereignty with no one geographical territory. The sovereign and his laws moved with the tribe, as did their possessions. Among stationary populations, the concept of sovereignty became tied to the territory the population inhabited. Yet sovereignty was exercised over the territory, not derived therefrom.

Even though state sovereignty is incomplete without a people, it does not require that the people be the custodians of sovereignty. This is an important distinction. For Grotius, the existence of a people is a prerequisite for state sovereignty But this idea is not the same as mandate for popular sovereignty. Popular sovereignty requires that the people determine the ruler and the ruler derive his authority from the people. In contrast, state sovereignty is tied to the mere presence of a permanent population. It vests no automatic authority in the people to select a government. So state sovereignty has no logical or legal relationship with popular will. It can exist with or without a popular government. Yet, the people are essential in that no state can lawfully come into existence in an uninhabited territory.[13]

The joining of territory and people into the definition of the sovereign state was innovative. This does not imply, however, that ancient tribes had no concept of territorial boundaries. The acquisition of land had been a constant human drive at both individual and collective levels. From time immemorial, thousands of wars have been waged to conquer people as well as land. The era of feudalism elevated land to the ultimate organizing principle of social, military and political hierarchy. Similarly, the enterprise of colonialism was partly driven by the desire to capture distant territories. If newly found territories were uninhabited, colonialism imported people to inhabit them. To control even more territory, the native people who previously held the land were often dispossessed.

In this ancient and continuing liaison between people and land, the sovereign state further deified the bond between people and territory. Tied to specific territories rather than universal unity of the entire earth, sovereign states were ready to break loose from the era of empires. Territory rather than theology became the new source of authority. No longer could people be sovereign without a territory. In fact, a people without territory, the so-called stateless people, have fewer rights respecting life and liberty. The nomadic era was also

13. Antarctica, with no permanent population, for example, does not qualify to be a state.

over; gypsies and other transient people were distrusted and mistreated, in part because their commitment to a fixed territory was tenuous at best.

Even if the era of sovereign states comes to an end, land will continue to be the chief source of human sustenance; our land defines who we are. Human cultures are rooted in the topology, character and resourcefulness of land. That is why estates and states mark out the land they control, often to the precision of an inch. Fences, walls and borders demonstrate a highly possessive attachment to land, the urge to define and delineate the scope of our respective authorities and identities. They tell a still-evolving story in which, at the present time, estates are used to seclude owners from strangers and states provide a basis to separate nationals from aliens. The sovereign state simply codifies the possessive-compulsive correlation between people and territory.

To highlight the other two elements of the sovereign state, effective government and foreign policy competence, Grotius uses a simple analytical framework under which state sovereignty is correspondingly composed of two distinct attributes. One is the internal attribute, which requires that the sovereign state possess civil power "having its own laws, courts and public officials." Jean Bodin, the French jurist, states that the first and the chief mark of a sovereign prince is the power to give laws to all his subjects. The ability to give laws presumes enforcement authority without which laws lose their efficacy. Citing several Greek sources, Grotius uses examples to explain the scope of civil power that the state may possess: it may render judicial decisions, administer criminal justice, confiscate property and impose the death penalty. The state's authority to institute an effective domestic legal order is thus an essential attribute of internal sovereignty. No state can claim sovereignty if it lacks formal or actual power to make laws; nor can it meaningfully exercise internal sovereignty if it lacks the means to enforce its laws. That is why both Grotian theory and international law require that a territorial entity claiming sovereign statehood have the means of instituting an effective government that can both create and enforce a normative order within the territory it controls.

The other attribute is external, requiring that the sovereign state be able to independently conduct its own foreign relations. Grotius states that the "actions of the sovereign state are not subject to the legal control of another." This simple and elegant definition of sovereignty fully defines the freedom a sovereign state has over its foreign policy. No entity can claim sovereignty if its external relations are dictated by another nation. To make this point clear, Grotius further asserts that a sovereign state must have decision-making authority with respect to "war, peace, the making and abrogation of treaties." Bodin also identifies the external attribute essential to sovereignty: The second mark of sovereignty, he states, is the power to "denounce war or treat of peace." Internal sovereignty alone is thus insufficient to constitute a sovereign state. Only when a piece of territory, whether a new island or a component of an existing empire acquires both internal and external sovereignty can it become a sovereign state.[14]

The combination of internal and external sovereignty was a great theoretical leap toward the era of sovereign states. The idea of internal sovereignty was already available in ancient Greek literature, particularly in the works of Aristotle. The historical events of the seventeenth century dictated that the notion of external sovereignty be added to the brew. The new mixture of internal and external sovereignty provided a simple formula that would eventually be used to divide up the world into sovereign states.

With respect to internal sovereignty, Grotius embraces Aristotle's idea that most perfect state is an association in which families unite into a single people. For Aristotle, the polis (the state) was the final and perfect association. The building blocks in the formation of the Greek state are families and villages; individuals join to make households, households form villages, villages unite and become a polis. This natural progression from the individual to the community is the foundation of the Greek state, which exists for the sake of the good life lived at "the height of full self-sufficiency." Only within the polis could individuals fulfil the promise of their lives. Hence the Greek state, shaped by its own historical dynamics, had already acquired internal sovereignty. Grotius borrows several ideas from the Greeks, including the concept of perfect association and the concomitant idea of internal sovereignty, the capacity to make laws, enforce order and establish courts.

Nonetheless, Grotius adds external sovereignty to the Greek definition of the sovereign state. The sovereign state is not only internally perfect, it is also externally independent. This new attribute is critical in freeing the state from the prevailing notions of imperial and papal supremacy. So historically as well as theoretically, the Grotian state is a further refinement of the Greek state. But the difference is critical. The Greek state is built up from the solitary life of the individual, whereas the Grotian state is built down from the colossus of the empire. The Greek polis is designed to forge a community by aggregating individuals, households and villages; the Grotian state is designed to free such communities from foreign rule by segregating them from the mass of the empire, alien domination and the supremacy of distant lords. The medieval concept of universal empire, still lingering in the seventeenth century, was as big a threat to the idea of "the most perfect society," as were atomistic and tribal tendencies in ancient Greece. The threat to the Greek state came from within, from tribalism; the threat to the Grotian state came from without, from imperialism. Each theoretical construct represented a different historical need. But when the Grotian idea joins with the Greek idea, the sovereign state is complete in both inward and outward forms.

To further clarify the nature of sovereignty, Grotius examines several different scenarios. No state, for example, loses its juridical personality simply

14. Recall that the Peace of Westphalia (1648) authorized each major territorial unit of the empire to make alliances among themselves and with foreign nations.

because its constituent parts have separate governments. Such is the case in a federated state, which exists in a conceptual twilight zone between sovereign states and confederations. A federated state is not a unitary sovereign state, since each federating unit retains at least some self-government and a significant degree of political, social and economic autonomy. Nor is it a perfect association since the people and their mores may vary from one federated unit to another. However, a federation is much more cohesive than a confederation, since each federated unit concedes to the central government more authority than just the power to provide a common defense and regulate commerce. Most important, a federation stands as a single, unified sovereign state to the rest of the world, willing to be counted as a single member of the community of sovereign states.

To distinguish a federated state from a confederation, Grotius depicts the latter as an alliance of many distinct peoples. No confederation is a separate sovereign entity; it is a union in which no participant parts relinquish the right "to retain the status of a perfect state." Ordinarily, legal agreements between sovereign states for war, peace, commerce and trade do not diminish their individual sovereignty. Mutually beneficial treaties among states do not automatically merge the parties into a new state. Sovereign states may therefore combine their efforts to pursue a unified defense or to establish a mutually beneficial economic relationship without compromising their sovereignties. It is unclear, however, whether states continue to retain their individual identities if they pool their sovereignties to institute a single economic market, allowing the free flow of goods, services, capital and labor.

The most intriguing dimension of the Grotian theory is its flexibility. As a theoretician concerned with practical reality, Grotius presents elastic concepts that can withstand both historical and jurisprudential changes. He presupposes a dynamic world in which events determine the fate of sovereign states. Accordingly, Grotius does not argue that once a sovereign state comes into existence, it will continue to exist forever. No sovereign state is a static entity, an inanimate object placed in an immutable world. Rather, it is a dynamic organism in the process of change. It changes in size, character, prestige and influence. In this interminable process of evolution, new states are born; some grow, some decay, and some die. The states' life cycles are rarely identical, but all share a common vulnerablity to the unpredictable upheaval of events.

Grotius offers many examples to explain the dynamic character of the sovereign state. A state grows in size if different communities join to create a larger single state. A true union of two peoples occurs when they voluntarily merge into a single state.[15] But the creation of a larger state is not always founded upon the mutual consent of merging communities. A community may be forced into the fold of a sovereign state by a treaty of cession. A state

15. The recent unification of East and West Germany is a case in point.

may grow in size if its ruler acquires a territory and a people that previously belonged to another sovereign.

Similarly, a single state may be divided either by mutual consent or by the violence of war.[16] "When such a division takes place several sovereignties exist in place of one, with their respective rights over the individual parts."[17] Grotius mentions several ways in which a state will cease to exist. A state may peacefully be dissolved if the people so decide. A forcible extinction of the state occurs if the people are expelled from their state and become so scattered they cannot reunite. Since no state can exist without its people, a state will come to an end if the people are physically exterminated. Similarly, a state will perish if its territory disappears due to natural disaster.

Ordinarily, internal constitutional changes do not extinguish a sovereign state. Yet in some circumstances, if these changes are imposed by an external authority, they do signal the end of the sovereign state. As a result of foreign occupation, for example, state sovereignty ceases to exist if the internal government is discarded, the people are subjugated, and a foreign hand rules the territory. Even if the occupied territory is not merged with that of the occupier, a forcible dissolution of its form of organization indicates that "not even the shadow of statehood" has been left intact. In this prophetic observation lies the general principle that not even the sovereign state is an immutable entity. Whether the sovereign state can mutate into a new entity is a question discussed in part three of this book. For now, suffice it to say that the sovereign state is an organism in the process of change.

The dynamic character of the sovereign state has allowed it to survive not only historical changes, but outlive jurisprudential changes as well. Since natural law dominated jurisprudence in the seventeenth century, Grotius based his theory of state sovereignty in the legitimacy of natural law. While natural law remained the authoritative jurisprudence for many centuries, it nevertheless began to lose prestige with the advent of legal positivism. The positivist revolt against natural law, however, did not challenge the basic concept of the sovereign state. In fact, legal positivism elevated the sovereign state to new heights of prestige and political power, vesting the state with the authority to fashion domestic legal order and participate in the formation of international customs and treaties.

All four elements of the sovereign state remained intact under legal positivism. The weakest link in the elemental structure of the sovereign state was the exclusion of popular will from the notion of effective government. As discussed earlier, Grotius does not require that popular will be the basis of governmental authority. One would think that legal positivism, with its emphasis on

---

16. A case in point is the division of Czechoslovakia. Through a peaceful method, the state was split in two, becoming the Czech Republic and Slovakia. Contrast this with the forcible division of the two Koreas.
17. The dissolution of the Soviet Union, for example, gave birth to fifteen independent states.

human will as the ultimate source of authority, would have sought to correct this normative flaw. But after rejecting the meta-human sources of natural law, legal positivism refused to embrace popular sovereignty as the final, legitimate source of authority. Positive authority instead was lodged in the construct of the sovereign state itself. Consequently, effective rather than popular government continued to be the norm under legal positivism, as it was under the Grotian theory.

Hans Kelsen (1841-1973), for example, describes the sovereign state as a legal order under which individuals are subject to a certain, centralized coercion. He distinguishes the state from pre-state communities by arguing that in the pre-state community rules are made by mutual consent of the people, while laws in the sovereign state are made by a centralized authority that possesses the coercive power to enforce them. The only relationship the people have with the state, Kelsen argues, is based on coercion. Any attempt to find another bond is destined to fail. In the Grotian theory, the state derives its sovereignty from the law of nature; in the Kelsenian theory, which rejects "metaphysics and mysticism," the state derives its sovereignty from the effectiveness of its coercive order.[18] Thus the rise of legal positivism reinforced the concept of the sovereign state.

State sovereignty began to assert itself in the letter of law. While customary international law has long recognized the concept of state sovereignty, eminent treaties of the twentieth century began to preserve the characteristics of the sovereign state in the written word. In 1933, three hundred years after the first publication of Grotius's book on *The Law of War and Peace*, the Montevideo Convention on the Rights and Duties of States reasserts the Grotian doctrine that states are sovereign and juridically equal, regardless of their might. The Convention specifically enumerates the four elements required to establish a sovereign state. It also recognizes the existence of a state as an objective fact independent of recognition by other states. More important, it insists that the territory of a state is inviolable. Ergo the Grotian theory of the sovereign state assumes the character of codified international law.

In 1945, the Charter of the United Nations, the founding treaty of modern international law, reaffirmed the Grotian principle of the sovereign state. According to the Charter, membership in the United Nations is open only to sovereign states. The principle organs of the United Nations, including the General Assembly, the Security Council and the Economic and Social Council, all consist of sovereign states. Furthermore, only states may appear as litigants before the International Court of Justice. Even the many specialized agencies in economic, social, cultural, educational, health, and related fields are established by intergovernmental agreements among sovereign states. To preserve the existing partition of the earth against forced mer-

18. South Africa, under apartheid, dramatically demonstrated an extreme example of the Kelsenian state. But even under the Grotian system, this morally repugnant form of government remains compatible with the concept of territorial sovereign.

gers, the United Nations Charter prohibits the threat or use of force to extinguish the existence of a sovereign state.

Inspired by the United Nations Charter, regional charters of America, Africa and Europe reaffirm similar principles, enshrining the sovereign state as an inviolable international person. The Bogota Charter of the Organization of American States (1951) preserves the territorial inviolability of member states and maintains that although each state has a right to self-preservation, the right does not extend to committing unjust acts against another state. Likewise, the Charter of the Organization of African Unity (1963) establishes "respect for the sovereignty and territorial integrity of each state and for its inalienable right to independent existence." The Charter further avows absolute dedication to freeing African territories that are still dependent. Since the proclamation of the African Charter, many African territories have won independence.[19] The Final Act of the Conference on Security and Cooperation in Europe (1975), also known as the Helsinki Final Act, proclaimed that the frontiers of all states in Europe are inviolable that must not be assaulted. In addition, the Final Act bans the use of force to induce participating states to renounce the full exercise of their sovereign rights.

Over a period of three hundred and fifty years after the Peace of Westphalia, sovereign states gradually began to replace empires. Universal sovereignty faded away, paving the way for the emergence of a polytheistic international order in which sovereign states would appear in all parts of the world and assert their separate identities, free of emperors, popes, caliphs and colonists. In the early seventeenth century, not a single sovereign state existed in the world. The four elements of the sovereign state provided a legal formula to deconstruct large empires and convert their pieces into sovereign states. In 1995, more than one hundred and eighty states share the surface of the earth. The United States, currently the most powerful sovereign state, did not even exist at the time Grotius presented his theory. The Vatican, once a claimant for the entire universe but now a ministate, has a small population of about 400 citizens.

But what are the attributes of a sovereign state? How does the concept of state sovereignty become compatible with international law? May states make international law? May they invoke their sovereignty to disregard international law whenever they please? To answer these and other related questions, Grotius provides a complex normative framework. In his legal theory, he not only identifies the four elements for the formation of the sovereign state but also describes the state's prime attributes, explaining how sovereign states participate in international life.

---

19. In 1990, Namibia won independence. Zimbabwe, formerly Rhodesia, won its independence from White minority rule in 1980. Algeria, Uganda, Swaziland, Nigeria, Kenya, and Zambia won independence after 1960.

Chapter Three

Prime Attributes of the State

An entity acquires statehood under international law when it possesses four elements: territory, people, government and foreign policy competence. Once a state comes into existence it assumes international rights and obligations, a concept more easily understood when analyzed in terms of the state's prime attributes. A prime attribute is the state's inherent trait, its fundamental capacity to perform certain tasks – just as flying is a prime attribute of a bird. According to the Grotian theory and classical international law, the state possesses three prime attributes. First, the state is sovereign. It is internally sovereign in that it is free to establish a domestic legal order by virtue of which the government rules the people and the territory. It is externally sovereign in that it may forge relations with other states. Second, the state is the subject of international law. That is, the state as an international legal person respects international law, performs international duties and claims international rights. Third, the state in union with other states is the maker of international law. By virtue of the third attribute, states join their political wills to develop rules of international behavior. They may make rules to regulate or prohibit war, to resolve disputes, and to settle conflicting claims. They may also, at a higher degree of cooperation, make rules to gain mutual advantage in trade and commerce.

These attributes of the sovereign state turned the entire infrastructure of the middle ages upside down. No longer was the so-called universal empire above nations and no longer was the papacy the most superior law-giver, not even in the Christian world. Despite its repudiation of imperial and papal institutions, the Grotian theory is not designed for European states only. Its conceptual scope is global, allowing nations from all over the world to lawfully participate in constructing a legal order without first having to submit to any one superpower. The success of the Grotian theory is evident from the fact that many aspects of his theory later became the norms of international law.

At the outset, one must distinguish between the sovereign state and the nation-state. The sovereign state is essentially a porous entity. It is no more than a legal concept, form without substance, an empty shell, a device that even nations with diametrically opposite views on religion, government and social justice willingly accept as a mechanism for participating in international affairs. A nation-state, on the other hand, is a concrete embodiment of the sovereign state. A nation-state most frequently has a specific religion, a specific form of government and a specific internal legal order that spells out individual rights and duties, notions of justice and norms of good behavior. Each nation fills the empty shell of the sovereign state with its own religious, political and cultural values. Despite their diversity, nation-states are nonetheless sovereign states. The internal sovereignty of nation-states protects the unique heritages that distinguishes them from each other. Their external sovereignty allows them to participate in international life.

1. STATE AS SOVEREIGN ENTITY

To understand the attribute of state sovereignty, recall the distinction that both Bodin and Grotius make between internal and external sovereignty. Briefly, internal sovereignty is the legal authority that a nation-state possesses over the people and the territory. By virtue of internal sovereignty, the nation-state institutes a domestic legal system to freely pursue its political, economic, social and cultural aspirations. Grotius does not contend that internal sovereignty is always absolute or indivisible, immune to any legal control. He points out several scenarios in which internal sovereignty might be restricted. "It may happen," for example, "that a people, when choosing a king, may reserve to itself certain powers but may confer the others on the king absolutely." Grotius also puts forth the idea of divided sovereignty, used in a federation in which the powers to govern are divided between the center and its provinces. These restrictions on internal sovereignty, however, arise from domestic constitution of the nation-state. Neither the Grotian theory nor classical international law places limits on how internal sovereignty ought to be exercised or allocated among different constituent units of the nation-state.

In contrast, both the Grotian theory and classical international law subject external sovereignty to the rule of law. This is so because when a nation-state exercises external sovereignty, it affects other nations. Without rules, the exercise of external sovereignty becomes arbitrary and lawless. It is important to note that external sovereignty is not asserted *over* foreign peoples or territories. It is invoked either *against* or in cooperation *with* other sovereign states. A nation invokes its external sovereignty *against* other nations to protect its lawful interests and territory against foreign aggression. External sovereignty, however, is not simply a defensive legal mechanism. It is also a cooperative tool. Nations may join their external sovereignties to enter into cooperative enterprises, such as mutually beneficial trade or defense agreements. Thus external sovereignty allows the nation-state to establish diplomatic relations with other states, to engage in international trade, to exercise the right of self-defense and so on. Contemporary international law regulates both internal and external sovereignty of the nation-state. Right now, however, it is important to understand that while the Grotian theory and classical international law placed no limitations on the state's internal sovereignty, they did offer rules to limit and regulate the state's external sovereignty.

Under classical international law, the notion of internal sovereignty evokes images of absolute authority because the state is free to organize itself as it sees fit. Ironically, however, the theoretical construct of internal sovereignty, which Grotius conceives and classical international law protects, is normatively barren and vacant. Since classical international law provides no rules to regulate the state's internal sovereignty, it reduces the sovereign state to an empty shell. There are good reasons to do so. If the sovereign state is to be a useful entity for diverse nations of the world, it must be content-neutral. It must accommodate various forms of government and differing conceptions of justice. Yet despite its vacant nature, the sovereign state must also be strong enough to withstand domestic upheavals, coup d'etats and other disruptive changes. The international legal system will be thrown into disarray if every domestic upheaval alters the state's international rights and obligations. To meet these challenges, Grotius offers a concept of internal sovereignty that accommodates religious, governmental and social diversity of nations but yet allows the state to remain a durable entity, durable enough to outlive rulers and revolutions. Let us examine why Grotius constructs the empty but durable shell of the sovereign state.

To understand its vacant nature with respect to diverse religions, the sovereign state may be contrasted with the papacy. Unlike the papacy, the sovereign state embraces no one specific religion. The sovereign state is compatible with all religions; so a nation with any religion or no religion at all may institute a sovereign state. Access to the papal order was limited to Catholic nations. But under the Grotian theory, no nation is required to embrace any particular religion as a prerequisite for joining the community of sovereign states. Once any religious or secular nation institutes a sovereign state, its access to international law is not prevented on account of its religion or lack thereof. Nor does a state lose its sovereignty by adopting a new religion. All states, regardless of diverse religious populations they contain, participate in the international legal system on an equal basis. However, one need not conclude that the Grotian theory of internal sovereignty promotes secularism. Just as the sovereign state is tied to no one specific religion, so it is wedded to no form of secularism. The state is under no obligation to disassociate itself from religion. The religious or secular nature of the state's legal order does not diminish or enhance its external sovereignty. If the state decides to separate its legal order from religion, this decision does not affect its status as a sovereign entity in matters of international law. Likewise, if the state's legal order is theocratic, its external sovereignty remains unaffected.

The neutrality of the sovereign state severs international law from all religions. This severance is necessary to expand the community of nations willing to participate in the international legal system. Seeking support from Vitoria, Grotius argues for this severance by declaring that any wars waged against those unwilling to accept Christianity or against those who "misinterpret" Christian doctrines are inherently unjust. Grotius further argues that it is lawful for Christian states to enter into relations with non-Christian states. These doctrines establish an international legal system in which no nation-state may lawfully go to war to impose its religion on others. These norms are now fully entrenched in international law. Yet in the seventeenth century, a religiously empty notion of sovereignty was a bold leap into an imaginative world in which papal claims of universal sovereignty would lose their force and legitimacy. This new notion of internal sovereignty paved the way for non-Catholic, indeed non-Christian, nations to join the international legal system, nations that the papacy would have condemned as heretical.

In addition to religion, the sovereign state is neutral with respect to diverse forms of government. The Grotian theory correctly assumes that not all nations wish to institute the same form of government. Some would choose monarchy, some democracy, some theocracy. Therefore to successfully solicit the cooperation of diverse nation-states in building a secure international legal order, international law must be neutral to diverse models of political organization and forms of government. Again, this assertion of neutrality may seem commonplace today. Yet, this assertion was brave at the time Grotius proposed it. The ability of states to take part in the international legal system without having to adopt a particular form of government was a decisive break from the rigid medieval theory touting monarchy as the best form of government.

To further drain content from the notion of state sovereignty, the Grotian theory dictates no international standards of social and other forms of justice that each nation-state must adopt. Instead, it treats questions of justice and individual rights as matters exclusively within the domestic jurisdiction of the state, having no effect on its external sovereignty. Consequently, each nation-state is purposefully set free to institute its own conception of justice in accordance with the values of its community or even those of the ruling elite. In fact, the Grotian theory would even tolerate extreme cases in which a government made no effort whatsoever to provide justice. But regardless of even appalling moral indifference to the plight of its people, no nation-state loses external sovereignty under classical international law.

Accordingly, the nation-state may invoke its internal sovereignty to practice an oppressive caste system that divides the community into rigid social classes. It may practice slavery or deny fundamental rights to women or minorities. The state's ruling elite may refuse to share its opulence with the common people. The people may starve. The state's criminal justice system may be arbitrary or unjust. Prisons may be subhuman and prisoners may be subject to official torture. On the other hand, the state may establish a domestic constitution, prohibiting such acts and providing a more humane and equitable legal system. Either way, the state's discretion is absolute. Classical international law provides no relief for the people who suffer from abuses by the government. What a state does within its territory and how it treats its citizens are matters belonging to the state's domestic jurisdiction. Classical international law does not regulate the state's internal sovereignty.

Having devised such a morally vacant concept of internal sovereignty, Grotius may be condemned as a moral relativist with no sense of right and wrong. Bear in mind, however, that in the seventeenth century no universal standards of justice existed for Grotius to intellectually impose on all nations. The papal order did offer a systematic moral system, but it was no longer acceptable to many nations in Western Europe, let alone the world. So to build an all-inclusive international order, Grotius invents a non-theological, pragmatic, content-neutral concept of the sovereign state that most nations of the world could willingly embrace.

The next conceptual challenge that Grotius faced was to make the sovereign state a durable legal entity that could survive palace coups, political upheavals, constitutional changes, rebellions and revolutions. To achieve this durability, the Grotian theory makes a useful distinction between state and government.

This distinction declares that external sovereignty is an attribute of the state and not of its government. Therefore a change from one ruler to another does not alter the sovereign status of the state in the eyes of international law. Likewise if the state's internal constitution is changed, for example from monarchy to democracy, its external sovereignty in matters of international law remains unaffected. The state, acting in the image of a corporation that continues to function even when shares change hands, survives changes in government. External sovereignty of the state is tied neither to any particular ruler nor to any one form of government. The governments come and go, but the state remains.

Durability of the state makes international law a more predictable legal system. Although the government represents the state in foreign affairs, it is the state and not the government that contracts international rights and obligations. Therefore, the state is bound by international law despite internal changes. If international rights and obligations were tied to current rulers, international law would be reduced to an interpersonal system. Moreover, international law would suffer uncertainty every time a government was overthrown or the form of government was changed. It would then be unclear whether the new government would carry on international obligations assumed by its predecessor. To avoid this confusion, the Grotian theory designs external sovereignty to minimize the impact of internal changes on the international legal system. It uncouples the state's external sovereignty from its internal legal order so that internal changes have little effect on the states' rights and obligations in international law.

Furthermore, the Grotian theory detaches the notion of external sovereignty from the state's self-sufficiency, material resourcefulness or military might. It sets no minimum criteria of wealth or military superiority for a state to be eligible for sovereignty. Accordingly all states, rich and poor, strong and weak, are joined into the system on equal terms. This egalitarian principle of sovereign equality, however, faces difficulty when powerful states claim or assert authority in proportion to their economic and military strength. To resolve this difficulty, the notion of external sovereignty must be severed from the state's prosperity, wealth, influence or weapons. This was a difficult task in the seventeenth century. And to a large extent it still is. It is therefore instructive to examine how the idea of sovereign equality among undoubtedly unequal states finally assumed the character of law.

First, however, it is important to understand how states embrace the notion of self-sufficiency, believing that no state dependent on others is truly sovereign. In classical literature, particularly in the works of Aristotle, the state is conceived as a perfect association of families and tribes. One characteristic of such a perfect association is its self-sufficiency: the state must have sufficient resources to stand as a self-sustaining unit idependent of all external sources. In a perfect state, families and tribes join their resources to acquire a sufficient degree of economic autonomy and defensive capability to assure the state's survival and safety from internal or external threats while at the same time promising good life for its citizens. This construct of *communitates per-*

fectae reflected the aspirations of the ancient world to weld together families and tribes that, often locked in conflict with each other, wished to preserve their familial or tribal autonomy. Accordingly they resisted shifting their loyalty or resources to support the state. Moreover, since early means of transportation were too undeveloped to facilitate contact even among neighboring communities, a self-sufficient state was a practical necessity more than a theoretical construct. What a nation could not produce at home it often had to do without.

The idea of *communitates perfectae*, when introduced in the discourse of law, merged with the notion of sovereignty, causing confusion and conceptual difficulty. The merger implies that sovereign communities must marshall sufficient resources to establish their independence. It further implies that communities lacking self-sufficiency are consequently less sovereign. The ideal of the perfect community had over the centuries become so entrenched in literature that it was hard to dismiss it outright even in the sixteenth and seventeenth centuries. Hence classical scholars of international law, including Suarez, Vitoria and Grotius, relied without much critical reflection on the idea of perfect communities, causing confusion between sovereignty and self-sufficiency.

At least some self-sufficiency is important; an entity lacking all means to preserve its people, maintain law and order and pursue foreign relations will most likely fail to exercise any bit of sovereignty. That is why the law of decolonization required that a territory muster the wherewithal for self-government before lawfully claiming the status of sovereign statehood.

When self-sufficiency is viewed as the opposite of interdependence, however, it distorts the concept of state sovereignty. If nations are indeed self-sufficient, they have little or no incentive to participate in the global system other than to repel foreign aggression. Additionally, if self-sufficiency also requires the accumulation of sufficient weapons to resist and repulse every possible attack, each sovereign state must be perpetually war-ready. If sovereignty necessarily entails self-sufficieny, the human world turns into a predacious jungle in which everyone hunts for self-sufficiency and consequently everyone's sovereignty is vulnerable. This equation offers another insight into the era of colonization.

Additionally, if "might makes right" is the ultimate principle governing interstate relations, as it was for many centuries and as some contemporary realists still believe it is, respect for international law is further reduced. If the world must be defined in terms of constant conflict among warring nations, international law is at best useful to distinguish between lawful and unlawful use of force. This is one reason why classical writers on international law, including Grotius, devoted so much effort to clarifying the law of war and peace.

In the seventeenth century, long after Europe first made contacts with Asia and the Americas, the world had begun to shrink. The idea of a self-sufficient state was disappearing in the wake of increasing international commerce and colonization. Not even the Holy Roman Empire at its apex under Charles V was truly self-sufficient, since its wars were financed by gold and silver shipped from the Americas. So to separate "sovereignty in law" from "self-sufficiency in fact" became a key conceptual challenge. This separation declares that lack of domestic resources to meet internal and external needs and consequent interdependence through international commerce do not diminish sovereignty.

Paying lip service to Aristotle, Grotius defines the state as the most perfect association. But to dispel the notion that the sovereign state is necessarily a self-sufficient entity, Grotius explains that most nations lack actual sufficiency: "There is no state so powerful that it may not some time need the help of others outside itself, either for purposes of trade, or even to ward off the forces of many foreign nations united against it. In consequence we see that even the most powerful peoples and sovereigns seek alliances, which are quite devoid of significance according to the point of view of those who confine law within the boundaries of states."

A bolder approach to repudiating the notion of self-sufficiency would have required a frontal assault on the very idea of perfect community, specifically attacking the false presumption that somehow a self-sufficient state is also a superior state. After all, no nation is superior just because it is self-sufficient. To equate self-sufficiency with perfection or superiority is to ignore that an affluent but unjust nation is far from being morally perfect or socially superior. Even in amoral terms, to equate perfection with self-sufficiency is to rely on a transient criterion since self-sufficiency is rarely a permanent condition. The rise and fall of nations demonstrate how wealthy nations fade away into the shadows of history, some without leaving a monument to their wealth.

With hindsight, one can easily distinguish sovereignty in law from self-sufficiency in fact. If, for example, a nation lacks the resources to be self-sufficient and borrows funds from external sources to balance its budget or feed its people, it may nevertheless be fully capable to exercise its internal sovereignty by maintaining an effective legal order. If a nation is militarily weak, it may still be capable of exercising its external sovereignty by participating in the evolution of customs and in the making of treaties. Thus, sovereignty in law does not require self-sufficiency. Interdependence and lack of self-sufficiency are indeed the reason for instituting the international legal system in the first place.

Nonetheless, the ideal of self-sufficiency continues to confuse even contemporary debate about international law. Any nation striving for self-sufficiency is likely to behave as if it can survive on its own. Instead of seeing the world as a complex web of interrelationships, it sets itself psychologically apart, abhorring complex relations with other states. It may chase the phantom of economic independence, forcing its people and corporations to produce and manufacture all necessary goods at home. It may raise tariffs to discourage the inflow of foreign products. It may protect its domestic producers from foreign competition even when domestic products are expensive and inferior. If a state can indeed attain self-sufficiency, its attitude toward the global order may radically change. To maintain its atomistic existence, a self-sufficient state may generate national paranoia founded on the fiction that other states are jealous of its wealth and hostile to its good life. Even when a self-sufficient state engages in trade with other nations, it may assert its superiority based on the idea, sincerely held though objectively false, that other states will suffer a greater damage if mutual trade is lost.

Since the main purpose of a self-sufficient state is to maintain its separate existence, it may refuse to play by international rules, particularly when its national interests are threatened. To ward off real or imagined enemies, the self-sufficient state may build a strong military defense. If it is already militarily strong, it may disregard international law to promote its national interests. Grotius chides "those who, while unwilling to allow any one to exercise authority over themselves except in accordance with law, yet are quite indifferent as to whether foreigners are treated according to law or not." This dual attitude toward the rule of law often stems from the arrogance of self-sufficiency.

The logic of self-sufficiency carries within it the old adage that the poor more than the rich need the protection of law, a concept that carries some element of truth. Since affluent and powerful nations possess more leverage to promote their national interests, they do not feel the need for international law in the same way as poor and weak nations do. Even if powerful nations treat each other in a mutually beneficial way, they may still be disinterested in a global rule of law in which all nations, rich and poor, strong and weak, are treated fairly.

To repudiate self-sufficiency as a basis of sovereignty, international law espouses the concept of sovereign equality under which all states, powerful and powerless, are equal in the eyes of the law. This *de jure* equality does not repair the *de facto* inequality that exists among states. Some states are still rich, others poor. Some are still strong, others weak. Yet by instituting formal equality, the legal system moves away from reliance on self-sufficiency as a measure of sovereignty. The idea of state equality is a principle of formal equality that post-Grotian natural law writers introduced into the theory of international law. Samuel Pufendorf (1632-94) and Emerich de Vattel (1714-69) anchor the doctrine in the mythical "state of nature" – a fictitious pre-legal world in which no nation has legal superiority over the other. Accordingly, they assume that when independent nations submit to the rule of law, they retain their preexisting equality. Alternatively, the theorists presume that only on the basis of sovereign equality would natural states enter into a social contract to institute an international legal order. The norms of this social contract made among equal states, indicating how states ought to behave toward each other, embody the principles of international law.

The principle of state equality, though derived from the awkward and unbelievable construct of the original state of nature, reverses the medieval conviction of papal or imperial supremacy. In fact, this secular postulate of state equality made sense only after divine law itself was separated from natural law, as was church from state and God from man. "One Empire under One King under One God" is derived from divine law. "Sovereign states are independent and juridically equal" is rooted in the respectability of natural law. The bond between natural law and state sovereignty is simple. Natural law presupposes a concept of freedom under which each constituent unit is independent and sovereign. State sovereignty relies upon natural law to assert that each state acts on an equal basis with other states. Thus natural law and the sovereign state become mutually supportive, almost collusive, witnesses to testify against the supremacy of any universal superior created by divine or any other law.

As papal supremacy was a theological belief, so the principle of state equality is a legal fiction, perhaps a useful one. In reality, states vary in the size of their territory and population, in prestige, in the form and efficacy of their government, in economic and military resources and in the influence they wield when dealing with each other. Nonetheless, in law all states are equal.[1] Theoretically, all states are entitled to the same rights and have equal sovereignty. Furthermore, the sovereignty of each state does not depend upon the power which it possesses, but upon the simple fact of its existence as a person under international law. Thus the smallest state is coequal with the most powerful state in the world.

Grotius does not explicitly invoke the fictitious state of nature in which all nations are sovereign. However, he does refer to a primitive state in which all things were the common possession of all men, and each man could take whatever he wished for his own needs. Idealizing "the simplicity of the state of the first men," Grotius paints a picture of the fall of man from innocence to ambition, from abundance to scarcity, and from common inheritance to private ownership. When families began to appropriate land for their exclusive use, Grotius argues, the first state of common ownership was dismantled. As a result, "men divided off countries, and possessed them separately."

Nor does Grotius specifically assert the sovereign equality of states. Nonetheless, his definition of sovereignty includes the equality principle. Maintaining that the state is the common subject of sovereignty, Grotius states: "That power is called sovereign whose actions are not subject to the legal control of another." If every sovereign state is in control of its actions, all sovereign states are equally independent in the community of states, a scenario resembling the mythical state of nature. Moreover, Grotius distinguishes between sovereignty and influence or prestige. If a state has less influence or prestige, it does not lose its sovereignty. Nor does a state lose sovereignty, Grotius further states, if it is "by treaty placed under the protection of a state which is superior in prestige." This is so because protection is not the same as subjection. "Just as private patronage in the case of individuals does not take away individual liberty, so patronage in the case of a state does not take away independence."

To further clarify the notion of sovereign equality, Grotius offers a powerful distinction between formal and functional sovereignty. "In the case of political power not less than in that of private ownership it is necessary to distinguish between the right and its exercise." To explain this, Grotius provides

1. Enshrined in the United Nations Charter, the sovereign equality of states is a founding principle of international law.

the example of an infant king who possesses political power but is unable to use it. This illustration clarifies a broader distinction between formal and functional sovereignty. Formal sovereignty vests in the state a bundle of legal rights by which it may institute a domestic legal order and conduct an independent foreign policy. When the state exercises these rights and accordingly institutes a state constitution, establishes an economy and conducts foreign policy, its sovereignty becomes functional. Functional sovereignty is thus the actual exercise of formal sovereignty. If an armed attack occurs, the target state has the formal right to defend itself. In reality, however, the target state may lack the military resources to repulse the attack. If so, the state suffers from a discrepancy between its formal right to self-defense and its functional capability to use that right. Similarly, a state may lack the means to exploit resources present in its territorial sea. Such a disability, however, does not diminish the state's formal right to exercise complete sovereignty over its territorial sea. Such incongruity may also exist with respect to the state's internal sovereignty, where the state possesses the right but lacks the resources to exercise it. A state may fail to exercise its internal sovereignty when, for example, it lacks sufficient law enforcement resources to protect lives and liberty of its people.

Gaps between formal and functional sovereignty do not *ipso facto* undermine the independence or equality of a state. Even though all states are theoretically vested with equal formal sovereignty, they need not be equally functionally sovereign. The degree to which a state may actually utilize its sovereignty varies from state to state. If an entity aspiring to be a sovereign state lacks the means to exercise control over its internal and external affairs and consequently fails altogether to establish an effective government and loses the capacity to enter into international relations, it lacks even formal sovereignty and therefore is denied statehood. However if a state temporarily plunges into anarchy or cannot conduct international relations, it does not automatically lose its formal sovereignty.[2] As a practical matter, powerful and rich states seem to better able to exercise the rights of sovereignty. Formally, however, all states remain equally sovereign. Thus law triumphs over reality.

Consistent with the ideas of Grotius, the notions of internal and external sovereignty are fully incorporated in classical international law. The Convention on Rights and Duties of States, a treaty among the nations of North and South America, articulates the Grotian theory in vivid language. Article 3 defines internal sovereignty: the state has the right to "organize itself as it sees fit." This means that a state is free to choose its form of government. The state is also free to embrace secularism or an official religion. It may likewise choose a specific conception of social justice, a distinctive regime of civil and political rights. Principles of territorial integrity and political independence, codified in the United Nations Charter and other eminent treaties, protect important

---

2. Somalia, for example, retained its formal sovereignty despite anarchy, starvation and temporary occupation by the United Nations armed forces.

aspects of internal sovereignty. Article 2(4) of the Charter instructs member states to refrain in their international relations from the threat or use of force against the territorial integrity or political independence of any state. To further protect the state's internal sovereignty, the principles of non-interference and domestic jurisdiction, also recognized in the United Nations Charter, bar foreign interference in the internal affairs of any state. Article 2(7) of the Charter prohibits even the United Nations from intervening in matters that are essentially within the domestic jurisdiction of the state. Although the contemporary international law of human rights has modified the scope of internal sovereignty, nation-states continue to invoke provisions of the Charter to defend their domestic laws and policies against foreign criticism.

Article 4 of the Convention on Rights and Duties of States describes the state's external sovereignty: States are juridically equal, enjoy the same rights and have equal capacity in their exercise. The rights of each state depend not upon the power that it possesses but upon the simple fact of its existence as a person under international law. Likewise, Article 2(1) of the United Nations Charter states that the United Nations Organization is based on the principle of the sovereign equality of all its members. These norms recognize that states are theoretically equal in their external sovereignty. Even though states may exercise their formal sovereignty in unequal amounts, the concept of state equality has serious implications in law. No state, for example, may be lawfully compelled to enter into an agreement with another state, nor can a state be lawfully forced to give up its right of self-defense against another nation.[3] This is so because no sovereign state is under the legal control of another sovereign state. Thus, the sovereign equality of nation-states serves as a useful conceptual tool to construct many rules of international law.

Both the Grotian theory and classical international law place few constraints on the exercise of internal sovereignty. Limitations on internal sovereignty arise only from domestic constitution, and these limitations may vary from state to state. The state's external sovereignty, however, is regulated directly by international law. No state may lawfully claim that by virtue of its sovereignty it can do whatever it pleases in the domain of international matters. An undivided notion of sovereignty may confuse states to make such claims. But when sovereignty is divided into its internal and external aspects, it becomes clear that classical international law ignores the state's internal sovereignty but places considerable constraints on its external sovereignty. The entire enterprise of international law will collapse if the state's external sovereignty is unlimited. To sort out this confusion, Grotius explains why the state is therefore a subject of international law.

---

3. This inherent right of self-defense has been explicitly recognized in article 51 of the UN Charter. Whether an arms embargo imposed by the Security Council violates the right of self-defense raises a serious question.

2. SUBJECT OF INTERNATIONAL LAW

To demonstrate that the sovereign state has no lawless authority to conduct foreign affairs, Grotius identifies two distinct sources of international law: natural law and positive law, the same two sources that classical expositors, including Aristotle and Thomas Aquinas, have examined in their analysis of the state's internal sovereignty. Relying upon the testimony of philosophers, historians, poets and orators, Grotius defines natural law as standards of behavior drawn from the principles of nature, the immutable and universal principles that are the same at different times and in different places. These principles are discovered by moral intelligence.

Most ancient writers on natural law assert that national legal systems ought to be in harmony with the principles of natural law, but rarely do they extend these principles to regulate international relations. Even the great Greek and Roman philosophers had little to say about international law. This is so because ever since the dawn of human civilization warfare has been so prevalent that nations have devoted more time to developing weapons and skills of warfare than to making a concerted effort to institute a system of laws in which nations with diverse backgrounds could live in peace. Thus most philosophies of politics, law and justice are confined to clarifying the legal relationship between the people and their ruler. Questions of interstate behavior are often omitted on the assumption that nations, in their dealings with each other, are and will remain in a state of perpetual conflict.

In building his theory of international law, Grotius repudiates the popular and philosophical views of his era. In the opening paragraph of *The Law of War and Peace*, Grotius laments the fact that many scholars have commented upon the municipal law of Rome but few have touched upon the body of law concerned with mutual relations among states. Deploring the general opinion that international law has "no reality outside of an empty name," Grotius identifies two fundamental impediments in the evolution of international law: armed force and national interest. He proposes to subordinate both to the rule of international law.

Arguments derived from armed force suggest that international law consists only of the dictates of powerful nations imposed upon weaker ones. Even well-informed, thoughtful men hold the mistaken view that injustice is inevitable in conducting the affairs of a state and that wealthy and powerful nations operate on the simple basis of "might is right." Nothing is more common, Grotius further points out, than the dogma that law and war are mutually exclusive. Those who argue for justice in the conduct of war are ridiculed, since "deception, harshness, and injustice are the regular business of battles." Accordingly, the proposition that international law ought to regulate the use of armed force is dismissed.

Arguments derived from national interest further confuse the need for law in building global order. Many opponents of international law, Grotius states, contend that national interest is and ought to be the supreme value in the conduct of foreign relations. The concept of national interest is often justified in drawing a parallel between human beings and other natural creatures. Advocates of the concept assert that all creatures, men and animals alike, are motivated to defend and advance their own advantage. It would therefore be foolish for any nation to uphold justice or the rule of law at the expense of its own interests.

The founders of international law, including Grotius, equate such assertion of might and pursuit of national interests with lawlessness. They fear that powerful nations, whether their power is derived from superior military strength, wealth or some other source, will use their power as a basis for seizing the resources of the world and deciding disputes in their favor. They correctly maintain that the use of armed force without legal constraints cannot construct a legal world. They argue that if each nation pursues its national interests without the guiding hand of law, the global order will cease to function, giving rise to lawlessness. If nations invoke both armed force and national interest as a combined strategy in foreign matters, the formation of an international community founded on law seems even more difficult.

To counter arguments derived from armed force and national interest, the founders insist upon the rule of law under which all nations ought to be able to participate in the system without unfair advantage or disadvantage. They wish to establish not only law but justice among nations. But why is this necessary? From an analytical viewpoint, justice and lawlessness are not the only two choices available. If international law is inseparable from justice, an assumption valid under natural law, the term "lawlessness" refers to a situation either of global anarchy or global injustice. If international law and justice are severable, a thesis valid under legal positivism, an international legal system can be established to serve only the national interests of powerful states.

Grotius makes no essential connection between law and justice with respect to domestic legal systems, as he has no conceptual difficulty with a type of government that institutes laws primarily serving the needs of persons in power. Such a government is unjust but not lawless, an argument that Grotius would willingly concede. If a national order can be instituted to serve only the interests of the rulers, a global order to protecting the interests of a few powerful nations ought to be permissble too. Once the bond between law and justice becomes expendable, a theory of international law can be conceived to support a system favoring wealthy and powerful nations and maintained by superior armed force.

Despite tolerating injustice within domestic legal systems, however, Grotius is unwilling to separate law from justice in his theory of international law. A theory supporting a global system maintained by armed force would allow a single world government, reinforcing the notion of universal sovereignty and the concomitant ideal of One Empire under One King. Proponents of the universal empire would willingly allow the use of armed force to subdue nations reluctant to submit to the authority of the single superpower. And that is precisely what Grotius opposes. Hence he envisions a global order in which the rule of law would bridle the might of powerful nations, most of all that of the single superpower. Law allows all nations, large and small, acting as sovereign states, to participate in the global order derived from the principles of natural law and common consent.

To subject states to the rule of law, Grotius first invokes the ancient theory of natural law championed in antique Greek, Jewish and Roman literature and examined in the works of Spanish jurists Suarez and Vitoria. Accordingly, Grotius presents a view of international law under which an act must be right, not merely lawful, "because law in our use of the term here stands related to matter not only of justice...but also of other virtues." Invoking St. Augustine and Suarez, Grotius argues that what is done according to law is done justly and what is unjustly done cannot be done according to law. Thus a symbiotic fusion of law and justice is the foundation of natural law, which in this fused state becomes a dictate of right reason, a way of analyzing human acts to determine whether they are in conformity with rational nature.[4]

To further argue that states ought to behave in accordance with law, Grotius points out that inherent in rational nature are two mutually supportive impulses: the longing to do good and the reason to act in an intelligently consistent manner, that is, in accordance with the rule of law. This combination of compassion and reason is the proper foundation for instituting an international legal system that preserves both order and justice. Thus these two principles offer a counter-thesis to the thesis of armed force and national interest.

Compassion, the disposition to do good, is not always compatible with national interest. Presuming that international life is a web of intricate relationships, compassion emphasizes sustaining global networks without which few people would be able to realize their full potential. Distinguished from charity, which flows from the affluent to the needy, compassion is a universal sentiment rooted in human intelligence, harmony and equality. Compassion rejects the psychology of self-interest that first creates and then sharpens the contradiction of individual *qua* society and nation *qua* nation. "Compassion is a difficult virtue to practice; it tests the limitations of our egotism, insecurity and inherited prejudice."[5] But human society without compassion remains defective and unfulfilled. Citing Cicero, Alberico Gentili (1552-1608), an Italian jurist, argues that "man was born for fellowship, and it is his duty to aid others, not to live for himself alone." To do good to others rather than always protect your own interests is the core principle of compassion.

"The assertion that every animal is impelled by nature to seek only its own good," Grotius argues, "cannot be conceded." Not even animals are always motivated by appetite, since most do at least care for their offspring. Dog does

4. Grotius's aim was to construct a system of laws independent of theological presuppositions. Accordingly, Grotius argues that natural law is valid even if there is no God. This separation of natural law and God supported a rational basis for universal ethics. A. P. d'Entreves, Natural Law (2nd ed. 1970) p. 54-55.

5. "The prophets insisted that cult and worship were useless unless society as a whole adopted a more just and compassionate ethos." Karen Armstrong, A History of God, (New York, 1993), pp. 391.

not eat dog, says Gentili, concluding that we are by nature all akin. Compassion as a natural trait is most visible among children who, even before their socialization begins, show disposition to do good to others. As children develop into adults they begin to gather knowledge that, Grotius argues, reaffirms the natural sympathy for others that comes spontaneously at an early age.

To further support his theory, Grotius argues that the innate human disposition to benefit others gains support from rational nature, also called moral intelligence. In other words, reason derived from knowledge strengthens the human instinct to do good to others. Likewise, moral intelligence is a blend of human inclinations rooted in instincts and intelligence derived from experience and moral knowledge. Moses Maimonides (1135-1204), an authority on the Talmud whom Grotius frequently invokes, says that the person most suitable to preside over a law court is the one whose heart is full of grace, i.e., in whom wisdom is united with humility and meekness. Thus compassion is not a childlike practice that only unenlightened adults continue to pursue. Nor is it an erratic instinct that reason wishes to suppress. The longing to do good, rooted in moral intelligence, is supported by both instinct and reason. Therefore, all the peoples of the world are predisposed to institute a gracious world.

A strident pursuit of national interest, in contrast, is not based on moral intelligence. Even if it is conceded that preservation of the state is a human inclination, reason opposes national interest as the predominant source of international law.[6] Reason tells us that no legal system, national or international, will survive if the individual or the state, motivated by immediate advantage, is free to violate the law with impunity. Thus rational nature weighs human inclinations against human intelligence "in an effort to control more effectively our more violent impulses and to restrain them within proper limits." Maimonides asserts that the perfection of man's moral principles is given to man for the benefit of mankind, since moral principles are only necessary and useful when an individual comes into contact with others.

Thus compassion and moral intelligence dictate that states act in accordance with law and justice. When states pursue their national interests supported by armed force, they act not only without compassion but also against moral intelligence. Just like a domestic legal system is oppressive and unjust if those in authority lack compassion and moral intelligence, so the international legal system will fail to create a gracious world if states use their superior armed force to pursue narrow national interests. Relying on the Greek tradition, Grotius cites Thucydides: "It is fitting that those who have the leading place in an alliance should arrogate to themselves no privilege in relation to their own interests, but should make themselves conspicuous above the others through their careful management of common interests." This command,

---

6. One may define self-interest to include compassion, as others may define compassion to include self-interest. Nonetheless, the emphasis and the moral direction of the two concepts are different. Self-interest begins with the self; compassion begins with the other.

derived from rational nature, dictates that powerful states practice wisdom rather than pursue narrow national interest.

Whether rational nature is moved by compassion, self-interest, or both in an elusive blend, is a centuries-old controversy, which will no doubt continue to stir debate for many more centuries to come. But two general points are clear: one, the source of law determines the nature of law; two, the legal system immersed in compassion is markedly different from the one rooted in narrow self-interest. Many people claim that the system based on compassion is more humane. Suarez, for example, argues that the human race preserves "a moral and political unity enjoined by the natural precept of mutual love and mercy; a precept which applies to all, even to strangers of every nation." Others of course disagree. Like Suarez, Grotius chooses to build the global system on compassion and moral intelligence rather than narrow national interests and armed force.

Despite the rooting of classical international law in compassion and moral intelligence, the arguments derived from the logic of armed force and national interests continue to bedevil relations between nations. The most conspicuous argument emphasizes that in reality powerful states do whatever they please regardless of international law. Another argument suggests "that right is that which is acceptable to the stronger" nations, which means that international law must protect the national interests of powerful states or it will not work. From another perspective, this argument implies that an international legal order exists only when powerful states, which can successfully undermine the law, are somehow induced to uphold it.

Associated with these views is another commonly-held belief that laws must be backed by sanctions, since the fear of punishment is the only sure motive for obedience. Thus no international law is worthy of the name if effective sanctions are unavailable to assure state compliance. This line of argument raises a difficult question: Why do states obey international law?

The logic of sanctions, if taken seriously, points toward the establishment of a world government, a single superpower or a coalition of well-armed states with efficacious enforcement means to impose global law and order. Such a view resurrects the norms of a paternalistic system in which the mighty father maintains order in the global household. Such a view is also rooted in the memory of many nations ruled by strong men. Moreover, a sanctions-based system easily captures the minds of those not versed in history. Grotius, for one, opposes instituting one paternalistic government over all nations of the world. He knew full well how the idea of universal sovereignty, despite repeated attempts at implementation, remained dysfunctional and in fact engendered the Thirty Years War in Western Europe, among many others.

To counter the idea of a sanction-based international order, Grotius again invokes the nobler side of human nature and a justice-oriented concept of law. Relying upon Plato, Grotius argues that states would rather obey just laws than violate them, since sentiments for justice are in harmony with rational nature. So in order to institute a fully functional global system, international law must stem from broadly-shared sentiments of justice rather than the fear of punishment.

Furthermore, the concept of law derived from rational nature dictates that laws ought to be obeyed even if no sanctions are available for enforcement. This view of law appeals to intelligence rather than fear, persuading rather than coercing states to do the right thing. In fact, just systems work precisely because they mirror rational nature, for no legal system can successfully function if every member has to be constantly coerced to comply with every single law. Most people willingly obey laws in a just system, while the cost of law enforcement escalates to maintain an unjust system. An over-reliance on sanctions in articulating the concept of law misses the point that a just legal system functions at a minimum cost of law enforcement.

That is why Grotius anchors international law in moral intelligence, proposing that if the global system is just, most nations will willingly obey the law. Moreover, a just global system requires no one superpower to enforce the laws, nor does it rely on sanctions as the primary means to seek compliance. Instead, it establishes a universal legal culture in which promises are kept, unjust wars are forbidden, and what belongs to others is not arbitrarily taken away from them. Such idealism, however, fails to persuade nations and peoples raised to believe that a perpetual state of war is an inherent part of the human condition. Such idealism also fails to persuade the so-called realists, who hold the view that compassion and moral intelligence are good concepts that fail to perform as promised in the real world. Therefore, they argue, smart states waste no time in forcibly appropriating the scarce resources of the world, establishing a sphere of influence and accumulating weapons to protect their supreme national interests. Some even suggest calculated aggression, preemptive strikes and even the use of weapons of mass destruction when necessary to preserve and enhance national interests. The world they see is completely predacious.

Legal regulation of the predacious world is a major focus of the Grotian theory of international law. War has been a constant feature of human civilization; sometimes it is waged to conquer the world, sometimes to destroy the enemy however defined, and sometimes to simply loot the riches of another nation. Vitoria, Bodin, Suarez, Gentili and Grotius, the theoreticians of classical international law, wished to transform the arbitrary and dangerous norms of the predacious world into a more gracious system.

The predacious world is founded on a set of morally dubious assumptions derived from the logic of war, national interest and self-righteousness. It ennobles war and warriors, devaluing those who cannot fight. It supports a view of human civilization in which warrior nations glorify their capacity to kill, often on the presumption that those who win are religiously, racially or nationally superior to those who lose. War, mythologized in classical literature as the opposite of cowardice, is considered the ultimate act of valor at both individual and collective levels. Bodin reports how Athenian men were bound to go to war at fourteen and remained in the military until they were thirty, and how the ancient Romans also aspired to excel in the art of war. Consequently, states prepared to take arms are traditionally celebrated as master nations, whereas those without skills in the use of arms are dismissed as weaklings and slaves. This cult of war reinforces a predacious world in which nations aspire to be powerful and powerful nations wage wars to rule the "inferior" nations of the world.

While self-preservation justifies defensive wars, self-righteousness provides the intellectual basis for offensive wars. In classical literature, Aristotle's idea that some people are inherently inferior bolstered the norms of the predacious world, romanticizing war and equating the superior with the powerful. Some theological beliefs of the middle ages added a dimension of righteousness to the logic of war, vesting in the "truthful" the right to inherit the earth. Vitoria reports how, relying upon the authority of St. Augustine, theologians developed the idea that "the barbarians were not true masters because they were continually in a state of mortal sin." A universal and peaceful religion was thus twisted to support aggressive wars by which the "truthful" dispossessed the "sinful" of their land and other assets.

To counter the cult of war, the world the architects of international law wished to create condemns the intellectual infrastructure that sustains predacious norms. Vitoria argues that neither difference of religion nor the enlargement of empire can be the cause of a just war. He further states that the "barbarians" cannot be robbed of their property on the grounds that they are irrational, sinners or unbelievers. Suarez also condemns wars waged to expand temporal domain against those who profess a different religion. Arguing that the king is obligated to seek arbitration to prevent war, Suarez places a moral duty on generals, particularly when consulted, to give an honest opinion about whether or not a war is just. Gentili distinguishes between military science and the morality of warfare, suggesting that good skills in the use of weapons may not be confused with good morals in choosing to go to war.

Consistent with the teachings of Vitoria, Suarez and Gentili, Grotius appeals to natural law to distinguish between just and unjust wars. Quoting St. Augustine, Grotius denounces wars prompted by "the eager desire to injure, the cruelty of vengeance, the unappeased and unappeasable mind, the savagery of rebellion, the lust of ruling." Since he equates law with justice, Grotius states that a lawful war must be a just war. Hence Grotius declares that predacious wars designed to loot the vulnerable, to conquer the "inferior," to obtain richer lands, to fullfil divine prophecies or to convert the followers of another religion are inherently unjust.

Not only should the cause of war be just, but the way the war is conducted must also be lawful. The raping of women in time of war, Grotius states, ought to be unlawful, an act "not held honorable even among barbarians." In view of past practices of the predacious world, however, Grotius permits the destruction of enemy property, including harbors, cities, ships, crops, temples and cemeteries. Moreover, quoting Plato and others, Grotius upholds "the eternal law" that all goods of the conquered become the property of the conqueror.[7] Criticizing the law of war as it existed, however, Grotius advocates caution and moderation in pillaging, arguing that what is permitted in law is not always prudent or morally appropriate.

To create a more peaceful world in which predation is no longer a supreme value, Grotius imagines a gracious world in which nations treat each other in accordance with laws. To further clarify the obligation of states under international law, Grotius draws an important distinction between a state and a union of brigands. No union of brigands is a state, Grotius argues, even if such a society practices equality and is internally just. This is so because what distinguishes a state from a union of brigands is not their internal system but their external viewpoint regarding the outside world. A union of brigands refuses to render justice to foreigners whereas a state assumes the obligation to treat nationals of other states in accordance with international law.

Grotius makes but does not fully develop this important distinction. What he calls a union of brigands is in fact a rogue state that refuses to be bound by law in its relations with other nations. The example of the pirates that Grotius uses illustrates this point. Pirates, even if they are fair to each other, as they often are in order to maintain their enterprise, share a predacious viewpoint with respect to the rest of the world; they have no sense of law when they encounter strangers. So no nation, even if it institutes a just legal system for its own people, becomes a state in the true sense of the word unless it accepts the rule of law in dealings with other nations.

In sum, the gracious world refuses to idealize war as glorious enterprise. Nor does it show any contempt for the people who cannot or do not fight. Moreover it disowns ideologies, religions and intellectual systems that legitimize subjugation, dispossession of the vulnerable or the superiority of one group over others. That war knows no law has been the practice of the predacious world; that war should be subject to law is the aim of the gracious world. Rooted in compassion and moral intelligence, the gracious world promotes minimization of conflict and resolution of disputes through peaceful means.

Consistent with the norms of the gracious world, the United Nations Charter outlaws offensive war as a lawful means of conducting foreign policy. Planning, preparing, initiating or waging a war of aggression or war in violation of international treaties, agreements and assurances constitute *crimes against peace*. The Charter further mandates that the parties to any dispute, the continuance of which is likely to endanger the maintenance of international peace and security, seek a solution by peaceful means including negotiation, mediation, arbitration and judicial settlement. Recognizing the inherent right of self-defense, Article 51 of the Charter nonetheless requires in such situations the involvement of the Security Council. Thus even defensive wars are

---

7. Some of these practices, which dominated and defined the predacious world, were declared unlawful only after the devastation of the Second World War.

brought into the institutional framework so that no state may threaten international peace and security.

To eradicate the brutality of the predacious world, the humanitarian law, the law governing the conduct of war, deviates even from the Grotian theory. It prohibits attacking of towns, villages, dwellings, hospitals, historic monuments and buildings dedicated to religion, art, science or charitable purposes. It outlaws starvation of civilians as a tool of war, proscribing the destruction of food supplies, water installations and irrigation works. Genocide of a national, ethnic, racial or religious group is now universally prohibited, a restriction elevated to the level of *jus cogens* from which no derogation is allowed. To humanize wars for members of armed forces, the humanitarian law protects soldiers incapacitated by injury, sickness, shipwreck or capture on the basis of a fundamental principle that human dignity must be respected even during armed hostilities. The law also limits the legitimate scope of military action, proposing to outlaw the use of chemical, biological and nuclear weapons.

These legal norms created by contemporary international agreements seek the evolution of a gracious world in which war and concomitant inhumanity will be minimized if not totally eradicated. Given the atrocities committed in recent regional wars, few take solace in the simple fact that paper rules would protect the weak and the vulnerable in time of crisis. We are still in an early stage of moral development and our elementary mind is not yet fully schooled in the higher ideals of compassion and peace. Therefore, the teachers of the world carry individual and collective obligation to disseminate the norms of the gracious world, as do nation-states in their role as law-makers. Law is a powerful force in shaping human behavior and therefore what nation-states legislate makes a difference.

3. Maker of International Law

The final prime attribute of the sovereign state is its inherent capacity to make international law. In addition to natural law, to which all nations must submit, Grotius focuses on the positive law that nation-states themselves make through mutual consent. This concept is consistent with the teachings of Suarez, who states that the law of nations is derived from the authority of all and cannot be annulled without universal consent. Such positive law, embodied in customs and treaties, "solemn agreements" in the words of Homer, can be found even in ancient texts and among primitive nations. It is by positive law, Grotius explains, that a truce is arranged, a safe-conduct is granted or ransom for a captive is paid. So positive law, the rules of international behavior made through a deliberative exchange of promises, is ancient in both theory and practice, and Grotius would seek no credit for its invention.

Even though Grotius advances the notion that international law is rooted in "unbroken customs created by common consent of nations," he does not fully develop the idea of nation-states as makers of international law. At least two factors may explain this shortcoming. First, Grotius views international law primarily as a body of customs that have already developed. Practices of international behavior, which develop over time and gradually assume the character of binding customs, reflect a slow moving global life. Most national legal systems, in which the process of change is sluggish and innovative situations infrequent, rely upon customs. Such has also been the condition of international law. The world in which Grotius lived experienced dramatic changes, including wars of national liberation and colonialism. Yet the body of existing customs, most dealing with questions of war and peace, constituted a comprehensive international legal system.

Second, Grotius does not regard treaties as tools for manufacturing international law. He presupposes that treaties are made according to custom, which means that treaties are the product of international law, not its source. The law of treaty he examines focuses on the formation and breach of treaties. Grotius states, for example, that treaties should be made by order of the highest authority, and that it is permissible to make treaties with non-Christian nations. He further states that if one party breaches a treaty, the other may withdraw from it. The terms and the subject matter of treaties, Grotius says, may be classified on the basis of fairness, since some treaties "oppress the other party more than is just." In the Grotian era, treaties were not yet a separate and distinct source of international law. This was so in part because treaties were always bilateral. The concept of a multilateral treaty was non-existent.

Grotius failed to foresee that in the future multilateral treaties would become the main source of manufacturing positive international law. But this omission is methodological rather than conceptual. It is methodological in the sense that Grotius views custom as the only method of making international law. Conceptually, however, the proposition that nations join their wills to create new rules of international behavior includes the possibility that nations would devise new methods to do so. He correctly identifies unbroken custom as the foremost mode by which nations expressed their collective will in past centuries. But whether nations of the world would develop the treaty as a law-making method was not yet on the horizon. Despite this omission, the important contribution Grotius makes is intact: his positivist notion that international law is the product of human will expressed through states as representatives of their respective peoples is not tied to any single law-making mechanism. This positivist enterprise, fully present in customary international law, has now been expanded to include multilateral and bilateral treaties as valid sources of new law.

If international law is the product of human will, must international law necessarily be subject to moral intelligence? International law, though rooted in rational nature, has a distinctive origin distinguishable from both natural law and divine law. Natural law exists *a priori*, constant and immutable. Divine law is given by the uncreated creator. In contrast, international law is a human product. It is the creation of time and custom: "whatever cannot be deduced from certain principles by a sure process of reasoning," Grotius says, "and yet is clearly observed everywhere, must have its origin in the free will of man." Even though international law may vary from natural law in details, it is nonetheless subject to the basic principles of natural law. For example, a rule of behavior that violates compassion or reason needs careful scrutiny before it is accepted as law. Accordingly, customs and treaties, the common sources of international law, should be harmonious with compassion and reason, for no rule of international behavior can claim the status of law if it opposes rational nature, which Grotius also calls the common sense of mankind.

International law may also be distinguished from national law, even when both are man-made positive law. This is so because the way in which positive law is made is of critical importance. National law flows from the power of a monarch, parliament or a majority of the people; it does not derive its validity from the consent of every member of the community. In contrast, international law repudiates hierarchical structures of law-making, under which law descends from top to bottom. It is derived neither from the authority of one superpower nor from the combined might of the most powerful nations; nor indeed can a majority of nations impose a new rule on all. For Grotius, international law is founded in common consent of sovereign states.

It is also instructive to distinguish international law from universal law. Grotius defines international law as "the law which has derived its obligatory force from the will of all nations, or of many nations." If a rule of international law is binding on all nations, either through custom or treaty, such a rule may properly be called universal law. But not all rules of international behavior are binding on all nations. Customs may vary from one part of the world to another. Even treaties may be regional in scope. Such regional customs and treaties are nonetheless international law, since the term international law includes both regional and universal laws. This conceptual clarity paved the way for the contemporary definition of international law under which a rule of obligation between two or more states would properly be called a rule of international law.

To examine why positive international law is binding on states, Grotius provides a theoretical framework to ensure that customs and treaties are not mere paper rules that nations may scrap at their arbitrary whim or by invoking their sovereignty. Grotius identifies three simple, related principles for the formation and observance of international law: common consent, promissory obligation and good faith. These principles provide a coherent basis to shape a law-oriented world in which sovereign states are not coerced but willingly develop, and in good faith follow, international law.

The Grotian principle that international law is anchored in the common consent of nations must first be understood in its historical context. Grotius wished to dismantle the idea of universal sovereignty, which had dominated philosophical and legal thought for many centuries. Both papalists and imperialists aspired to construct a vertical structure of authority under which the One King on top of the world pyramid dictated the norms of international behavior. Authority in such a global system was based on the concept of command, not consent. The consensual principle as a source of international law was, therefore, set in direct opposition to papal and imperial orders; it sought to dismantle the coercive order founded on the will of one superpower and replace it with a consensual order derived from the collaboration of many nations.

At an intuitive level the consensual principle corresponds closely with reality, since most treaties and customs in fact emerge from the common consent of participating nations. Treaties require explicit state consent at each stage of treaty formation, from the adoption of the text to final acceptance. State consent in the formation of customs occurs in diverse ways: a state may obligate itself by engaging in the actual practice, express *opinio juris* in straightforward official statements, or simply remain silent while the custom evolves.

A logical extension of the consensual principle requires that no nation-state be coerced into accepting a rule of international law. The concept of persistent objection – under which a state is exempt from the obligation of a new custom if the state has persistently objected to its formation – supports the consensual theory to the extent that a state may lawfully withhold its consent to a new rule. Likewise, a state cannot lawfully be coerced to sign a treaty. A state may even withhold its consent with respect to some provisions of a multilateral treaty, provided such reservations do not defeat the object and purpose of the treaty. Thus the doctrines of persistent objection and lawful reservation are compatible with the consensual principle.

Despite its conceptual charm, the consensual principle is problematic; it does not fully explain all rules of international law, including unequal treaties that Grotius mentions to show how one nation may impose hardship on another. Furthermore, a newly-born state cannot seek exemption from the obligation of established customs by withholding its consent. The argument that the state was not yet born when the custom developed and thus was unable to give its consent is rarely accepted.

Nor can states lawfully use the consent principle to violate fundamental norms of international law, called *jus cogens*. An agreement between two states to commit genocide, for example, is void *ab initio* since it seeks to permit what is fundamentally prohibited. Such constraints on state consent are consistent with the Grotian theory. Recall that Grotius derives his theory from the norms of natural law, stating rather boldly that "even God, then, cannot cause that two times two should not make four, so He cannot cause that which is intrinsically evil be not evil." This observation clarifies that the consensual principle cannot lawfully be invoked to violate basic values recognized by the international community. The free will of nations does not operate in a moral vacuum. State consent is and ought to be subject to constraints derived from moral intelligence, shared human experience and common sense.

One such constraint is the principle of *pacta sunt servanda*, which holds that promises made ought to be kept. The principle is as old as human sense of right and wrong. Yet its acceptance into international positive law has been problematic. The difficulty rests on the following simple logical confusion: If a sovereign state cannot be compelled to make a promise, then the sovereign state is equally free to break a promise. It is further argued that to deny that the sovereign state cannot break a promise would fetter its sovereignty. A strict rule that binds the promisor state to carry out its promise is considered incompatible with the notion of sovereignty. In the same fashion, one may also argue that if positive law is founded on the consent principle, a state should be able to disregard an existing rule by withdrawing its consent. To answer these questions, the relationship between consent and promise must be examined.

As a general principle, a state cannot be coerced to accept a new rule of international law. Yet the notion of consent considered apart from the concept of promise is misleading. When a state gives its consent to be bound by a rule, its consent is transformed into a legal promise. Grotius states that when a promise is made, the sovereign power is in a way limited. This is so because an act performed contrary to the promise is unjust and illegal. After making a promise, the promisor state cannot assert its sovereignty to break the promise. The promisor state cannot do so not because it is no longer sovereign and not because the promisee state is a superior sovereign but because to break a promise is unjust and ought to be a violation of law. In addition, a promise creates an expectation among promisee states that the promisor state will abide by the rule. Some promisee states may actually rely on the promise and accordingly act or refrain from acting in a way they would not have done without such a promise, a phenomenon known in the law of contracts as detrimental reliance.

Even though most promises create expectations and some create detrimental reliance, these consequences are not critical to the legal transformation of consent into promise. Once state consent is lawfully expressed, it turns into a promise. This transformative act is critical. A state is ordinarily under no obligation to express its consent to be bound by a new rule, but when it does so it promises to abide by that rule. To withhold consent is a matter within the authority of the state, but to break a promise is not; to coerce a state to express its consent is unlawful, but to coerce a state to keep its promise is not. Once state consent has been converted into legal promise, it becomes a matter of international law. Grotius summons the *Iliad* to make the point with poetic power: "The one to whom promise is made in some way captures and binds the promisor."

Although the distinction between consent and promise illuminates the basis of obligation, the question remains why states ought to perform their promises in good faith. Francois de Connan (1508-51), a French jurist whom Grotius challenges, argues against performing all international promises. According to Connan, promises can sometimes be worthless, some devoid of purpose, some more harmful to the promisor state than they are beneficial to the promisee state. He further argues that it is honorable but not obligatory to fulfill promises; only promises containing an exchange of interests ought to be obligatory. Thus Connan injects mischievous uncertainty in the regime of promises, vesting in the promisor state the authority to review the promise after it has been made and alter it if necessary to balance the national interests at stake.[8]

---

8. Thomas Hobbes (1588-1679), an English philosopher, argues that the promise means little in the state of nature. Benedict Spinoza (1632-77) denies that treaties have any binding force.

In addition to opposing Connan's specific arguments, Grotius announces a fundamental principle: "nothing is so in harmony with the good faith of mankind as that persons should keep the agreements which they have made with one another." Invoking the combined authority of Homer, Cicero, Solomon and the Scriptures, Grotius argues that good faith fulfillment of promises is the foundation of justice and that even God would act contrary to His nature if He did not make good His promises. All beings possessed of reason, he says, realize that the obligation to perform promises is the bond without which no legal system can successfully function. Once again Grotius invokes moral intelligence to make his point.

An additional dimension of good faith requires that promises ought to be performed truthfully. Technical and legalistic compliance, contrived to meet the letter of the law but not its spirit, is insufficient to satisfy the principle of good faith. According to Grotius, bad faith interpretations that distort the meaning of ordinary or technical language introduce deception to the regime of promises. Evasion or deceptive performance may likewise frustrate parties' intentions.

In advocating good faith performance of promises, Grotius focuses more on the aims of the gracious world than on tools of interpretation. Promises, he says, ought to be performed in order to avoid injustice and lighten the burden of odious agreements. Good faith seeks no pound of flesh, even if the text of the promise so demands. So interpretive rules to resolve disputes arising from the text of promises ought to be adjusted in each situation to obtain manifest fairness. Any formalistic use of the tools of interpretation, which frustrates the combined goals of reason and compassion, resurrects the predacious world in which promises are first extracted from weak states and then mercilesssly manipulated to optimize national interests.

Grotius offers the notion of good faith as the supreme principle that sustains the regime of promises called international law. Good faith is a principle of natural law in the sense that our intuitive intelligence tells us that no international system will function if promises are broken in the name of national interest or sovereignty. It is also a principle of positive law in the sense that it provides a legal basis to hold the promisor state responsible for its assumed obligation. So the principle of good faith joins positive law with our rational nature, facilitating the making of a decent and gracious world in which compassion and reason, not lawless national interest or willful sovereignty, guide relations among the nations of the world.

The promise of a gracious world remains unfulfilled. The Grotian legal positivism, however, derived from the principles of consent, promissory obligation, and good faith, was later codified in law. In 1927, the Permanent Court of International Justice reiterated the law-making authority of the nation-states in *The Lotus* case: "The rules of law binding upon states...emanate from their own free will as expressed in conventions or by usages generally accepted as expressing principles of law." Likewise, Article 38 of the Statute of the International Court of Justice codifies international custom and conventions and the general principles rooted in human civilization as the authoritative sources of international law. The preamble of the United Nations Charter states that one aim of the organization is to establish conditions under which respect for obligations from treaties can be maintained. The Vienna Convention on the Law of Treaties (1969) restates the customary rule that no state may invoke its domestic law as a justification for its failure to perform a treaty obligation. It also mandates that every treaty be performed in good faith. In the *Chorzow Factory Case*, the Permanent Court of International Justice states that it is a principle of international law that the breach of an international obligation must be fully compensated by adequate reparation.

In sum, the sovereign state emerges from the Grotian theory as a normatively empty entity exercising internal sovereignty without any external legal controls. In matters of internal sovereignty, it is tied to no one form of government, no one conception of justice, no one religion. Accordingly, nation-states with diverse political, cultural and religious backgrounds exercise internal sovereignty in accordance with domestic constitutions and design their internal institutions in response to the aspirations of all or some of their people. In matters of external sovereignty, however, nation-states are subject to international law.

The chief merit of the Grotian theory lies in its vision of a dynamic world in which states play an active role in constructing and preserving international order. As a pragmatist, Grotius recognizes the authority of states to make international law. But Grotius is not simply a legal positivist confined to statism. He ultimately anchors international law in the dictates of common wisdom. As an idealist, Grotius envisions a world in which the peoples of the world are tied together by bonds of compassion. He repudiates the doctrine of national interest as a basis of international law, for when nations are determined to advance their selfish goals or, even worse, to dominate other nations by the threat or use of force, the world order suffers instability. Grotius envisions a legal system in which the rule of law supplants the logic of force and moral intelligence replaces the theory of national interests.

Despite its great contributions to classical international law, some aspects of the Grotian theory are no longer valid. The rhetoric of national interest and state sovereignty continue to confuse the norms of moral intelligence. Vision of the gracious world still evokes criticism from hard-boiled realists. Yet contemporary international law has begun to place serious constraints on the state's internal sovereignty. Moreover, the fundamental structure of the sovereign state itself seems under distress as global forces pierce the veil of internal sovereignty. More and more it appears that the sovereign state may have to mutate and adapt to the changing landscape.

Part II:

Weakening of the Nation-State

Chapter Four

The Failure of State Structure

Classical international law provides a simple theoretical formula for establishing sovereign states: the sovereign state welds together four elements: a defined territory, a people, an effective government and competence to engage in foreign relations. For analytical purposes, the first three elements may be distinguished from the fourth. The first three elements constitute the *structure* of the sovereign state, through which the state exercises its internal sovereignty. The fourth element bears upon the state's external sovereignty, its ability to participate in international affairs, possess international rights and duties, and make and observe international law. The four elements together may be called the formula for creating a sovereign state. On the basis of this formula, colonial powers and other empires were broken into sovereign states. Few deny the total triumph of the Grotian theory and the concomitant sovereign state now that the era of empires, which placed the peoples of the world under a few crowns, has passed away into history.

Just like empires, however, nation-states cannot forever occupy the globe, primarily because no form of social organization is permanent. But now it appears that the era of nation-states may prove shorter than the era of empires. The structure of the sovereign state is inherently flawed, unable to withstand the contemporary strains of ethnonationalism, bitter historical memories that erupt into consciousness with vengeance, and state ideologies that impose cruel authoritarian governments. Many such forces challenge the territorial integrity of existing nation-states. Constituent units, including states or provinces within federated nation-states, assert their autonomy demanding the reallocation of internal sovereignty and in some cases even striving to break away. Secessionist movements, such as the ones for the independence of Quebec from Canada and the separation of Kashmir from India, rage in many nation-states, reminding the world that final boundaries are yet to be drawn.

This weakening of state structure from within is further aggravated when the regional and global forces of economics, the environment and information challenge the state's internal sovereignty and forcibly open its sovereign borders to the process of integration. Just as the middle ages were driven by the idea of One God, contemporary times highlight the meaning of One Earth. Increasingly, the prosperity of nations depends upon their ability to effectively participate in a rapidly changing international economic order.[1] Responding to highly competitive economic forces, nations have created both regional networks to pool their resources and global frameworks to facilitate interna-

---

1. That is why the economic sanctions imposed by the United Nations can be an effective weapon to modify the behavior of the target nation.

tional commerce with minimal national restrictions.[2] Corporations once loyal to the nation-state are now demanding more freedom to produce and invest in all parts of the world. They resent sovereign borders and internal sovereignties that impede the free flow of capital, goods and services. In addition, the creation of global legal mechanisms to protect the environment demonstrates a new consciousness among the nations of the world that, in many ways, they share the same destiny. Some environmental concerns are strictly local, but many others are regional and global. The recent explosion of information flow via satellites and computer networks has further diminished the significance of internal sovereignty as national events receive world-wide exposure and provoke international reactions. No longer may any nation-state live in isolation, for example, when satellite technology can pierce through the veil of internal sovereignty.

Thus a disruptive brew of ethnic, local, regional and global forces assaults the defective and artificial structure of the nation-state, raising fundamental questions such as which populations and territorial units are entitled to have separate states and which are not. No nation-state seems strong enough to withstand the conflicting but simultaneously active pressures of disintegration and integration. Nation-states created in the wake of decolonization show visible signs of weakness, since many are poorly equipped to repair the ethnic conflicts raging within their boundaries and some lack the means to effectively participate in and benefit from the new internationalization. Ancient countries, such as India, which for centuries held disparate communities together, are also experiencing the mixed impacts of provincialism from within and globalism from without. Even mighty nations such as the United States have begun to encounter the vortex of opposing forces unleashed by rapid internationalization on one hand and distrust of the central government on the other.

1. State as Defective Association

The Grotian state presupposes a state structure in which territory, people and government are in harmony with each other. A people who speak the same language, practice the same religion and share the same racial characteristics might arguably be able to institute a perfect association, provided they occupy a distinct geographical territory and submit to a single government, whether or not derived from popular will. In such a theoretical state, the territory contains a unified people and the people are at peace with their government. Consequently, each element of the state structure supports the others, maintaining the state's internal balance in both peace and war. In peace, the govern-

---

2. The North American Free Trade Agreement (NAFTA) among Canada, the United States and Mexico is an example of regional cooperation. Thee General Agreement on Tariffs and Trade and the associated World Trade Organization are the examples of global integration.

ment takes care of the people; in war, the people defend the territory. If all nation-states maintain such a structural balance, the Grotian theory of the sovereign state will survive and continue to be relevant.

No theory can be expected to perfectly mimic reality and therefore no theory may be discarded for its imperfection. However, a theory loses its efficacy if it substantially deviates from reality or if reality begins to deviate from the theory. In the case of the sovereign state, it appears that contemporary reality has substantially deviated from the Grotian theory. Even in the seventeenth century, the establishment of a balanced state structure was problematic. For example, the Dutch and Swiss struggles for independence from the Holy Roman Empire primarily sought local rather than national autonomy, since each Swiss canton and Dutch province was fiercely independent. That is why Grotius wanted Holland to be a separate sovereign state and resisted its inclusion into the Netherlands – an effort for which he had to go to prison. Historically, the consolidation of peoples and territories to build West European state structures had been tedious, slow and problematic.

Recall that Grotius repudiates popular sovereignty as a valid basis for demanding either independence or popular government. It is unclear, however, whether the people in the Grotian state ought to have a distinct identity derived from ethnicity, religion or language. Grotius embraces the Aristotelian notion of a perfect association, implying that the people of a state ought to have a common historically rooted identity. Yet Grotius leaves open the possibility that some of the people in the state, just like slaves in a household, may share little in common with the dominant people.

A balanced state structure in which territory, people and government are in harmony with each other is consistent with the Grotian theory. Since Grotius discards popular sovereignty as the mandatory basis of both state and government, a coercive state structure is also consistent with his theory. Accordingly, the Grotian theory suggests a hierarchical organization of three elements of state structure: territory emerges as the most superior element while popular government is the least important. The requirement that people have a shared identity falls somewhere in the middle.[3] Such a state structure may or may not be stable, it nonetheless simplifies the relative importance of elements.

Contemporary international law protects the territorial integrity of the state structure, a norm consistent with the Grotian theory. Accordingly, it rejects territorial secessions and outlaws territorial gains by conquest. The United Nations combined effort to evict the Iraqis from Kuwait demonstrates the superior value of territorial integrity in that the international community was willing to use any means necessary to discourage the forced absorption of a state structure. Existing sovereign territories may of course voluntarily reuni-

3. If the identity of a people is an insufficient basis to claim statehood, no people may lawfully seek independence from an empire except by force. That was precisely the case in the era of empires. The Swiss cantons and Dutch provinces had to fight the German and Spanish empires to gain independence.

te through valid legal procedures. The unification of Germany and the promised return of British Hong Kong to China are lawful territorial transactions. But forced mergers that destroy the separate existence of a sovereign territory are illegal.

As contemporary international law deviates from the Grotian theory, however, it injects confusion in the Grotian ranking of the elements. Despite continuing to emphasize the territorial integrity of the nation-state, contemporary international law resurrects popular sovereignty, which Grotius has painstakingly rejected. For example, contemporary law recognizes the people's right to self-determination, a right that dismantled colonial empires, foreign rule and alien domination. This right, granted to "all peoples," recognizes the preeminence of the people in the state structure. The emergence of more than a hundred new states carved out of colonial empires demonstrates that colonialism is no longer compatible with the norms of international law. Equally important, however, the right to self-determination upsets the structural equation of the Grotian state. It subordinates the territory to the people.

Furthermore, the law of human rights invokes popular sovereignty to subordinate the government to the people. The Universal Declaration of Human Rights and the International Covenant on Civil and Political Rights require that the government be based on popular will expressed in periodically held free and genuine elections, thus replacing the classical norm of effective government with that of popular government. This normative shift modifies the Grotian state structure under which the government may lawfully derive its authority from control over the territory and the people, without regard to the people's consent.

Thus when the right to self-determination is joined with the right to popular government, the Grotian ranking of three elements of state structure is radically changed. Now the people are the preeminent element. They may invoke the right of self-determination to carve out a new state and they may invoke the right to popular government to recall authoritarian government. Thus contemporary international law aims at subordinating both the territory and the government to the people. More important, this normative change, when successfully carried out, subjects the state's internal sovereignty to the people.

But even under contemporary international law, the preeminence of the people in the state structure is less than total. Contemporary international law recognizes no right of territorial secession against existing nation-states. And not all nations of the world have fully embraced the notion of popular sovereignty as the basis of government. As a result, many state structures are in disarray. It remains unclear which peoples are entitled to the right of self-determination and which are not. It is also unclear whether the people in each state have the right to popular government. International law still upholds the elements of the state structure. However, no agreement exists as to which element is the controlling factor in the formation and preservation of nation-states. Accordingly, three competing models of state structures have developed, each espousing the preeminence of a different element.[4]

First, the ethnic model advocates the preeminence of the people, asserting that the people ought to be the chief element in the making and breaking of nation-states. Deriving its vigor from the concept of self-determination, the ethnic model proposes to divide ethnic populations into separate independent territories, thus seeking and approving territorial secessions. Second, the civic model emphasizes the element of territory, asserting that the territorial integrity of the state ought to be maintained by enticing diverse populations to coexist in accordance with a broadly approved rule of law. This model proposes to unify diverse peoples by advocating loyalty to the territory in which they reside. Third, the authoritarian model relies upon efficacious government, uniting all the peoples in a territory by requiring loyalty to the state's ideology. It demands that the people submit to the authoritarian state structure, and it suppresses ethnic diversity, particularly when incompatible with the state's ideology.

Each model must ultimately embrace all four elements of the sovereign state – people, territory, government and the foreign policy competence – simply because no state can come into existence if any one element is absent.[5] The problem that arises, then, is that undue emphasis on any one element compromises the others, weakening the state structure. Thus a dynamic and unpredictable relationship between the elements is generated, rendering each model inherently defective and dysfunctional.

Emphasizing people, the ethnic model wishes to resurrect the Aristotelian concept of a perfect association. But what is a "people"? The ethnic model claims that a group of persons sharing a sense of belonging derived from shared ethnicity constitutes a people, providing a natural foundation for the state. Therefore, a people derived from common ancestors and with a shared sense of history, culture, language, religion, folk songs and music have a natural right to live in union without any external interference. To realize its vision, the model demands a liberal construction of the right of self-determination to establish, as far as possible, ethnically pure sovereign states. This demand at first seems reasonable in part because the formula for the creation of the sovereign state is simple and flexible. In theory, any people occupying a territory can establish a sovereign state if they can institute an effective government and demonstrate the competence to conduct foreign policy, a set of criteria not too difficult to satisfy. Practically, ministates such as Monaco,

---

4. Assume that under all models the capacity to conduct foreign relations is not in question.
5. The fourth element, the capacity to conduct foreign policy, may be more relevant for dependent territories seeking independence from parent states.

Nauru and Liechtenstein act as models for many peoples who seek independent statehood.[6]

The ethnic model highlights the artificial character of existing nation-states by pointing out how national borders do not correspond with the ethnic map of the world. Some states contain diverse ethnic populations; others partition the same ethnic population. States like Rwanda and Bosnia contain ethnic populations willing to dominate each other by genocide. Some, like Israel, are founded by imported populations. Some, like Iraq and Kuwait, are fragments of the same historic region. Furthermore, religious, cultural and linguistic populations that previously lived together in the same country without any marked sense of nationalism, such as the Kurds, have been forcibly scattered among two or more separate nation-states. This artificial and in some cases mischievous partitioning of ethnic populations is a constant source of political confusion, regional instability and global disorder.

The communist era further distorted the ethnic map. The Korean peninsula, populated by a single ethnic group, is still divided into two hostile territories. The ideological division of the peoples and territories of Vietnam and Germany for decades remained a source of conflict threatening world peace. The continual struggle between Afghans and Tajiks, two distinct ethnic groups in Afghanistan, for the control of government is a legacy of Soviet occupation. Capitalist Taiwan remains severed from Communist China, even though Taiwan has not yet claimed the status of an independent nation-state. China now wishes to absorb both Taiwan and Hong Kong, arguing that these scattered populations constitute one people who must live within a single state structure.

Inspired by the ethnic model, some artificially partitioned ethnic populations seek more autonomy within existing states, some assert the right of self-determination to found new, separate states, and some wish to be reunited with their kind in neighboring states so that they may jointly create a new nation-state.

In each case, existing nation-states usually resist these demands, frequently at the expense of serious human rights violations. For example, when Muslims in the Indian-held Kashmir assert their demand to join Pakistan, Indian security forces determined to preserve the borders of their nation-state use ruthless means to suppress what they call Pakistani-sponsored terrorism. The Kurds, divided among Turkey, Syria, Iraq and Iran, have suffered relentless repression that becomes even more brutal when the Kurdish call for an independent state involves armed insurrection. The forced expulsion and dispersion of Palestinians in states surrounding Israel have inflamed terrorism in the entire region as Palestinian refugees assert their right to return to their ancestral homeland, the same territory Israelis claim as their own.

---

6. Monaco is less than two square kilometers in size; Nauru's population is less than ten thousand; Liechtenstein's population is less than thirty thousand.

Even though the ethnic model provides a useful critique of existing nations, it has its own serious flaws. To begin with, the notion of ethnicity itself has no clear basis. The Aristotelian myth of perfect association has little bearing in contemporary global life. Even Aristotle knew full well that the human propensity to classify people will find some basis to divide even the most apparently homogeneous community. No wonder, therefore, that the criteria for ethnic classifications vary from place to place and from people to people, as defining criteria are most often tied to complex historical events and memories. At the crudest level of classification, ethnic populations may divide themselves on the basis of race or color.[7] But race and color are not the only factors for ethnic divisions, because even racially homogeneous populations may nonetheless find some other reason to form separate nation-states. So ethnicity also may be defined in terms of religious, cultural or linguistic differences. The movement for an independent Quebec is based on culture and language, not race or color. The movement for separating Kashmir from India is motivated by difference in religion, not race or language. Each ethnic classification, how arbitrary it may seem, assumes a real and forceful character.

It will be hard to defend that one type of ethnic group may lawfully claim a separate state but not the other. If each criterion of ethnicity is taken seriously, the ethnic model loses the guiding hand. If every ethnic group is granted the right to self-determination, many nations-states may have to be dismantled or rearranged – a proposal that seems overwhelming. Furthermore, many states contain minorities that share little in common with the dominant ethnic group. Sometimes, as in Bosnia, the ethnic populations are more or less equal in numerical strength or live in such intertwined cities and villages that they cannot be severed from each other. If ethnic populations cannot be severed into separate territories, the ethnic model does little beyond breeding intolerance that may lead to conflict, repression, forced homogenization, even genocide.

Finally, the ethnic model is doomed to fail because it seeks a world that simply does not exist. Ignoring the complex history of cultural and racial diffusion, ethnic statism pursues the ideal of homogeneity. It presupposes a static world in which ethnic populations are forever confined within closed geographical boundaries. In past centuries, primarily due to modest means of transportation, populations of the world sequestered in different parts of the globe were successful in preserving distinctive characteristics such as language, skin color, religion and culture – the bases of ethnic statism. But even in the relatively static world, however, migrations caused by conquests, famine and natural disasters occurred in many regions of the world, intermixing ethnic groups. Nonetheless, ethnic statism prefers and longs for a world in which ethnicity crosses no national boundaries – a plan that must fail under the dynamic stress of global integration.

---

7. In the United States, for example, racial classification is the dominant factor.

Reliance on fantasies of ethnic purity makes the ethnic model a dysfunctional social construct.[8] The model fails to cope with human movement, it resists diffusion, and it seals off territories. It prohibits inter-ethnic contact. It is narcissistic and self-righteous. It advocates segregation. It ignores the fact that moved by slavery, war and importation of labor, sizable ethnic populations relocate across states, regions and continents – a process of cross-migration that continues to alter the demographics of nations. Due to this constant migration, ethnic states, even if once homogeneous, experience tension with the arrival of new ethnic populations that wish to speak their own language, practice their own religion and form their own neighborhoods, often to the displeasure of existing ethnic populations. To re-establish ethnic purity, the ethnic state may resort to exclusion, deportation and harassment of foreigners, anyone who can be labelled as "the other."

Consider the example of Western Europe. The new ethnic complexity in some European states breeds cultural tensions and identity conflicts. The presence of North Africans in France, South Asians in the United Kingdom and Turks in Germany has disturbed the traditional cultural balance in these states threatening, some would say, the core values of Western civilization. Distinct in race, religion, language and living habits, these immigrants implant Islamic, Hindu, African and Asiatic values into the heart of Europe, challenging the norms of homogeneity, ethnonationalism and even the concept of the nation-state itself. Even though the European Convention on Human Rights, to which France, the United Kingdom and Germany are signatories, prohibits *en masse* expulsion of immigrants, many extremist groups in these states argue for the eviction of foreigners. For the time being, it seems unlikely that extremists will achieve their goal of "social decontamination." But the fury of ethnic nationalism, sustained in interstices of prejudice, will continue to apply pressure on the people and governments to define the nation-state in the Aristotelian terms of perfect association under which, for example, "Germany is for Germans only." Some fear, and rightfully so, that following the successful example of the Serbs, ethnic cleansing by which target ethnic populations are evicted from specified territories will be practiced in other parts of the world to establish or preserve the perceived purity of the ethnic state.

Repudiating ethnic statism, the civic model advocates the preeminence of territory in the state structure. To establish the territory as the basis of national motif, the civic state usually institutes popular government and a constitutional order in which diverse ethnic groups are promised fair and equal treat-

8. Remarkable trends distinguish older nations from newer ones. Migration toward older nations, such as India and China, despite the mystique of their ancient cultures, has been notably low. In contrast, newer nations, such as the United States, Australia and Canada, are essentially populated by immigrants. Economic opportunities and a liberal culture often attract immigrants.

ment. This gives all the people more or less the same stake in the preservation of the state. Furthermore, the civic state creates the concept of a "new people." This is achieved by merging loyalties of diverse groups into a new identity that attaches them to the territory. Since the civic state is formally identified with no one people, all peoples within the territory can develop the same respect for state institutions and the state structure. The citizens of the the United States are Americans, not Italians, Nigerians or Pakistanis. The civic state may even make an affirmative effort to socialize diverse populations, impressing them with the virtues of mutual tolerance and non-discrimination and providing them with equal access to political and economic opportunities. Thus the civic model attempts to develop structural harmony between diverse peoples, the territory and the government by emphasizing the principles of civic responsibility, patriotism and the rule of law.

The civic model retains the concept of territorial sovereignty but modifies the Grotian theory in one important respect. Instead of focusing on efficacy alone, the civic model espouses popular sovereignty as the sole legitimate basis of government. Recall that Grotius does not reject popular sovereignty but simply insists that popular sovereignty need not be the basis of every government. The civic model, however, elevates popular sovereignty to a level of preeminence required by no other form of government. It is unclear, however, whether the civil model necessarily allows popular sovereignty to be the basis of territorial partition. The peaceful partition of Czechoslovakia into two separate states suggests that the civic model may permit territorial partition if the ethnic populations inhabiting the same civic state mutually agree to do so. However, most civic states prefer that a new definition of "the people" be used to preserve territorial integrity.

Two distinct submodels exist within the concept of the civic model. One submodel, exemplified by nations like Canada, focuses upon multiculturalism. In addition to forging the sense of a new people, it encourages ethnic communities to preserve their old cultural heritages. Multiculturalism presupposes that the civic state is compatible with the simultaneous presence and protection of diverse communities. The other submodel, typified by the United States, emphasizes the integration of ethnic populations into a new cultural ethos that draws strength from diversity but discourages the retention of separate ethnic identities. The sense of a new people supposedly overrides the need for old identities. In both submodels, state institutions such as the legislature and the courts are expected to act as fair and neutral arbiters, consolidating the civic state structure. In both submodels, therefore, a temperate but persistent effort is made to homogenize diverse groups into a new national identity, forming a new people.

The civic state in some ways embraces the mystical meaning of *country*. The traditional meaning of country, as seen in India and China, was all-embracing; it was a formless concept suited to accommodate all diverse groups. Few countries had homogeneous populations. Most contained disparate ethnic populations that lived side by side, in adjoining territories but with open borders, sometimes in the same region, even within the same community. Though ruled by a single king, the country had no flag, no national anthem, no high court and no over-arching central bureaucracy – the symbols of modern statehood. No single legal order is required to found a country. In fact, a country is not actually founded but comes into existence through the action of complex historical forces spread over centuries. The civic state attempts to follow the example of an essentially formless country, but simultaneously invents a new artificial objectivity rooted in state symbols. Diverse populations derived from diverse cultures, races and religions are socially orchestrated to identify with state symbols and the civic state they represent.[9]

In theory, the civic state structure is preferable to the ethnic model. It accommodates ethnic diversity, severing the state's formal connection with any one ethnic, religious or linguistic group. The First Amendment of the United States Constitution, for example, prohibits the government both from establishing an official state religion and from denying diverse groups the right to practice their faiths. This state neutrality toward religion allows diverse religious groups to coexist with equal freedom and dignity. Furthermore, the rejection of racial segregation in the United States is also a legal attempt to minimize the gulf between ethnic groups. Current laws against discrimination on the basis of race, color, religion and national origin serve to further reinforce the structural balance of the civic state.

But despite its efforts and apparent successes, even the civic model cannot maintain a balanced state structure. The laws of the civic state tell one story, social reality tells another. The state structure looks balanced but only on paper. Even when the civic state is formally neutral in matters of ethnicity, state institutions are often dominated by a single ethnic group. Take the example of the United States. Despite a rich linguistic and cultural diversity, the domination of Anglo-Saxons is firmly established in the United States. Many ethnic populations willingly relinquish their languages and abandon their cultures in exchange for more complete participation in the civic order. Others resist. The Hispanic populations conquered by the United States in the 1846 war with Mexico continue to assert their linguistic and cultural identity. Even Chinese immigrants brought in the nineteenth century to build the railroad seem determined to preserve their language and culture. The native Indians who were once sovereign in the Americas live confused, isolated and resentful lives, partially as a result of resistance to "American" culture.

The plight of indigenous populations in the nation-state reveals the flaws of homogenization and the concomitant concept of a new people. Even in the

9. These objective symbols may sharpen the identity of a nation-state in the community of nations. Ironically, however, the process of state differentiation at the global level comes home to roost, inculcating among domestic populations a more pronounced sense of their separate ethnic selves. Consequently, many ethnic populations begin to dream of and demand a separate statehood. Thus, the process of ethnic consolidation triggered through superficial state symbols begins to work in the opposite direction of ethnic segmentation.

civic state, assimilation is often achieved by imposing on the entire nation the values of a specific ethnic population, whether in the majority or not. Even though most ethnic minorities are susceptible to both forced and manipulative assimilation, indigenous populations have been the most vulnerable groups. For decades, states containing indigenous populations adopted the policy of assimilation, with no respect for "aboriginal ancestral-historical territories." Advocates for indigenous populations, both in administering states and the United Nations, argue that indigenous peoples should have the right to self-determination by virtue of which they should be free to determine their own degree of autonomy. Few states, however, grant indigenous populations the right to secede. Sequestered in territorial reservations, indigenous populations continue to resent the authority and even the existence of the administering nation-state. Nonetheless, an eerie myth is maintained that such segregated indigenous populations constitute "sovereign nations."

This idea of sovereign nations within the sovereign state is unworkable both in law and fact. When conveneint, administering states find pretexts to encroach upon the promised rights of indigenous populations, particularly if the territory allotted to these groups turns out to be rich in valuable minerals or other natural resources. Indigenous populations themselves face the dilemma of choosing between the benefits of assimilation and isolation. A gradual and voluntary integration of indigenous populations into the mainstream culture might in some cases be acceptable, but indigenous populations are in principle as much entitled to preserve their culture as are other ethnic populations. Groups forced to assimilate will most likely pass their grievances on to posterity, sowing the seeds of future discontent.

When diverse ethnic populations willingly undergo a gradual and peaceful process of socialization for a significant period of time, they may merge and develop a shared sense of a new one people. A broadly-shared governmental system in which diverse groups are equitably represented may further nurture a legal and political culture that inhibits dissension and strengthens bonds across ethnic lines. But even in such cases, old identities can be resurrected to redefine historic relations. In the United Kingdom, the gradual process of socialization between the Scots and the English has been relatively less brutal. Even after four centuries, however, the bond between Scotland and England is weak in many ways. Recent Scottish demands for more autonomy exemplify the power of ethnicity to shape the dynamics of the nation-state. If ethnic statism continues to gather momentum, the separation of Scotland and similarly situated ethnic territories cannot be ruled out. If mistrust between ethnic populations is deeply entrenched and periodically erupts in bloody clashes, such as between Hindus and Muslims in India, even democratic institutions face difficulty in preserving the state structure against the forces of secession, violence and intolerance. These examples also show that even the rule of law and a relatively equitable legal system cannot always forge a new civic identity.

A further difficulty arises when, despite its formal commitment to equality and the rule of law, the civic state's actual commitment to fairness toward diverse ethnic populations is questionable. In the United States, most state institutions are designed to discourage discrimination on the basis of race, color, religion or national origin – the typical bases of ethnicity. Yet mutual distrust among ethnic populations, particularly in the area of race, continues to plague the society. Minority groups complain that they lack equal access to political and economic opportunities, while the dominant ethnic population believes that law unjustly favors minorities. These complaints are normal in any community and pose no danger to the civic state structure, provided ethnic populations remain within the limits of tolerance and resolve their grievances through law. If the distribution of civic benefits and burdens is itself unfair, mere formal equality cannot sustain the state structure. Injustice leads to violence and violence deepens mutual distrust. If the level of violence is a reliable indicator of the failure of the state to harmonize its people with each other as well as with the government and the territory, the United States must do more to achieve a more just and inclusive state structure.

The most vulnerable dimension of the civic state structure is the rather frail assumption that ethnic groups can indeed forget the past and join into a new civic enterprise. This is a noble mission without which no civic state can hope to survive. It may even succeed when the people are generally prosperous. Yet civic statism provides no assurance that ethnic injustices committed in the past can be erased from the memories of the oppressed. After all, the human condition is such that the past never ceases to shape the present. In the United States, slavery and segregation practiced in the past have left deep scars on both black and white Americans. Even though new laws prohibit any such degrading treatment, the memory of past events persists and the relation between blacks and whites remains tense. Likewise the memory of the holocaust persists as do the claims of those who believe it never took place, raising a troublesome question whether Jews and Germans have indeed reconciled with each other. In India, a thousand years of Muslim rule, which often brutalized Hindus, left a trail of uncomfortable memories.

In addition to preserving historical memories, the human inclination to avenge past injuries, real or assumed, has been astounding. Even the dynamics of civic statism fail to prevent ethnic groups from acting upon past memories. So what seems to have been forgiven, if not forgotten, resurfaces in new contexts, leading to conflict and even civil war. In Bosnia, the Serbs exhume past memories of five hundred years of Turkish rule to recall the ill-treatment of their ancestors. The dismantling of Yugoslavia and subsequent rapid recontextualization of ethnic relations in Bosnia have unleashed forces of hatred and genocide among the same people who for decades lived side by side in relative peace.

Ideally, the civic state structure ought to succeed despite its shortcomings, because fragmentation of the earth in accordance with the ethnic model would produce innumerable, small, dysfunctional nation-states. In reality, however, the civic model fails to recognize the force of ethnicity in the structural equation of the sovereign state. It pretends that diverse peoples can indeed be merged by common loyalty to the territory and that they will indeed develop a new common identity. History in general and the conflict in

Bosnia in particular demonstrate that ethnic identities can linger over centuries in periodic cycles of quietism and eruption. Founded on uninformed innocence, the civic model thus builds the nation-state on disproven idealism. Most important, it refuses to see that the very concept of the nation-state sharpens a sense of identity *vis a vis* other nations. It divides the peoples of the world rather than uniting them. So the creation of a new common identity by assimilating diverse groups, even if successful, will reinforce the same human inclination that causes ethnic conflict and partition to begin with.

This is most obvious when ethnic groups use peaceful and legal mechanisms to break up seemingly well-functioning civic states. The voluntary and legal partition of Czechoslovakia into two separate states is a case in point. Another such method to gradually weaken the civic state is the idea of *devolution* – a legal challenge to the central authority of large and powerful states. In contrast to revolution, by which internal sovereignty is seized in violation of existing succession rules, devolution is a legal mechanism by which state authority is decentralized. Based on the premise that government ought to be "closer to the people," devolution seeks to shift power to local governments. Opposed to powerful central governments under which decision-making authority is concentrated at the center, devolution repatriates the greater portion of internal sovereignty to constituent states or provinces. Consequently, local rather than central government regulates the day-to-day behavior of natural and juridical persons. External sovereignty, including foreign policy competence, however, remains at the center.

If constituent units contain distinct ethnic populations, the demands for devolution may coincide with ethnonationalism. The Scottish demand for peaceful devolution of authority from the central government in London to Scotland is partly inspired by ethnic consciousness, as subdued animosity continues to exist between the Scots and the English. Likewise, the demand for local autonomy in the ethnically disparate provinces of India is primarily inspired by ethnonationalism. In Indian Punjab, for example, the Sikhs strive to acquire more local autonomy, even a separate homeland, chiefly because they resent the Hindu-dominated central government.

The most intriguing demand for devolution has surfaced in the United States, which presently enjoys an unprecedented prestige not only as a successful nation-state but also as a formidable world superpower. The national government conceived in the constitution as a government of few enumerated powers has over the last two centuries augmented its authority in areas once belonging to constituent states. Devolutionists now wish to disassemble the national legal order, reallocating governmental authority to federated units.

Since the constitutional establishment of the United States as a union in 1789, both the federal legislature and federal courts have, jointly and severally, constructed a national legal order facilitating free trade among what were once "sovereign states" and harmonizing the laws regarding civil and political rights. This process of nation-building has been slow, often facing resistance from states that wish to retain the authority to shape life in their respective communities. Southern states, which opposed federal decisions to abolish slavery and racial segregation, have been the most persistent advocates of what is known as "state's rights." Originally, associated with segregation and racial discrimination, "state's rights" is a constitutional code phrase that refers to opposition to national intervention in the domestic affairs of constituent states.

In the past few years, however, the demand for reducing the size of the national government has reinvigorated the doctrine of state's rights. The criticism that "the national government is too big" implies that executive, legislative and judicial authority ought to be reallocated, giving more to the states. Southern politicians are once again among the most effective and outspoken advocates of the devolution of authority. In the changing political climate, however, the proposed devolution is no longer associated with racism but defended in the name of economic efficiency and the people's right to self-government. The national government, it is asserted, is too paternalistic, remote and bureaucratic. Familiar and accountable local and state governments, it is further argued, offer better democracy, better economic efficiency and a greater individual involvement in the affairs of the community.

In addition to peaceful political advocates of devolution, a small number of militant and armed right-wing groups across the United States challenge the authority of the central government. Protected by the constitutional rights of free speech and association, these groups assert the right to bear arms, conduct paramilitary exercises, and resent what they describe as an overly intrusive federal government. Some protest against federal incomes taxes, some against the mixing of races, some against perceived domination by Jews, some against the secularization of the state, some against the country's involvement in the United Nations, and some against environmental regulations. Equating the central government with an occupying army, these groups challenge the authority of federal officials and impede the enforcement of federal laws. Afraid that their freedoms will be taken away, some groups even advocate violence against the federal government and its officials.[10]

This devolutionary revolution in the United States, if successfully carried out, is likely to weaken the central state structure. Although the United States cannot be compared with the Holy Roman Empire, the phenomenon that dismembered the empire seems to have taken root in the United States. State and local "princes" in the United States are determined to weaken the authority of the central state structure. Though highly unlikely, some states may in the future collude with disgruntled groups to weaken the authority of the central government. A more serious and unintended consequence of such devolution might encourage states like California and Florida, which contain large Spanish-speaking populations and bear the massive expense of illegal immigration from Central and South America, to assert even more independence.

---

10. On April 19, 1995, a bomb blew up a federal building in Oklahoma City in the United States, killing about two hundred people. The bombers had close ties with right-wing paramilitary groups.

Ethnic relations between Hispanic and Anglo populations might deteriorate to further compound the struggle between states and the central government. If demographics continue to change due to increase of the so-called Latino population, the states carved out of the territory conquered from Mexico in 1846 might begin to claim the right to self-determination. While these events seem unlikely to occur in the near future, revived historical memories of forced assimilation and reckless demands for devolution jointly may over time weaken the foundation of the United States. It seems also unlikely that the United States will abandon civic statism and adopt the authoritarian model that proposes to suppress what cannot be cured.

Repudiating both ethnic and civic models, the authoritarian state structure emphasizes the element of efficacious government in the structural equation of the sovereign state. It employs the force of ideology, religion or national unity to fortify the nation-state against the centrifugal forces of disintegration. Authoritarian statism is the product of legal positivism run rampant, under which a coercive legal order is deemed essential to define the relationship between people and government. According to Hans Kelsen, a legal positivist present at the time of decolonization of the world, the state is a politically organized society held together by a coercive order called law; accordingly, an efficacious government, whether just or unjust, is the *sine qua non* of the nation-state. In contrast to ethnic statism, the authoritarian state structure does not require that the people share linguistic, religious or racial characteristics; authoritarian statism uses coercive power when necessary to weld even the most disparate communities into a single entity. The authoritarian model may be used to establish communist, fascist, theocratic and racist regimes.

Ironically, the authoritarian model is also consistent with the law of decolonization under which an entity, whether a portion of the empire or a colony, seeking independence could not obtain separate statehood unless it was able to institute self-government.[11] But self-government may not be confused with with democracy. Self-government, a term closely associated with decolonialism, was the opposite of foreign rule. Having no one precise definition, self-government primarily entails the ability of a people to govern themselves without foreign control. Many forms of government, not just democracy, are compatible with the notion of self-government. Influenced by the authoritarian model, the ruling elites of newly independent states instituted coercive state structures based on the questionable assumption that the people were not yet able to live under democracy. Consequently, the authoritarian model

11. The element of effective government often trumped the elements of people and territory. An ethnically homogeneous community occupying a geographically distinct territory could not become a state if it lacked the resources to institute self-government. It remained a dependent territory under the suzerainty of another state. Not all dependent territories, however, are incompetent to institute self-government; some are occupied or compelled to remain under the control of another state.

imposed on many new nation-states in Asia and Africa spawned dictatorships, military rule and one party "democracy."

The authoritarian model exploits the norms of classical international law to seek legitimacy. It invokes the principle of political independence enshrined in the United Nations Charter, asserting that sovereign states are free to institute any form of government as they wish. This interpretation of the principle vests the "state" and not necessarily the "people" with political independence – a position consistent with the Grotian theory. To further forestall legal criticism, the authoritarian model also invokes Article 2(7) of the United Nations Charter, arguing that not even the world has the authority to intervene in matters within the domestic jurisdiction of the state. Many authoritarian states continue to advocate these interpretations, ignoring the human rights law that now requires that the government be derived from the will of the people. Even some so-called civic states, such as India, adopt a similar legal position to deny access to human rights organizations.

Thus, the authoritarian state structure often denies the fundamental civil and political liberties guaranteed by the international law of human rights. The dynamics of the authoritarian model have different consequences in different states. In an ethnically homogenous state, the people often protest the authoritarian rule, demanding denied liberties and in some cases even a change in the form of government itself. Sometimes they resort to violence. In such conflicts between people and government, however, the survival of the state is rarely threatened. The people in most cases wish to bring about necessary changes in government without further insisting that the state itself be dissolved. In Iran, many groups oppose the theocratic structure of the state but rarely do they insist that Iran as a nation-state ought to be dismantled.

Authoritarianism in a multiethnic state must contend with the forces of ethnic fragmentation. However, the problem of ethnic division remains unresolved when the state structure itself is dominated by one ethnic population to the exclusion of others. In the Soviet Union, for example, the Russians formed the ruling elite. In such situations, groups excluded from participation in the state structure not only resent authoritarianism but may also contest the very existence of the state, particularly if these groups inhabit distinct and severable territories. The demand for secession gathers further momentum when the state uses harsh means to suppress the movement. Repression of diverse ethnic populations usually fails to build a stable state. If repression is carried out through the use of force, ethnic conflict may be temporarily quelled. The protection of the state structure through repression, however, brings more harm than good. Russia's recent use of force in Chechnya, which attempted to secede, brought world-wide condemnation and internal opposition. A defeated Chechnya may unwillingly embrace Russian statism. But the sentiments of self-determination and secession would continue to stir the republic of Chechnya toward independence.

The breakdown of the Soviet Union demonstrates how even authoritarian statism, driven by a powerful ideology, may prove insufficient to support an otherwise artificial state structure. The Soviet Union encompassed fifteen republics with disparate historical, sociological and cultural backgrounds. Islamic republics in the east shared little in common with Baltic states in the west. One might imagine that more than seventy years of ideological education, forced discipline and a shared pride of living together in a superstate with tremendous influence in the world would have welded the diverse ethnic populations into a new nation. The Soviet Union, however, remained an artificial state structure of disparate populations and territories.[12] Communism failed to replace religio-ethnic identities. When the authoritarian structure began to collapse, Christianity in the western republics and Islam in the eastern republics leaped out of suppressed memory of these communities, restoring their old, now revitalized, historical identities.

To avoid territorial fragmentation and localism, the authoritarian model may dissolve internal provincial boundaries imposing a single national state structure. Such a unitary state structure often fails to build a cohesive nation, particularly if its ethnic populations have previously lived in historically distinct territories and resist the concept of a new identity. In Pakistan the unitary state structure imposed in 1958 by the military government highlighted, not diluted, the separate provincial identities of Sind, Punjab, Baluchistan and Bengal derived from more than a thousand years of distinctive history. Indeed the ethnic divisions ran so deep that they led to the eventual secession of Bengal, which became Bangladesh. Likewise, the central control imposed on the Indian Kashmir is effective in temporarily suppressing the secessionist movement, but in the long run it strengthens the Kashmiri ethnic identity.

Just like the civic model, the authoritarian model underestimates the significance of distinct peoples in the structural equation of the sovereign state. The civic model recognizes the existence of diversity but attempts to create a new people. The authoritarian model may or may not recognize distinct peoples. In most cases, however, it assumes that separate identities will meld in the grip of a strong unifying ideology and under the pressure of a coercive government. Thus the authoritarian state structure remains unstable, as each element tears upon the other. The people are in conflict with the government and the government is in conflict with distinct territories. Still the authoritarian state structure, whether it is theocracy in Iran or as it was communism in the Soviet Union, insists on constructing a perfect association.

To overcome the weaknesses of the inherently flawed structure of the nation-state, many states use external enemies and appeal to patriotism to protect themselves against the disruptive forces of ethnonationalism and territorial fragmentation. Authoritarian states use external enemies, real or perceived, to merge the loyalties of ethnic populations or defend the repressive state structure. Even civic states sometimes use the same technique. The fear of commu-

---

12. Iran is also an ideological state but its national cohesiveness is derived from shared language, religion and culture, not exclusively from ideology.

nism generated in the United States, for example, sharpened its national identity in the world as the chief bulwark of capitalism and individual liberty. This was arguably a step in nation-building. During this same period, however, federal enforcement agencies became overly intrusive, seeking un-American activities, spying on writers, teachers and artists, the very people who nurture the soul of the civic state. The external enemy created the internal enemy, weakening the process by which citizens were supposed to come together. Without learning from past experiences, federal and local policymakers continue to periodically pick out an external or internal enemy to reinforce feelings of patriotism among citizens. Perceived threats from China, Japan, Iran and Cuba are exaggerated to demonstrate that the United States is vulnerable and needs the support of the people. The example of the Soviet Union proves that even the threat of an enemy is unable to save the artificial and defective state structure. It remains to be seen, however, whether such nation-building techniques will work in civic states.

Patriotism is another means to bolster a defective state structure. It functions because the borders of the nation-state are not merely geographical, they are also psychological. Geographically, natural barriers such as mountains, oceans and canyons divide few states. More often, leaders first draw boundaries on a map and then artificially protect them with fences and border police. For example, oceans border the United States in the east and west, but in the southwest the dividing line between the United States and Mexico is predominantly barbed wire rather than rock or river. Similarly, in the north only an artificial concept divides the vast stretch of nature that native tribes freely traversed for centuries before Canada and the United States even existed. All over the globe, states erect legal and physical fences to divide what nature has left united. Quite often, the geographical boundaries nation-states wish to develop are capricious from cultural and anthropological viewpoints. Boundary makers have partitioned ethnic, linguistic, religious and cultural populations that previously lived together for generations. But even where physical borders are capricious, psychological borders are concrete. The psychological boundary between the United States and Mexico looms large even if populations on either side remain substantially related, if not indistinguishable.

Geopsychological boundaries and patriotism are related to the legal concept of nationality, the primary relationship that binds the individual to the nation-state. Through the concept of nationality, the nation-state imposes burdens, such as military service, and confers benefits, such as diplomatic protection. Nationality, however, is not simply a legal bond that the state uses to control its nationals; it is also a social attachment by which individuals acquire sentimental pride in their nation-state. Nationals frequently favor their state over all others, work for its interests and betterment, volunteer for military service and even sacrifice their lives defending its honor. States that fail to create patriotic sentiments among their nationals remain unstable, break up, and even lose their existences altogether. Patriotic indoctrination, therefore, occurs in almost all states. Furthermore, states use their coercive power to protect themselves from subversion by imposing stiff penalties for treason, espionage and other offenses against state interests. In fact, some states go as far as to grossly violate the human rights of their nationals in order to stifle criticism.

Many nation-states have been successful in forging patriotism. In some cases, however, patriotic attachment to the nation-state fails to develop. Secessionist movements in India and Canada demonstrate the failure of patriotism to unite disparate peoples. But patriotic attachment to a territory can be worse than patriotism that fails. The conflict between Israelis and Palestinians stands as a tragic and bloody example of conflicting psychological loyalties to the same territory. The establishment of Israel forced hundreds of thousands of Palestinians from their ancestral territory, making them refugees in neighboring countries. Opposed to the existence of the state of Israel, Palestinian activists launched an armed struggle against the new state and its inhabitants, who migrated there to establish a homeland. The Palestinian National Charter declared that the "partition of Palestine in 1947 and the establishment of the state of Israel are entirely illegal." The Palestinians want to establish their own nation-state, which Israel opposes. This conflict demonstrates how a patriotic attachment to the same territory may invite a bloody feud between peoples who previously lived together in relative harmony.[13]

Patriotism may benefit the nation-state, but it acts as a wedge to divide the peoples of the world. The legal and psychological control a state exercises over its nationals disables many individuals from relating to "foreign" peoples and "foreign" lands. Attachment to the territory of the nation-state may preclude nationals from developing an interest in and concern for people in other parts of the world. Allegiance to the nation-state may prevent nationals from challenging incorrect and unwise state policies, particularly against foreign peoples and foreign lands. National narcissism may impede respect for other cultures and civilizations, causing ill-will, contempt, and even hatred. National fanaticism may lead to aggression and genocide. Such artifacts of the nation-state can therefore endanger the physical and spiritual well being of global life.

The structure of the sovereign state appears to be inherently flawed. Consequently, all models fail to create structural harmony among the elements of the state. Ethnic statism presents a view of the sovereign state in which territory must correspond with ethnic borders, a process that leads to fragmentation. Civic statism promotes the territorial unity of the state by persuading diverse populations to merge and create a new sense of the collective self, a difficult goal to achieve. Authoritarian statism relies on coercive government to safeguard territorial unity and cement loyalty of the people to the state and its ideology. Due to its repressive nature, authoritarian statism is bound to fail as it has in the Soviet Union and other Eastern European states. Even though civic statism appears to be best able to safeguard the territorial integrity of the nation-state, the demands for devolution and local government may eventual-

13. In article 6, The Palestinian National Charter recognizes that the Jews who had normally resided in Palestine will be considered Palestinians.

ly lead to the weakening of the civic state and increasing the concomitant risk of territorial fragmentation.

Even if the state structure is relatively successful in forging a balance among territory, people and government, the internal sovereignty and the sovereign borders may nonetheless be vulnerable to new forces of global dynamics. In the real world, the inherent weakness of state structure is further aggravated when forces of regionalism and globalism assault it from the outside, making a concerted effort to dismantle the state's sovereign borders.

2. Weakening of Sovereign Borders

National boundaries, even when arbitrary and artificial, are the most determinative feature of the state structure. They define the state structure in both geographical and psychological senses, demarcating one state from the other. Just like a fence around an estate, the borders of the nation-state define the enclosed territory, the enclosed people and the enclosed government. Most important, geopsychological boundaries provide states with the basis for exercising internal sovereignty, free of external control as promised by classical international law. Governments use borders of the nation-state as guide-posts to regulate national economy, national security, the environment, corporate conduct, technology and the flow of information. National borders also furnish a geopsychological enclosure, a box, within which individuals and communities organize themselves, thereby defining their vision, choices, loyalties and concerns.

Furthermore, governments use sovereign borders as barriers to define "foreign elements," that is, whatever lies outside the purview of the state structure. National boundaries provide a basis to monitor and exclude foreign nationals, foreign goods and services, foreign corporations, foreign currency, foreign investments, foreign culture, indeed anything that may be labeled "foreign." This power to exclude foreign elements is often used to protect internal economic, cultural and sometimes ideological institutions. Just as the Great Wall of China symbolizes ancient human attempts to erect barricades against conquerors and barbarians, so modern national borders provide a convenient fence to separate native from foreign. Walls satisfy an old and apparently primordial human inclination to maintain self-identity by continually creating "the other."

Sometimes ideologically related states build a common fence around themselves. The Iron Curtain around the Soviet Union and its satellite states interposed an ideological barrier to consolidate communism from within and screen capitalist goods and ideas from without. The Iron Curtain extended the theory of "the other" to a pathological extreme, turning the communist bloc into a virtual prison. But this effort exposed a simple truth: the stricter the borders, the more suffocating life becomes within the enclosure, breeding suspicion, self-doubt, neuroses and paranoia. The collapse of the Iron Curtain further demonstrates that no human society, despite the need for identity, self-preservation and cultural integrity, can successfully live apart from the rest of humanity.

Currently, three momentous phenomena challenge the traditional notion of sovereign borders. First, corporate transnationalism has created a global economy by interweaving national economies in such a way that exclusion of an economy from global markets is indeed a punishment. Second, the environmental unity of the planet defies national boundaries, forcing the recognition that human civilization, despite its ethnic and territorial diversification, is rooted in one nature. Third, the information revolution is in the process of transforming traditional notions of territorial communities tied to contiguous geographical areas. Information-driven communities require no geographical contiguity, threatening the core characteristic of the state structure. National laws seem inadequate to contain these phenomena as domestic matters.

Under the impact of these and other forces, nation-states experience difficulty in maintaining the traditional meaning of the sovereign borders. Moreover, a new familiarity among the peoples of the world, caused by tourism and migration, has accelerated the process of mutual contact and diffusion by which diverse cultures learn about each other. If these forces continue to shape global life, the boundaries of the nation-state will become progressively less obstructive to the free flow of goods, services, capital, labor, technology and information.

Among the forces that challenge the notion of sovereign borders, corporate transnationalism determined to achieve the global integration of national economies is the most commanding. Influenced by the global competition and comparative advantage, transnational businesses increasingly defy the internal sovereignty of nation-states. Once largely confined to the parameters of the nation-state, corporate practices have undergone radical changes. No longer is it always efficient or profitable for a company to produce goods and services within a single nation-state, particularly goods and services designed to be consumed in diverse regions and marketplaces. Corporate attachment to a specific nation-state counts as a bad business practice, since a state-bound company will have to market in foreign countries both its product and patriotism, a tough combination to sell. To reduce export shipment costs, conform more closely with regional needs and develop bonds with overseas consumers, companies are increasingly dispersing their production facilities among various nation-states.

Despite the complex network of free trade agreements, national leaders and even people continue to demand that corporations demonstrate loyalty to the nation-state rather than to profit from overseas markets. Governments resent the exodus of corporations to foreign countries, complaining that corporate flight causes unemployment and lowers the standard of living in the home state. They argue that if manufacturing plants are retained in the home state, the company will directly contribute to the territorial economy. This is so, they further argue, because manufacturing at home keeps investment capital within the national market, creating jobs and paying higher wages to workers at home. To make these assertions morally more persuasive, governments allege that corporations exploit foreign labor by paying substandard wages and cause environmental degradation, since many developing states lack effective legal regimes to protect their labor and environment.

National legal restrictions on the transboundary movement of corporate capital and manufacturing, however, distort the same regime of free trade that most nation-states are committed to maintain. If companies are legally coerced into remaining within the territory of the home state, they risk losing the ability to produce competitive products. In many cases such domestication of corporations raises the cost of production, diminishing corporate ability to compete in international markets. Patriotic corporations may even lose their share in the home market if competing products imported from foreign countries are cheaper, better or both. Moreover, domestication of corporations invites retaliation from other states, threatening the whole regime of free trade.

Thus a new corporate transnationalism has taken root, under which corporate decisions about investment and manufacturing in diverse regions and nations are dictated by business considerations rather than loyalty to nation-states.[14] Transnational networks of imports and exports, joint ventures, transfer of technology, shared manufacturing projects, portfolio investments, interlocked currencies, transboundary data broadcasting and scores of other corporate relations have transformed the nature of national economies formerly confined to the boundaries of the nation-state. No longer is any territorial economy self-contained, self-sufficient or sovereign – thus dismantling Aristotle's concept of the perfect state. Corporate transnationalism shapes all national economies, large and small, binding them together into an intricate web of interdependence.

Note a distinction between transnational corporations and corporate transnationalism. Transnational corporations are giant enterprises that control subsidiaries in many nations. To further maximize their flexibility and expand their global interests, they often combine manufacturing subsidiaries with finance, insurance and holding companies. One cannot deny that multinational corporations create a global culture in which the consumers of the world begin to share similar tastes and preferences. Corporate transnationalism, in contrast, is not confined to the conduct of transnational corporations. Even national corporations and local businesses promote corporate transnationalism when they buy and sell foreign products. By carrying imported products for local consumers, even small stores in remote villages participate in the grand enterprise of corporate transnationalism.

Most nations agree that the borderless economic order must flourish within the confines of a legal regime. Some still contend, erroneously, that the

---

14. When a nation-state extends its laws to regulate the acts of its national corporations in a foreign country, legal and political conflicts arise. This assertion of extraterritorial jurisdiction becomes even more problematic when the foreign state compels the corporation to defy the command of the home state.

legal regime, even if international in character, should be subject to their domestic constitutional orders. Most concede, privately if not publically, that no one national legal system, no matter how powerful, can control global markets. Multilateral treaties such as North American Free Trade Agreement and General Agreement on Tarrifs and Trade establish regional and global legal regimes for the promotion and protection of corporate transnationalism. These regimes facilitate transactions between global and regional producers and consumers, providing producers with new markets and consumers with new products.

International attempts are under way to draft laws for regulating the behavior of transnational corporations. The competing claims of national sovereignty and free trade continue to muddle the discussion about an appropriate legal regime that will both facilitate transnational transactions and restrain transnational exploitation. Historical modes of thinking pull toward the assumption that national laws are best suited to protect consumers, workers, shareholders and the environment against the excesses of corporate greed. The complexity and the rapid growth of transnational corporations, however, defy national attempts at regulation. A global corporate code is therefore needed to establish a normative framework within which transnational corporations may operate without fear of unfair treatment, but are nonetheless obligated to contribute to the development of national communities and avoid exploitation of labor and the environment.

Corporate transnationalism in its full sweep has become a formidable force beyond national control and even beyond comprehension, just like the proverbial elephant grasped only in parts. Thus even when nation-states attempt to control some facets of corporate transnationalism, others slip away from their control. For example, the political and economic cost of regulating transboundary flow of corporate data is prohibitive if not completely impossible. Even economic superpowers cannot afford to fully govern information-driven corporate transnationalism. Moreover, regulatory efforts by international institutions such as the International Monetary Fund and the World Bank, and nation-states caught in the intricate networks of economic forces, fail to control the rise and fall of currencies and trade surpluses or deficits. And despite patriotic indoctrination, nation-states also fail to reorient consumer preferences for domestic goods, especially expensive or inferior products. It appears as if corporate transnationalism is determined to erase the artificial boundaries that man has drawn on the surface of One Earth. Modes of analysis must therefore be readjusted from national to regional and from regional to global perspectives in order to establish a world economic order embodying the complex interplay of free trade, consumer protection, and labor and environmental concerns.

In any event, it appears that no territorial economy can survive on its own. The economic sanctions imposed on Iraq after the Gulf War demonstrate how a territorial economy, when isolated from the rest of the world, fails to provide even the basic necessities of life such as food and medicine to its citizens. Most nations, large and small, have joined the global network of lower tariffs and fewer national restrictions on imports and exports negotiated through the General Agreement of Tariffs and Trade. Many others, most notably China with its large and rapidly growing economy, are eager to join the World Trade Organization and financial networks, without which no territorial economy can prosper or harmonize with global financial and monetary markets.

Nonetheless, it is too early to pronounce economic nationalism dead or even dying. Trade wars between nations and blocs periodically erupt, endangering the regime of commercial and financial networks. Some nations advocate free trade to sell but not to buy. Some open their markets to foreign competition in theory but not in practice. Some manipulate the regime of free trade to advance national strategies, building their own economic power and establishing geopolitical leadership. Some institute public and private protectionist policies and encourage domestic cartels. Some require heavy local content in manufacturing. And some invoke cultural practices to exclude foreign goods and services, inviting retaliation from other nations that must then find a way to repair trade deficits.

In view of lingering economic nationalism, the globalized economy is an anti-utopia, carrying the seeds of discord and war, with or without the use of force. With luck, these seeds will not blossom. The danger looms, however, that globalization is likely to stratify the peoples of the world into rich and poor communities, instituting a rigid caste system under which some nations will occupy the top, some struggle in the middle, and some toil at the bottom. If the global economy creates an unjust system in which the distribution of benefits is unfair, the wretched nations grinding at the bottom, just like the untouchables in India, will be unable to protect their vital interests or change the system. Some states may accept their fates. Others will resort to rebellion, seeking to dismantle the unjust world that abuses them.

The challenge to the global economy may or may not come from the bottom. Even frustrated trade partners losing a higher standard of living may fall back to economic nationalism, unravelling the web of interdependence. If military superpowers fail to draw substantial benefits from the global economy, they may resort to the use of force to tilt the balance in their favor. Indeed, the ways in which the global economy may fall apart are legion. Unless the nations and the peoples of the world establish a gracious world in which compassion and moral intelligence rather than predacious national interests guide the forces of global economy, interdependence will assure neither peace nor prosperity. Whichever way the future unfolds, the sovereign borders are presently under distress.

Though economic concerns have for years commanded the most international attention, widespread damge to the world's environment has changed the debate about unrestrained economic development. Since the 1972 Stockholm Declaration of the United Nations Conference on the Human Environment,[15] major legal and practical efforts have been made to develop global environmental regime that would ultimately reorient the way we think about ourselves. Realizing that the One Earth, our home, is indivisible and civilization is rooted in nature, the nations and peoples of the world have begun to develop a legal framework, integrating economic growth with the protection, conservation and restoration of natural resources, the degradation of which endangers the vitality and even the survival of life. This environmental ethic provides a new legal and existential vocabulary to reimagine the seamless unity of life, the common destiny of all creatures of the world. It also exposes the inherent flaws of analytical modes that confine human compassion to artificial borders and national interests. Rejecting the Hobbesian world in which everyone is constantly at war with everyone else, environmental consciousness envisions a gracious world in which human beings are in harmony with nature and with themselves.

In contrast to environmentalists, some realists view nature as an adversary that human beings must subdue in order to live in safety and comfort. Natural forces such as earthquakes, storms and droughts, and natural agents such as bacteria and viruses, are indeed inimical to human life. Moreover, predation is common in nature, in which the weak and the careless are most vulnerable. By observing nature and the behavior of predators, some realists conclude that even the human world is made in the image of the jungle, in which predation is the key to survival. This norm of predation is then elevated to an elaborate sociopolitical framework, as in the works of Thomas Hobbes (1588-1679), generating both offensive and defensive responses. The offensive response legitimizes predation as a mode of acquiring land and other resources by dispossessing the weak and the vulnerable, exploiting women and children, imposing slavery and engaging in merciless economic opportunism. The defensive response argues for the creation of military might, including chemical, biological and nuclear weapons, to deter and even destroy "the other" predators.

Furthermore, predacious beliefs provoke a hostile attitude toward nature itself. Instead of living in harmony with nature, human communities founded on the norm of predation destroy those parts of nature that seem unfriendly or obstructive to economic development. Many life forms are jeopardized or extinguished; whole ecosystems, including organisms, land, marine and atmospheric resources are utilized in ways that endanger the integrity of natural systems. Excessive consumption, another attribute of predacious ideology, causes rapid depletion of natural resources, some of which are non-renewable. In this unrelenting pursuit of consumption and accumulation, human communities often fight with one another over the ownership and use of natural resources. The resulting warfare brings the process of predation to the bitter end of self-destruction, degrading the utility and the beauty of the One Earth.

---

15. The Second U. N. Conference on Environment and Development was held in Rio de Janeiro from 3 to 14 June 1992, which produced the Rio Declaration on Environment and Development.

To counter the norms of predation, the environmental ethic envisions the One Earth in its full complexity. No longer is life defined in terms of human life only, nor is the norm that human beings are God's best creation overemphasized. Rather, life on One Earth is seen as a seamless web in which all life forms must be safeguarded. The World Charter for Nature declares: "Every form of life is unique, warranting respect regardless of its worth to man, and, to accord other organisms such recognition, man must be guided by a moral code of action." This recognition that human beings must learn to respect other life forms rejects the predacious norm under which human utilitarianism determines which life forms will live and which will not. Indiscriminate violence against other forms of life, originating in fear, ignorance and unchecked utilitarianism, is incompatible with the gracious world.

The environmental ethic proposes to reverse all ideologies of supremacy by nurturing a web of interdependence. Yet the doctrines of sovereign borders and national interests continue to offer opposition. National appropriation of natural resources to the exclusion of the rest of the world continues to set the rule of capture against the principle of conservation. The division of One Earth into over a hundred and eighty nation-states has resulted in the grossly uneven distribution of natural resources such as land, oil, gas, minerals and water. Furthermore, this ownership of resources has no proportionate link with the size of the population deriving the benefit. Small states such as the United Arab Emirates and Kuwait have tiny populations but huge supplies of oil; some states occupying vast territories, such as Canada and Australia, have vast resources but small populations, especially when compared with India and China, which together contain almost two fifths of the world's people but nowhere near two fifths of the world's resources.

This uneven distribution of natural resources is legalized under several precepts of international law. First, each nation-state possesses permanent sovereignty over its natural wealth and resources. Second, the state is free to exercise its control over natural resources in the interest of national development and for the well-being of its people. Third, states undertake to respect each other's sovereignty over their respective natural resources. These rights were initially designed to reverse colonial exploitation, which drained natural resources from colonized territories often for the exclusive benefit of colonizers.

Since many states in possession of rich natural resources lack the means to exploit them, they often seek the assistance of technologically advanced states to extract and market these resources. While this partnership works for both naturally and technologically resourceful states, raising their standards of living, nations without such resources remain in a vicious cycle of poverty as their underdeveloped economies fail to vigorously participate in, and benefit from, the global economy. Although international cooperation for the economic development of poor nations is periodically emphasized in moral and quasi-legal commitments, states with no natural or technological resources, frequently dependant on subsistence agriculture, continue to suffer severe economic hardship resulting in civil strife and even famine.

Just like colonial exploitation, the doctrine of permanent state sovereignty over natural resources obstructs the emergence of the gracious world. It provides a legal basis for resourceful states to appropriate the natural resources of the One Earth for the benefit of the few. In the realm of compassion and moral intelligence, however, such exclusive and permanent sovereignty over natural resources, which were created by the forces of indivisible nature over a span of millions of years, is indeed selfishness, a predacious norm defended on the morally thin basis that those who live outside the artificial boundaries of the resourceful state have no claim to benefit from the natural wealth of the One Earth.

Even the living and non-living resources of the high seas and the Area over which no single nation state can lay claims of sovereignty are increasingly falling under the de facto control of the few states that possess the means to catch or extract them. Negotiated over fifteen years, the 1982 Law of the Sea Convention extends the control of nation-states over thirty-five percent of the ocean's surface by establishing the two hundred mile exclusive economic zone. Nonetheless, egalitarian legal norms incorporated in the Convention have been undermined. The principle that "activities in the Area shall be carried out for the benefit of mankind as a whole" has failed to muster approval of many technologically-sophisticated states, including the United States. Instead the predacious rule of capture has taken hold allowing the taking of resources of the Area on a first-come, first-served basis. This rule further entrenches inequities in the allocation of natural resources, since poor nations lack the means to compete for their share of the loot.

Furthermore, a serious dilemma undermines the environmental ethic. Developing nations, jointly containing the majority of the people of the world, insist on economic development without the strict environmental controls that developed nations now advocate. They argue that developed states have already done substantial damage to the environment in their pursuit of economic development, a charge that developed countries acknowledge in view of the pressures their societies place on the global environment. In advancing the right to development, developing states support the general principle that sustainable development cannot be achieved by ignoring environmental concerns. They also undertake not to damage the environment beyond their national borders. Nonetheless, they assert "the sovereign right to exploit their own resources pursuant to their own environmental and developmental policies."

This nation-by-nation approach to protecting the environment, though understandable in view of the need to eradicate poverty and disease in developing states, compartmentalizes the natural unity of the One Earth. To counter this artificial segmentation, the environmental ethic emphasizes a spirit of global partnership to conserve, protect and restore the health and integrity of the Earth's ecosystem. A global partnership to safeguard the environment, however, will not materialize in the foreseeable future if states continue to pursue selfish and foolish development policies in the belief that economic growth is a higher priority and that conflicts between developmental and environmental goals must, in the short run, be resolved in favor of achieving national prosperity. A fascination with consumption and an ever higher standard of living dictates political priorties in many nations of the world as politicians strive to produce tangible economic results at the expense of environmental degradation, frequently to bolster their own political futures.

Hence the dynamics of national interests continue to distort the environmental ethic. Poor nations striving to solve basic problems of survival lack the means, and often the inclination, to protect the environment. Politically unstable nations are often preoccupied with pressing economic problems and thus fail to pursue environmentally conscious economic development on a consistent basis. Even developed states in which the public is aware of environmental concerns frequently institute trade policies that merely transfer environmental damage to foreign states. Some even unabashedly relocate their hazardous waste to poor nations. Some resist the need to create global institutions for monitoring environmental concerns and coordinating national policies toward protecting the environment. Given budget deficits and other domestic socioeconomic problems, many nations lack the political will to allocate funds for solving the environmental problems of the One Earth that affect us all.

Meanwhile, the exploration of outer space further expands our horizons even beyond the Earth. The nation-state as a geopolitical unit is primarily tied to the landed surface of the Earth. For centuries, the oceans and outer space were mystical entities that lay on fringes of human knowledge and outside the sovereignty of the nation-state – inspiring awe, incomprehension and reverence. Proposals were made in the early seventeenth century to divide the oceans of the world. Grotius, however, ably argued against private ownership of both air and oceans, contributing to the emerging custom of freedom of the seas. But beyond the basic principle that some assets of nature should not be allocated to nation-states, no question was raised about whether the nation-state was indeed a practical concept to partition the universe into distinct parcels of national sovereignty.

The exploration of the moon and other celestial bodies and the discoveries of outer space have undermined the epistemological foundation of the nation-state. Originally, a state's sovereignty over the airspace above its territory was thought to extend *usque ad coelum*, but recent scientific discoveries and the development of space technology exposed the impractibility of enforcing such a conception. Even if nation-states can appropriate airspace, they cannot partition the incomprehensible and infinite horizons of the universe. Using the predacious rule of capture, nations may of course "colonize" reachable celestial bodies, but such appropriation would be a new human phenomenon, a quantum leap in the notion of territorial sovereignty that can in no sense be labeled as a natural extension of the nation-state, a conceptual creature affixed to the surface of the Earth.

In contemporary international law, states have relinquished the concept of national sovereignty in the exploration and use of outer space, including the moon and other celestial bodies. Nations also undertake to facilitate and encourage international cooperation and the use of outer space for the benefit of all mankind. They regard astronauts as envoys of mankind, required to render all possible assistance to each other without distinction on the basis of national origin. The law also prohibits nation-states from placing nuclear and other weapons of mass destruction in orbit around the Earth, on celestial bodies or in outer space. All these measures contribute to a gracious world in which sharing rather than seizing is the preferred norm.

There is no indication, however, that the doctrine of national interests has been effectively abandoned from the legal regime bearing upon the exploration and use of outer space. The nation-state continues to be the organizing principle behind the rhetoric of universality. In theory, free access to all areas of celestial bodies and outer space is available to all states. In practice, however, only resourceful states are able to conduct such exploration. If a treasure trove is found in outer space, the finder state will probably refuse to share it with all mankind. Just like natural assets retrieved from the high seas, treasure troves in outer space are likely to be appropriated on a first-come, first-served basis. Contemporary international law assures only equal access to the exploration and use of outer space, not equal benefits.

Even if economic integration and the environmental ethic fail to unite the peoples of One Earth, the information revolution is determined to defy the confines of the state structure. The information age may even change the very meaning of the term "community." The concept of the nation-state defines communities in terms of territorial fellowship. Even before the era of nation-states, physical proximity was vital to the development of communities. Traditional communities sharing the same language, culture or ethnicity often occupy the same territory that assures close physical proximity. If a community, such as the Jews in the past and the Palestinians in the present, is forced to disperse among different regions and nations, it loses its territorial basis. The Zionist movement to unify scattered Jewish populations was in part motivated by a territorial concept of the community, seeking a geographically contiguous space for otherwise ethnically distinct Jewish populations. *Diaspora*, which shatters territorial contiguity, is thus considered the negation of traditional community and, of course, the nation-state.

The information revolution is expanding the definition of community beyond territoriality. Physical proximity is still an important ingredient in the formation of communities and will continue to be so regarded. But its importance is likely to diminish as the flow of information links distant lands and peoples. A shift from territorial to information communities is already taking place in professional and political circles. Professional groups sharing the same interests and research objectives, such as astronomers, can build vibrant transnational communities through information networks. Similarly, a vigorous discourse among political allies and opponents living in different cities and states can occur through electronic media, a method most convenient and productive in a regional setting such as the European Union. In many ways, information communities may use their time, resources and interactive dynamics in a more efficient and productive manner than do territorial communities.

In any event, the territorial state is no longer an over-arching limitation on building communities. Cities and states founded upon the model of territorial organization will continue to furnish tangibility to the sense of community, but their limiting role in the formation and preservation of social, economic, political and cultural groups is undergoing a significant change. If the information revolution can successfully create transnational networks for scientists, doctors, bankers, brokers, lawyers, politicians and academics, it will bind even the ordinary peoples of the world into meaningful transnational communities, far beyond the sovereign borders of the nation-state. It is in this sense that the information revolution will reinforce regional and global links.

The information revolution, however, is likely to strengthen localism and ethnicism as well. In fact, territorial and ethnic communities may become even more cohesive and permanent. Communication resources in many nation-states are already decentralized, creating local and provincial print media, radio and television. Pluralistic and alternative viewpoints in national discourse are protected by allocating radio and television resources to ethnic, linguistic and cultural minorities. Territorial and ethnic communities whose language, folk music, art and history have previously been suppressed or ignored may thus be better able to assert their distinctive identities. This resurgence of territorial and ethnic identities may weaken those nation-states that are built by joining disparate historic provinces, localities and ethnic populations.

The tension between information-based localism and globalism raises important concerns. If the state controls the means of communication, information disseminated is often partial or distorted, the aim of which may be none else but to further entrench the political and social control of those in power. If the means of communication are privately owned, information may be influenced by the biases of the owners of news agencies or the personal leanings of the reporters. Even when owners and reporters seek to eliminate conscious prejudice and the law safeguards free and fair reporting, information remains tainted as it filters through the shared norms of a culture – the supreme blinder that most people, including owners of news agencies and reporters, wear in most communities.[16] When people receive information from both national and foreign sources, they are more likely to be better informed even when, because of their cultural conditioning, they view foreign news and opinions with suspicion.

A free and fair global press, however, is not yet fully in place. News agencies and reporters, due to lack of understanding of foreign cultures, regularly misinterpret the deeper layers of foreign events. Most media are tied to the interests of their own nation-states. Even when the national media are professionally committed to honestly and objectively report news and events within the nation-state, the same media, out of loyalty to the state and sensitivity to its foreign policy show reluctance, if not outright cowardice, in robust inter-

16. Noam Chomsky, Towards a New Cold War: Essays on the Current Crisis and How We Got There (New York: 1982), pp. 80-81 (under capitalist democracy, the same fundamental assumptions are insinuated, though rarely expressed. They are presupposed, but not asserted).

national reporting, fearing that such journalism might be considered contrary to the interests of the state. Frequently national laws prevent and punish reporting detrimental to national interests. Particularly in war situations, the national media are frequently prohibited to contradict the official news, indeed the propaganda. Accusations of treason or disloyalty endanger the work and lives of reporters who dispute the official version of transnational hostilities. Even in less coercive situations, news agencies and reporters often show restraint in criticizing their own nation's role in transnational disputes. Sometimes the national media play an unreflective role in demonizing foreign states, their leaders and cultural practices, and sometimes they even help prepare the general public sentimentally to support a war the government has already decided to wage, openly or covertly, against a foreign state.

However, the information revolution of the last few decades has increased protection for a globally free press, changing the dynamics of international reporting. A global press is better able to overcome government censorship originating in any nation-state. It will also educate reporters in accurate and reflective reporting beyond the interests of any one nation. Transnational news agencies and reporters whose first commitment is to free and fair reporting are in the process of breaking out of the legal, political and cultural framework of the nation-state. Some make sincere efforts to demand and obtain full and free access to the facts before disseminating what might otherwise be false or biased information. Some insist on applying the fairness doctrine and the personal attack rule to foreign figures.[17] Professional ethics are also in the making to prohibit covert inclusion of biased international propaganda in news services.

A free and fair global press would encourage a global society as news and events, both good and bad, occurring anywhere on earth are instantly broadcast to the entire world. When the people of the world simultaneously experience the horror of genocide in Rwanda, the pain of starvation in Somalia, the anguish of ethnic cleansing in Bosnia as well as the joyous festivities of Christmas, Chinese New Year, successful launches of space ships and the sprouting of democracy in Haiti and South Africa, an emotional foundation is laid for the building of a global society. Such shared experiences clarify and reinforce universal values; they also build shared memories for the people of the world living in different nations and continents. This ever-increasing proximity among peoples creates a web of complex relations, giving birth to new sentiments of global harmony and bracing the existential bond among communities of the world. In addition to their local and communal history, the people of the world now have shared memories to pass on to future generations. Thus the information revolution weakens the primacy of national histo-

17. Acral Metra, Free Flow of Information, (Greenwood Press, 1986). The author argues that national media should extend the fairness doctrine to foreign figures, who should be invited to reply to charges made in the media by the national government.

ries that view global events as part of local history rather than the other way around.

In addition to exchanging information with other nations and peoples, physical exchanges of persons, such as tourism and migration, are powerful forces that erode rigid loyalties to nation-states. The Universal Declaration of Human Rights recognizes that individuals have the right to leave any country and return to their own country. Yet freedom of movement across national borders is available only to rich individuals who can afford to travel and migrate at will and whom foreign nations allow entry into their territories. If the freedom of cross-national movement is fully granted, rich nations fear that individuals from poor countries will arrive in swarms, destabalizing their economic, political and cultural communities.

Notwithstanding the restrictions most states place on freedom of movement, the scope and speed of cross-national movement has increased in the past few decades in part because of rapid means of transportation. Moreover, nations realize that tourism is a lucrative source of revenue. However, the fear that more open borders may cause mass-scale shifts of populations seems exaggerated, at least judging from the experience of the European Union. Freedom of movement may in fact slow down the process of migration, since most people wish to spend their lives in territorial communities where they were born and where their families and friends live. This propensity is most vividly seen within nation-states in which the people enjoy the right to freedom of movement but nonetheless continue to live in the same communities generation after generation.[18]

Freedom of movement across national borders serves an important purpose in bringing down the traditional physical and psychological barriers that separate peoples of the world. It reduces the degree of cross-cultural paranoia, prejudice and stereotypes that often lead to hostility and even war. A vivid example of the forging of common bonds among diverse communities of the world is the Islamic institution of the *Hajj*, the pilgrimage to Mecca. When Muslims from all over the world congregate for a few days in the same place, everyone wearing the same standard garment, they forge a universal bond with each other beyond their ethnic and national identities. Likewise world games, festivals and trade shows bring diverse peoples together in healthy and playful settings. If these global gatherings continue to flourish and multiply, the peoples of the world may begin to appreciate the value of a global society unfettered by the geopsychological borders of the nation-state.

Despite the impact of the global economy, environmental unity, information revolution, and tourism and migration, it still remains to be seen whether individuals will shift their geopsychological orientation from the nation-

18. For example, not everyone in France lives in Paris. Nor do all Kansans move to San Francisco though they have the right, freedom and in some cases the desire and resources to do so.

state to a global society. Most people are still loyal to territorial communities, which they see as the most natural entities. Widespread patriotism, including psychologically charged phrases such as "my country", "the fatherland" and "the motherland," reveal that many peoples maintain an attachment to the idea of the nation-state. Just as some individuals make human sacrifices to please their gods, others stand ready to die for their states. National anthems, patriotic songs and the stories of local heroes killed in wars with other states bring tears to the eyes of many who sincerely believe that national boundaries indeed separate good from bad and heroic from brutal, with the good and the heroic almost always on their side of the border. Such deep sentiments cannot easily be overcome.

The nation-state as a geopsychological entity is in no immediate danger of dissolution. Nor is localism or ethnicism in any danger of extinction. Gradually, however, the forces of global integration may evolve, dismantling sovereign borders of the nation-state. Corporate transnationalism weakens the nation-state as a viable economic unit, while the information revolution spawns information communities beyond national borders. A global environmental consciousness emphasizes natural unity of One Earth. A free and fair global press is likely to develop loyalty to accurate and fair reporting, resisting both the temptation and compulsion to distort stories for the benefit of any single nation-state. Tourism and migration will promote contact among diverse cultures and communities; regional and global festivals, games and other events may strengthen cross-cultural ties. All these forces already pressure the nation-state to relax its sovereign borders for the free flow of capital, goods, services, labor, tourists, athletes, guest workers and permanent residents. The people would continue to live in small territorial communities, cherishing their unique ethnicity. Just as communities are free within the confines of the nation-state, so they would be on One Earth without sovereign borders.

Chapter Five

The Impact of International Enmeshment

The traditional notions of state sovereignty and independence are progressively losing efficacy and legitimacy in the enmeshed world. The phenomenon of enmeshment interweaves the shared interests and reciprocal rights and obligations of the nations of the world into numerous legal networks. These networks vary in scope and size. Some enmesh states into a single economy, some into a common armed defense, and some into a single human rights regime. Some networks are subregional, some regional, and some global. Moreover, no network stands alone. Just as states are interwoven into networks, so networks are enmeshed with each other in complex institutional patterns. As a result, now no state is completely sovereign or independent. Instead, all are simultaneously tied by a thousand strings. By joining each network, the state surrenders a portion of its sovereignty, its freedom to act independently. Since the benefits of enmeshment are substantial, most states willingly accede to the corresponding loss of sovereignty and independence. The phenomenon of enmeshment, however, is not always completely voluntary. States that resist enmeshment not only lose the attendant advantages, but also may be criticized, reprimanded, or ostracized by regional or global networks.

Due to this inescapable enmeshment, contemporary international law diverges from the Grotian theory in two significant ways. First, it places more extensive controls on the exercise of the state's external sovereignty, its classical authority to conduct independent foreign policy. The term "external sovereignty" is at least a partial misnomer, since no state enjoys an unfettered authority to act without legal controls in their external relations with other states. Even the Grotian theory placed serious constraints on the exercise of the state's external sovereignty. In fact, no international law can exist if states are completely sovereign. The whole enterprise of international law aims to define and restrict the state's external sovereignty, requiring the state to fashion its behavior in accordance with customary or treaty obligations. Hence the state's external sovereignty, if this notion is still useful, must be coterminous with the state's authority to conduct interstate relations in accordance with international law.

In its initial stages, classical international law placed few constraints on the state's external sovereignty. As international law developed and states began to benefit from the legal regime, more laws in diverse areas of interstate activity were added to further subject interstate behavior to the rule of law. Contemporary international law, which focuses on state cooperation, is in some ways qualitatively different from both the Grotian theory and classical international law. Originally, classical international law was the law of coexistence, which regulated war and peace; contemporary international law is primarily the law of cooperative enmeshment. Before, states had fewer beneficial contacts with each other. Now they often pool their resources and act jointly in many areas of regional and global life to pursue shared goals.

Accordingly, states have established numerous international networks to forge cooperative enmeshment – just as extended families unite the resources, strengths and even weaknesses of individual members and family subunits into a common household. And just as individual members and family subunits surrender their wilful autonomy to the intricate web of the extended family, so nation-states and state coalitions relinquish their wilful independence in exchange for the benefits of cooperative enmeshment at the regional and global levels. This *institutional enmeshment* has transformed the nature of international legal theory and practice, primarily because the tasks that were previously the exclusive domain of the nation-state are now performed by a complex legion of interstate institutions.

The second way in which contemporary international law diverges from the Grotian theory is even more dramatic and highly consequential because it subjects the state's internal sovereignty to international law. Recall that under the Grotian theory as well as classical international law, the state's internal sovereignty was almost total. Classical international law placed no constraints on the state's form of government, the state's choice of religion, the state's treatment of its citizens, or the state's conception of social justice. The state was truly sovereign, completely free to organize itself as it saw fit, a norm explicitly recognized even as late as in the 1933 Montevideo Convention on Rights and Duties of States. The state was of course free to promulgate a constitution limiting its internal sovereignty. However, if no such constitution existed, the state was free to mistreat its citizens, deny them fundamental civil and political rights, and oppress women or minorities. Classical international law stood outside the state structure as a silent spectator. But this unfettered internal sovereignty is now under increasing international scrutiny and regulation.

Consequently, states have forged networks of common values at both regional and global levels, giving rise to a new and powerful phenomenon of *normative enmeshment*. The law of human rights and obligations, for example, not only regulates the state's internal sovereignty but establishes a legal regime of common values. Classic arguments that each state's sovereignty allows it to freely pursue its social, cultural, religious and political values are now intertwined with contemporary arguments that the state is under an international legal obligation to uphold the law of human rights. No longer may the state totally disregard foreign criticism aimed at the state's internal policies and practices in violation of individuals' and peoples' basic rights. No longer is the individual at the total mercy of the state. Thus the law of human rights has made it progressively more difficult for states to impose oppressive legal orders. Numerous regional and universal treaties place an affirmative duty on the state to adapt its internal legal system to conform with the law of human rights and obligations.

Normative enmeshment however is not confined to human rights. Even in trade and commerce, common values have emerged that restrain the state's independence to arbitrarily change its national laws to discriminate against foreign corporations and products. States' commercial, trade, financial and monetary interests are so intertwined at the regional and global levels that most willingly join the international economic order to draw the attendant benefits. Common standards arising from normative enmeshment certainly facilitate the exchange of goods and services. They also assure that the capitalistic order of free trade and commerce would protect the people's health and safety. Regional and global environmental concerns have further underscored the need of forging common standards.

Thus a legal culture of normative enmeshment has taken root, which respects political, cultural and religious diversity, but at the same time imposes common values on states. This normative enmeshment is almost completely contrary to classical international law; some states still invoke the dying notion of internal sovereignty to deviate from the regime of human rights and obligations and to resist common commercial values. Some still hold on to the supremacy of their domestic constitutions to prevent normative enmeshment with the region or the world. But as contemporary international law continues to deviate from the Grotian theory, nation-states are likely to more willingly relinquish the norms of sovereignty and fantasies of independence. If this normative transformation proceeds unimpeded, the peoples of the world and not the nation-states would become the direct beneficiaries and trustees of international law.

Here, an important historical parallel may be noted. In the Grotian era, some nations objected to classical international law on the ground that it obstructed their freedom to settle questions of war and peace as they pleased. Notwithstanding state criticism and even defiance, classical international law resolutely placed serious legal constraints on states' external sovereignty. Presently, some nations object to contemporary international law on the ground that it lessens their sovereignty and normative freedom to act as they please within their own borders. Notwithstanding state criticism and even defiance, the law of normative enmeshment seems determined to construct a legal culture in which no state may oppress its people or isolate itself from regional and global enmeshment in the name of cultural diversity or in the disguise of internal sovereignty. Normative enmeshment may or may not succeed in forging common values. However, the present trend suggests that it will.

Under the impact of institutional enmeshment, states are losing their classic independence to conduct foreign policy. Normative enmeshment, on the other hand, is weakening their classic authority over internal matters. Thus the norms of classical international law, some of which are incorporated in the United Nations Charter, may have to be reexamined to adjust to the realities of a changing world. Since the European Union offers a unique example of institutional and normative enmeshment and has evolved into an entity *sui generis*, it is examined separately.

1. Institutional Enmeshment

At the outset, alliance may be distinguished from institutional enmeshment. An alliance is a compact among independent states to pursue shared goals.

Thus a defense pact or a trade agreement between two or more independent states may properly be called an alliance. Grotius points out that states making an alliance may be of unequal strength. In fact, one state in a defense alliance may be so powerful that it undertakes to defend all its allies. Grotius also examines a situation in which an alliance vests a permanent superior advantage to one state over the other states in the alliance. Despite their different strengths and varying advantages drawn from the alliance, the participating states nonetheless retain their independence and sovereignty. This is so, Grotius argues, because unequal treaties or alliances simply recognize the unequal prestige and power of the participating states.

An institutional enmeshment is a higher form of alliance. Just like an alliance, an institutional enmeshment may be organized by a treaty. The most notable feature of institutional enmeshment, however, is the establishment of interstate institutions that coordinate the efforts and resources of the member states. These interstate institutions frequently have a permanent headquarters, a technical and bureaucratic staff and a separate budget, funded by its member states. The United Nations, for example, is not merely an alliance; it is an institutional enmeshment. This is so because the United Nations has its own institutions, such as the General Assembly and the Security Council, which carry out specifically authorized functions. These institutions play a critical role in formulating common policy and coordinating joint action among member states. Thus the strength of an institutional enmeshment depends directly upon the effectiveness of its institutions. An alliance that begins with mere cooperation among states may gradually develop into an institutional enmeshment – a phenomenon that further deepens as its institutions gain more extensive authority to formulate policies and act on behalf of the member states.

As nation-states experience the forces of integration, a new set of creatures has arisen to perform the functions that once exclusively belonged to the state's prime attributes. Known as international organizations, these creatures are the prime weavers of institutional enmeshment.[1] Since the Second World War, cooperative enmeshment has spawned hundreds of international organizations in almost all areas of international life. In fact, the proliferation of international organizations in the second half of the twentieth century has been astounding. Often founded by a multilateral treaty, called a constitutive instrument or simply a constitution or charter, an international organization establishes important institutions to manage its affairs. Most international organizations have a plenary organ in which all member states are represented and a smaller executive council vested with authority to carry out the goals and policies of

1. "Institutional cooperative plans and experiences between politically independent entities go far back in history, at least to ancient Greece. But the modern concept of international organization is the outcome of a century and a half of evolution in the cooperative practices of states in response to a rapidly changing world." Abdullah El-Erian, Special Rapporteur (1963).

the organization. Larger organizations like the United Nations have additional organs and subsidiary bodies, such as commissions and agencies.

Not all international organizations are composed of states. When the term international organization is used in a broad sense, it includes both interstate and private organizations. Interstate organizations are created by nation-states themselves and are often described as intergovernmental organizations. Note that the phrase "intergovernmental" does not mean that an international organization is a union of governments. Notwithstanding terminology, an interstate organization is almost always comprised primarily of states, though nonstate actors such as national liberation movements or quasi-independent territories have also been admitted as observers or associate members. Ordinarily, an interstate organization is established through a multilateral treaty, a constitutive document that defines the scope of the organization's authority and institutes its internal organs. Among interstate organizations, the United Nations is by far the most powerful organization vested with a broad scope of authority. It is also the most universal in affiliation as almost all states are members.

Private international organizations, also known as non-governmental organizations, monitor the development, implementation and violation of international law. As distinguished from interstate organizations, non-governmental organizations are primarily composed of individuals having no official ties with any government. They are involved in all areas of global activity, including human rights, health, hostilities, famine, professional and scientific matters. Amnesty International, for example, is a world-wide organization that monitors the criminal justice systems of nation-states, exposing violations of defendants' rights, inhumane prison conditions, police brutality and other state practices in violation of human rights. Article 71 of the United Nations Charter allows its Economic and Social Council to make suitable arrangements for consultation with non-governmental organizations. Thus many non-governmental organizations play a critical role in presenting evidence of human rights abuses by nation-states before appropriate official bodies established by the Economic and Social Council.

Interstate and private organizations act at both regional and global levels. Global organizations, such as the International Labor Organization, are interstate organizations of a universal character whose membership and responsibilities are on a world-wide scale. Though open to all states, these organizations nevertheless require the consent of the majority of current members before a new state is admitted. Membership in regional organizations is restricted to states in the geographical region. The Organization of American States, for example, is a regional interstate organization whose membership is confined to states in North and South America. Just like interstate organizations, private organizations may also operate either at the global or regional level.

Global and regional interstate organizations cover a wide range of activities ranging from economic cooperation to mutual defense to establishing a common human rights regime. Global finance organizations such as the World Trade Organization, the International Monetary Fund and the World Bank administer the international economic order; the World Trade Organization provides institutional enmeshment for the promotion of free trade, the Fund provides stable exchange rates and the Bank furnishes development loans and other economic assistance. Some interstate organizations, such as the North Atlantic Treaty Organization, are established for the mutual defense of specific regions. Likewise, the Council of Europe provides a regional institutional framework to protect fundamental individual rights.

Institutional enmeshment in diverse areas of interstate activity is a relatively new phenomenon. It is, therefore, important to understand how classical international law changed over the centuries to facilitate the enmeshment process. In this regard, three related changes may be noted, of which the first two are technical in nature and the third is more fundamental. The first technical change, introduced in the nineteenth century, brought about the concept of a multilateral treaty, modifying the archaic rule that only two states could be parties to any one international agreement. Under the old rule, when several states agreed to a common peace settlement, like the Peace of Westphalia, a series of bilateral treaties with identical content were drawn between each pair of parties. This strict bilateralism, anchored in historical practice, became cumbersome as nations increasingly assumed identical obligations. In addition to removing transactional inefficiencies, the multilateral treaty provides a pluralistic legal tool that can simultaneously bind several nations, indeed the entire world, to the same regime of rights and obligations. Furthermore, this tool is compatible with the convening of international conferences at which state representatives may come together and conduct multilateral negotiations in the hope of constructing a common legal regime.

The second change, related to the first, adds a legislative dimension to the character of the treaty. For centuries, international law was created exclusively through custom; treaties were merely transactional documents containing the terms of territorial settlement, trade and commerce, joint action in war or resolution of other bilateral matters between parties. Treaties were not used as a means to make new rules of international conduct.[2] The development of multilateral treaties was a critical step in the evolution of the treaty as a law-making device. This was so because the formation of a multilateral treaty is conceptually analogous to the custom-making process: If many states mutually consent to make a new international rule, simultaneously assuming the obligation to fashion their actual practice in compliance with the rule, the critical ingredients of making a custom are joined. When such a shared commitment is codified in a multilateral treaty, the treaty itself becomes the evidentiary as well as generative source of the new rule.

The third change transformed the nature of international affairs by introducing the concept of multinational cooperation. Even though cooperative ties among nations for trade and defense have existed from time immemorial,

2. Recall that Grotius did not mention treaties as a distinct source of international law.

the antique world was nonetheless a conglomerate of isolated communities having minimal contact with each other. The idea of self-sufficiency was still the driving paradigm of the perfect state, and legal independence was synonymous with economic independence. Whatever minimal contact existed was often dictated by war. Therefore, the bulk of classical international law consisted of customary norms of conflict management bearing upon the regulation of the use of force and the minimization of causes of war. Beginning in the nineteenth century, however, a great attitudinal change occurred. States began to cooperate to solve ordinary, practical transnational problems such as the delivery of mail across borders. Ever since, increasing contact among nations has further underscored the need to establish beneficial multilateral ties, laying the foundation of contemporary enmeshment.

This reorientation among nations to establish mutually beneficial networks created the milieu for the burgeoning of the first international organizations, which were mostly of administrative character, such as the Universal Telegraphic Union established in 1865 and the General Postal Union established in 1874. But the nineteenth century world, controlled by a few powers, was still predominantly predacious, a world in which empire-building, acquisition of foreign natural resources and other forms of colonialism determined the content and character of international affairs. The first half of the twentieth century witnessed an inconsistent mix of cooperative multilateralism and destructive wars. Eventually, the scourge of war which brought untold sorrow to humanity set the machinery of collaborative multilateralism in motion. The formation of the United Nations in 1945 was a momentous leap toward the era of international organizations and institutional enmeshment. By one estimate, more than five thousand interstate organizations now function at global and regional levels.

Interstate organizations are the prime weavers of cooperative enmeshment. They maximize their members' abilities to set and achieve shared goals. They also help states formulate common values. Even though nation-states themselves have established international organizations to promote interstate cooperation and to pursue shared goals in a more orderly and informed manner, they nevertheless resist the authority of these organizations. International organizations assert their authority to influence, direct and even determine international and national policies. In many ways, they subordinate nation-states. Thus a tension exists between the new phenomenon of institutional enmeshment and traditional notions of sovereignty and state independence. This tension becomes most visible when the state's national interests conflict with the purposes of the interstate organization.

Tied to the concept of external sovereignty, the state's independence to assume or not to assume international rights and obligations was the principal characteristic of the classical era of international law. The significance of the state as the chief player in international affairs is contained in its constitutive definition: no entity is a state under international law unless it has the competence to conduct foreign relations. This competence is thus the most exceptional definitional element of the state. It distinguishes the state from other entities, such as provinces within a federated state and dependent territories.[3] By virtue of this competence, the state assumes international rights and obligations and participates in the formation of new international law. On the basis of this competence, moreover, states have traditionally determined almost all aspects of international life, including questions of war and peace, treatment of prisoners of war, making and breaking of customs and treaties, management of the air and oceans, and the rights and obligations of individuals.

The competence to conduct an independent foreign policy is so entrenched in the theory of classical international law that even today states continue to assert their independence by taking disparate positions on international issues. Even when states develop a common foreign policy, they often retain the authority to opt out at their discretion and pursue a different course of action. Weaker nations resent the hegemony of powerful states when dictated to pursue or not to pursue a certain foreign policy. Some states regard the authority of the United Nations as a direct limitation on their right to conduct foreign affairs. Some are reluctant to accept the jurisdiction of the International Court of Justice, fearing a loss of control over the resolution of international disputes.

This classical state independence, however, is gradually undergoing a major transformation in the web of institutional enmeshment. Globally, international organizations diminish the state's decision-making authority in diverse areas ranging from the production of nuclear weapons to the resolution of interstate disputes. Nationally, they pierce through the veil of internal sovereignty exposing abuses of state authority, such as the mistreatment of women, minorities and political dissidents. They also expose national discrimination against foreign corporations and misappropriation of foreign intellectual property. Many regional and global organizations require member states to bring their laws into compliance with the supreme norms of organizations' charters. Even national constitutions, once considered sacred and beyond external scrutiny, are now subject to criticism, review and amendment.

Caught in the web of institutional enmeshment, states lose their formal and functional sovereignty. Recall that formal sovereignty is the cumulative legal authority, the bundle of powers, vested in the state to institute its own domestic legal order and conduct foreign relations, and functional sovereignty is the actual exercise of formal sovereignty. This distinction is important because, due to complex reasons, the state may or may not be able to fully

---

3. A federated unit such as Kansas in the United States, which is constitutionally incapacitated to conduct foreign policy though it has the political, technical and financial means to do so, has no separate statehood under international law. The competence to conduct foreign policy has been constitutionally reserved for the United States, which acts as a single state representing all constituent states and dependent territories of Guam, Puerto Rico and others.

exercise its formal sovereignty.[4] In the legal world, formal sovereignty claims more authority than any nation-state can actually exercise. Thus in the real world functional rather than formal sovereignty is a more accurate measure of the state's independence and ability to act. This gap between formal and functional sovereignty has legal consequences. In accordance with the concept of *desuetude*, an aspect of formal sovereignty left unexercised over a period of time may forfeit its legal basis, just like a statute not enforced over a long period of time can become a dead letter. The phenomenon of institutional enmeshment, on the rise in the past few decades, is thus rapidly changing the dynamics of international legal theory and practice.

In the institutional enmeshment of regional and global life, most nation-states voluntarily transfer numerous bits and pieces of their traditionally-held sovereign powers to hundreds of interstate organizations. A remarkably large transfer of authority from nation-states to interstate organizations has occurred by way of specialized agencies. These agencies are established to promote institutional enmeshment in technical areas such as international aviation, health, shipping, food and agriculture. Linked in a cooperative network with the United Nations, a specialized agency comes into existence when member states agree to establish a special area of cooperation. Although contemporary international law compels no state to join any specialized agency, the advantages of joining agencies are so substantial that few states choose to retain their sovereign powers and forego the benefits.

Most specialized agencies deal with issues of a technical character. The Food and Agricultural Organization promotes scientific and technological research relating to nutrition, food and agriculture. The International Atomic Energy Agency assists members with development and practical application of atomic energy for peaceful uses. It further assures that approved nuclear reactors comply with health and safety standards and advance no military purpose. To carry out their functions, most agencies employ resident experts. Even state representatives in these agencies are most often technical experts rather than career diplomats. In addition, each agency has its own technical and administrative staff composed of individuals well-trained in their fields. Political organs of each agency possess the formal authority to approve regulations and practices. Therefore, some politicization of even highly technical issues is inevitable. In most cases, however, agency experts and bureaucrats with technical rather than political agendas remain the real decision-makers.

The International Civil Aviation Organization provides a good example of how nation-states trade pieces of their sovereign authority for benefits drawn from a specialized agency. The aviation agency ensures the safe, orderly and economically efficient development of international air services. By joining the organization, member states benefit from the uniform standards the agency

---

4. The state, for example, has the formal right to self-defense. However, the state fails to exercise this right if it lacks the adequate means to repulse an attack.

develops for aircraft, technical personnel, airports, airways, communication systems, air navigation facilities and the collection and exchange of meteorological information. These uniform standards allow the civil aircraft of one member state to fly through the airspace of other members and use their airport facilities based on shared knowledge, expertise and expectations and without fear of erratic or unpredictable rules and results.

Without the aviation agency, international aviation would be difficult and dangerous. If each state exercises complete and exclusive sovereignty over the airspace above its territory, it might insist on setting its own aviation standards without consultation with other states. If every nation acts independently, standards of safety and navigation will change from state to state, causing confusion, complexity and inefficiency. And if each state individually bears the prohibitive expense of aviation development, states will lose the cost-effective benefits of shared research and information. If no mutual rights and obligations are negotiated, a state exercising airspace sovereignty may arbitrarily deny foreign civil aircraft permission to fly in its airspace. To assert its sovereignty over its airspace, a state may even resort to the use of force against civil aircraft in flight.

To avoid these difficulties, a cooperative institution such as the aviation agency becomes indispensable for carrying out safe and efficient international civil aviation, not only for poor nations that otherwise lack the technical means to provide international air service but also for rich nations whose civil airlines engage in world-wide air service flying over or into the airspace of other states. In fact, the benefits ensuing from such an institutional enmeshment are so significant that their withdrawal constitutes an economic sanction. When Libya refused to surrender two men allegedly responsible for the bombing of a United States civil aircraft in flight over Scotland, an attack in which all on board were killed, the United Nations Security Council imposed economic sanctions that included termination of air traffic and a prohibition on sale of aircraft and related components to Libya.

The benefits of joining the aviation agency, however, exact a cost in terms of traditional sovereignty. Even though the constitutions of most specialized agencies reiterate the concept of national sovereignty, as does the aviation agency's constitution, in almost all cases they obligate member states to do or not to do certain things, thus restricting the state's sovereign authority to act independently. The aviation agency proscribes member states from using civil aviation for any purpose inconsistent with the aims of the agency's constitution. Accordingly, member states undertake both to abrogate existing obligations and to refrain from assuming future obligations inconsistent with the terms of the aviation agency's constitution, a clear limitation on the state's traditional sovereignty.

In addition, the aviation agency's constitution authorizes the Council, a permanent institution of the agency, to adopt international standards and practices to facilitate and improve air navigation, simultaneously obligating member states to collaborate with the Council. Although the Council is composed of state representatives, often aviation experts, it works in close cooperation with the Air Navigation Commission, a body of resident experts trained in the science and practice of aeronautics. The commission possesses the primary authority to initiate, consider and finally propose the rules of international civil aviation, thus shifting in principle and practice the decision-making authority from constituent member states to the specialized agency.

A specialized agency restricts not only the external sovereignty of member states but may also restrict a portion of their internal sovereignty, their power to regulate behavior within the state's national boundaries. For example, by an amendment passed in 1984, the aviation agency's constitution prohibits member states from resorting to the use of weapons against civil aircraft in flight.[5] This prohibition diminishes the power of member states to exercise their internal sovereignty by using deadly force against civil aircraft. A member state may still lawfully exclude foreign civil aircraft from flying over security-sensitive areas within its territory. It may also lawfully force the landing of civil aircraft engaged in spying or merely flying above its territory without authority. But no member state may adopt rules and practices of interception that endanger the lives of persons on board civil aircraft. This important limitation on the state's traditional national sovereignty is designed to protect the safety of international civil aviation, a goal for which most states are willing to accept the proposed restriction.

Just like the aviation agency, scores of other specialized agencies linked with the United Nations system assert their constitutional power and technical expertise to regulate international behavior in their respective fields, with each agency thus seizing pieces of sovereignty that previously belonged to member states. These bits and pieces of sovereignty disbursed among diverse agencies cumulatively cover a significant area of international relations in which agencies set agendas, make rules and monitor state behavior for compliance. Thus, though the advantages of institutional enmeshment exact a cost in terms of the state's traditional sovereignty and independence, most states willingly accept the exchange in order to enjoy the benefits of institutional enmeshment.

However, it would be a mistake to assert that institutional enmeshment is always completely voluntary. The need for interstate cooperation in many areas of global life is so great that most states have no choice but to join regional and global networks. This is most evident in the areas of international trade and finance. Even a cursory examination of international economic organizations reveals how some states, by joining these organizations, have lost most of their traditional autonomy in economic matters. And yet these states seem to have few alternatives, just like the poor members of an extended family who may not have equal influence in the dynamics of the family

5. Article 3 bis was added on May 10, 1984 to the Convention on International Civil Aviation after the downing of a Korean aircraft in the former Soviet Union.

but yet for the purpose of their own survival and possible future improvement nonetheless remain in the group.

Presently, three major organizations are responsible for enmeshing national economies into a global capitalist network: the International Monetary Fund, the World Bank and the World Trade Organization. Instituted to enhance economic cooperation and competition among states, these organizations in their individual and joint efforts promote market economies at national, regional and global levels. They also strive toward dismantling national barriers that obstruct the free flow of goods, services and investment capital across borders. They jointly discourage protectionist policies, like those of the 1930s, when states erected high tariff barriers in the vain hope of boosting domestic manufacturing against foreign competition, policies that precipitated a world-wide depression. Although each organization performs complex tasks, at least a brief overview of their prime purposes may inform an understanding of how this institutional enmeshment forges a global capitalist order from which few states choose to live apart.

The Fund provides the machinery for consultation and collaboration on international monetary problems, such as the manipulative exchange depreciation that nations foolishly use to try to gain an unfair competitive advantage over other nations. The Fund assures an orderly balance of payments among members and "exercises firm surveillance over the exchange rate policies of members" with a view to providing exchange stability, a set of monetary policies conducive to the expansion and balanced growth of international trade. Separate but related to the Fund is the International Bank for Reconstruction and Development, also known as the World Bank. The Bank facilitates the investment of capital for productive purposes. It encourages private foreign investment by means of guarantees and if private capital is unavailable on reasonable terms, the Bank offers its own capital for approved development projects in member states.

The third entity, the World Trade Organization, is designed to foster free trade among member states. This interstate organization seeks to bring down tariff and non-tariff barriers among its members. Consistent with the free market policies of the Fund and the Bank, the World Trade Organization has successfully interlocked the national economies of member states into an intricate legal order of trade and commerce. Based on the general principles of most-favored-nation treatment and non-discrimination between domestic and imported products, the organization plays a leading role in suppressing trade distortions and unfair trade practices.

The Fund and the Bank encourage individual states to adopt market-oriented policies conducive to sustained, non-inflationary economic growth. They also provide technical assistance and training for the officials of member states in a wide range of economic and financial areas, including economic policy, debt management, exchange and trade issues, accounting, statistics and data processing. Periodic consultations between these institutions and member states focus on the states' compliance with previous commitments and on the need for further reforms. If these institutions view a state's economic policies favorably, they may extend financial assistance to the state. "An important characteristic of this assistance is its catalytic effect in generating additional financing from other sources, both official and private." In other words, the Fund and the Bank serve as "character references" on behalf of member states. Thus, whether or not a state gets foreign investment capital depends to a large extent on the state's record with these institutions.

In terms of traditional sovereignty, the impact of economic enmeshment on the state's decision-making autonomy is momentous. Since most states need foreign investment capital, they work in close cooperation with the Fund and the Bank. A state's creditworthiness with the lending institutions of the world is greatly damaged if the Fund or the Bank "impeaches" the state. But if the state is obligated to obey the Fund and the Bank, it loses substantial control over its economic policies. The investment capital sponsored or approved by the Fund, the Bank or its affiliates comes with conditions that the receiving state cannot disregard. The Fund's mechanisms regulating the stability of national currencies further limit the state's discretion to unilaterally alter the scope or size of its international trade, since no member state may arbitrarily manipulate its exchange rate to increase exports. The Fund and the Bank often work in close cooperation with each other to harmonize their policies, further tightening the noose around the state's decision-making authority. The policies dictated by these institutions are not confined to exchange rates, loans and free trade. Often they directly determine what the state must do when managing its national economy, sometimes including micro details such as whether or not the state must raise utility rates in order to qualify for another needed loan.

Moreover, the economic enmeshment brought about by global economic institutions has eroded the traditional principle of state equality, a principle under which each state has equal sovereignty. The Fund and the Bank have no internal organs in which each member state has equal voting power. In both institutions, the state's voting power is directly proportionate to its allocated quota. Though no scientific basis exists for the allocation of state quotas, a number of economic variables are taken into account. Developed states are assigned higher quotas based on their relative economic strength. For example, the United States' current quota in the Fund is 17.8 percent of the total whereas twenty five African states have a combined quota of 1.55 percent. Existing quotas cannot easily be modified because the constitutions of both the Fund and World Bank require a supermajority (85% in the Fund) of the total voting power for any change in the allocation of quotas. Existing quotas have been modified to reflect the states' improved economic strength. However, higher quota states have little incentive to dilute their voting power. The voting inequality in most regional economic institutions is similarly structured, though some regional organizations are more egalitarian than others.

Related to the issue of unequal voting power is the majoritarian principle of law-making within these organizations. Classical international law requires that a nation-state give its consent before it may be saddled with an international obligation. This concept repudiates the majoritarian principle by which a majority of states may legislate for all members or even the entire world. If international organizations were structured in accordance with classical international law, unanimity among member states would be required to create new rights and obligations within the organization. The principle of unanimity, however, vests each member state with veto power, since even a single negative vote disables the decision-making process. This principle also defeats the purpose of unequal voting power since poor states would be able to effectively block proposals made by states with higher quotas. Thus, in order to establish organizations more in tune with reality, the unanimity principle has been discarded by many international institutions in favor of the majority principle.

The majority principle in the context of unequal voting power, however, assumes a new character. If each member state has equal voting power, such as in the United Nations General Assembly, where each member has one vote, outcomes are determined by a majority of states. But if member states have unequal voting power, a majority of voting power, not a majority of states, determines outcomes. In an organization with unequal voting power, even a handful of states that jointly possess the majority of the voting power can prevail over the rest. Unequal voting power may create a single hegemonic state or a coalition of like-minded states that effectively control the organization. Thus, the exclusion of weaker states from the decisionmaking process is almost complete.

Since most economic institutions require a supermajority to make organizational decisions, even a coalition of many poor states may have little say in the decisions and dynamics of economic enmeshment. On the surface, the idea of a supermajority seems egalitarian. In reality, however, it is often just another name for veto power. In the Fund, an eighty-five percent majority of the total voting power is required for any changes in quotas and for making many other important decisions. A member state such as the United States, with more than sixteen percent of the voting power, can therefore veto any decision because the entire remaining membership of the Fund lacks the combined voting power to pass a measure. Even if the organization is redesigned to deny such substantial authority to any single state, a coalition of states, like the European Union, could still pool their voting power to block any decision of which they disapprove. If such a coalition is maintained on a consistent basis, it becomes dominant and marginalizes the majority of member states within the organization. Thus what might appear to be a global institution may be reduced to a league of a few dominant states.

If the dominant coalition resorts to predation, poor states can pool their voting power to oppose unacceptable policies only if the combined voting power is sufficient to constitute a veto. Such a veto, however, is likely to be ineffective, because rich states control the resources and available funds. So in reality the high quota states shape the policies of economic institutions. Rich states are unlikely to accept a voting structure under which they pay the bills while poor states write the checks. Thus the rejection of state equality in important world economic institutions reflects reality. It confers disproportionate authority on rich states to design an international economic order supportive to their own economic interests. These institutions will continue to reflect the inequality that exists among states. Even though poor states benefit from membership in these institutions, few would deny that such states pay a higher cost in terms of relinquishing their traditional sovereignty and state independence. In addition to sacrificing their right to an equal say in international economic matters, poor states lose control over their own social and political autonomy. Decisions made by economic institutions may even directly encroach upon the state's cultural and religious practices.

From the viewpoint of a single poor state, global economic enmeshment is tantamount to extinction of the state's sovereignty. A state with insignificant voting power in regional or global organizations cannot even pretend to be autonomous. In need of the investment capital and technical assistance essential for its economic development, a poor state has little choice but to submit to these organizations. Within the organization, however, its inconsequential voting power has little or no impact on the decisionmaking process. It is not treated equally. Its consent is almost irrelevant to the decisionmaking process. Its domestic economic policies are subject to the dictates of lending institutions. If its external politics or internal social and cultural policies displease the dominant coalition in a lending institution, the state has no choice but to change its ways; otherwise it risks losing even normal borrowing benefits. Thus in the web of economic enmeshment the poor state practically ceases to exist as a sovereign entity.

In view of this helplessness, poor states might feel inclined to leave the capitalist network and rely on their domestic resources and national pride to make necessary headway. But this course of action may prove imprudent, because non-member states frequently end up even worse off. The Soviet Union serves as an example. Even though the reasons for the collapse of communism in the Soviet Union and other East European states are legion, the inability of communist states to successfully sell their products in the so-called free markets played a key role. Since most communist states did not join the capitalist network of economic enmeshment, they could claim no benefits ensuing from capitalist organizations. Consequently, international lending institutions extended little or no foreign investment capital to communist states.

Nor were capitalist states under any legal obligation to open their markets to communist goods. Even when they did, they refused to treat communist goods on par with like products imported from states that joined the capitalist network. Due to quantitative restrictions and high tariffs imposed on products originating in communist countries, communist goods could not compete in international markets. So despite their rhetoric, alternative economic theories and trading blocs, communist states ultimately failed to compete with capitalist institutional enmeshment. Moreover, they lacked the favorable exchange rate needed to buy goods in the free markets, nor could they produce their goods cheaply enough to overcome the high tariffs imposed on their products. These rates and tariffs were imposed in part because the communist states were not part of the capitalist network and in part because some capitalist states were determined to subvert communism if and when possible.

Thus the fall of communism in general and the extinction of the Soviet Union in particular may, among many other factors, be attributed to their exclusion from the capitalist network.

Other international organizations not concerned with economic matters have also weakened the traditional notion of sovereign equality. Even the United Nations, the most universal organization, does not fully embrace the principle of sovereign equality. The United Nations Charter is based on the principle of sovereign equality and accordingly allows each member of the General Assembly one vote. Yet each of the five permanent members of the Security Council has the power to veto the decisions of the Council. The oligarchic structure of the Security Council, consisting of the victorious nations of World War II, is defended on the pragmatic basis that the permanent members, each a nuclear-weapons state, jointly constitute a powerful executive coalition, best suited to maintaining international peace and security. The oligarchic structure of the Security Council is incompatible with the principle of sovereign equality. It even fails to reflect the real balance of power, since two large economies of the world, Japan and Germany, do not have permanent seats in the Council. But even if the Security Council is reorganized, as many states insist it should be, state equality is unlikely to be the guiding principle for its reformation.

Whereas unequal voting power diminishes the autonomy of poor states, equal voting power reduces the authority of rich states. That is why rich nation-states like the United States often insist on having the veto or unequal voting power in most organizations. The recent establishment of the World Trade Organization, after years of multilateral negotiations, freed international trade from national protectionist barriers. The World Trade Organization is founded on the principle of equal voting power; each member state, large or small, has one vote in internal organs, including the dispute resolution body of the organization. This equalitarian principle is consistent with sovereign state equality. However, it offends many groups in the United States who wish to allocate voting power in proportion to the relative economic strength of member states. These groups argue that the United States has no special mechanism to protect its national interests if other states pool their votes to shape the policies of the organization. They further fear that the United States, having just one vote in the World Trade Organization dispute resolution panels, has no assurance that its trade policies would be upheld; in fact, the World Trade Organization might strike down federal or state laws considered incompatible with the organization's constitution. This, these groups point out, is a sacrifice of sovereignty.

The emergence of international organizations thus challenges the autonomy of both small and large states. If these organizations are structured in a way that establishes the oligarchic rule of few states, the majority of states lose control over their internal and external sovereignty. If they are instituted on the equalitarian principle, powerful states risk losing their superior negotiating leverage and their ability to maintain the system in their favor. A more equitable formula could perhaps be designed to accommodate complex and even inconsistent state interests in international organizations. But the logic of contemporary international life is such that no state, large or small, can successfully transact its internal or external affairs without joining these organizations. This inevitability forces a re-evaluation of the assumptions derived from the classic sovereignty of the nation-state.

By transferring authority from states to international organizations, the phenomenon of institutional enmeshment has both bureaucratized and professionalized international law, thereby weakening the traditional authority of state diplomats to shape international policy. Just like national governments, most global and regional organizations maintain bureaucratic structures and staffs charged with the duty to carry out the constitutional functions of the organization. The bureaucratic power to conduct and even shape the affairs of the organization is a new and powerful phenomenon. It has transformed the traditional role of state diplomats, from time immemorial the chief architects of international law-making. While state diplomats still play a critical role in international affairs, organization bureaucrats and international civil servants are gaining ground. In addition to their formal authority, resident bureaucrats draw functional power from their experience with and superior knowledge of the organization. State diplomats live in their national capitals and must be summoned for international conferences. In contrast, organization bureaucrats are in permanent session, occupying the institutional milieu and studying the problems and proposals that affect international life. Consequently, in many cases the initiative to affect international policy has shifted from state diplomats to organization bureaucrats, thereby diminishing the power of the nation-state and enhancing that of international organizations.

In this shift of diplomatic authority some states have lost more than others: many developing states lack personnel qualified for appointment to many organizations. Most constitutive instruments require recruitment of organization bureaucrats on a broad basis, giving due consideration to geographical and cultural diversity. Nonetheless, standards of efficiency, competence and integrity are the paramount considerations in the employment of staff and determination of the conditions of their service. These standards favor developed nation-states that can supply global and regional organizations with a pool of well-qualified nationals. As a result, international secretariats are predominantly staffed by individuals recruited from, or, at least educated in, a few developed states.

International bureaucrats serve in their personal capacity and are thus distinguishable from state representatives, who work on behalf of their states. They undertake to neither seek nor receive instructions from governments or any other authority outside the organization. They are also required to refrain from any action that might reflect on their positions as international officials responsible only to the organization. Furthermore, customary as well as treaty law binds states to respect the exclusively international character of organization bureaucrats and prohibits attempts to influence them in the discharge of their duties. These mutually supportive undertakings by international officials and states are designed to foster bureaucratic loyalty to regional and global organizations rather then native lands.

In the real world, however, it is difficult to separate a person from his or her cultural formation, moral viewpoint and national attachment. Despite formalistic commitment to the organizations they serve, international bureaucrats remain cultural and ethnic beings often sharing the same prejudices that divide communities of the world. Many international bureaucrats are recruited from national bureaucracies and therefore may have mixed loyalties. If the socialization process in support of international organizations is weak, national loyalties remain intact. The personal views of a bureaucrat on such basic matters as whether sovereignty is transferable may also influence the socialization process. Likewise, personal circumstances such as family and friends continue to remind international civil servants of their ethnic and national origins.

Therefore, states that dominate international organizations through their voting power receive further support from an international bureaucracy predominantly comprised of their own nationals. Since most global organizations are headquartered in dominant states, even international bureaucrats recruited from developing and culturally diverse communities tend to adapt the cultural and ideological mores of dominant states. Despite the norms of neutrality and formal loyalty to the organization, existential ties to dominant states play a critical role in enhancing the influence of the dominant coalitions in international bureaucracy. The impact of such an international bureaucracy on the traditional concept of the nation-state thus can be profound. The shift of decisionmaking authority from the nation-state to international organizations expedites the extinction of weaker states, a logical step in the dynamics of any evolution.

The idea of epistemic communities provides yet another way to analyze the role of the international bureaucracy in the evolutionary extinction of the nation-state. Earnst Haas defines an epistemic community as a body of persons sharing the same normative or analytic system derived from a common knowledge base. Technical bodies such as the physicians of the World Health Organization or the aviation experts of the International Civil Aviation Organization are epistemic communities. An epistemic community is not a robotic population of automatons who agree with each other on every normative or analytic standard. It is a human community in which difference of viewpoint and even some conflict among members is inevitable. Nonetheless, epistemic communities are distinguished from other associations by the common basis of knowledge that members acquire as well as the broad consensus they forge with respect to primary assumptions and policies within the scope of that knowledge.

Since specialized agencies and financial and trade organizations employ experts to carry out their constitutional functions, these organizations may be viewed as epistemic communities of experts rather than political bodies of state representatives. Even though the formal constitutional power to adopt policies is usually vested in the political organ of the organization, the epistemic community within the organization enjoys considerable knowledge-based authority to shape policies. If state representatives are themselves experts in the specialized field, they become part of the epistemic community. Moreover, the tension between national and international interests diminishes if both national and international experts belong to the same epistemic community.

Thus the rise of epistemic communities transforms many aspects of international law. The traditional desire of each nation to protect its interests in the calculus of international policy misses a fundamental point: not all regional and global problems involve conflicting national interests. In fact, many national, regional and global problems demand knowledge-based, collaborative solutions. Increased interdependence among the peoples of the world further demands the involvement of epistemic communities in policymaking, because no piecemeal or interest-based solution will work for what is indeed a regional or global epistemic problem. The failure of a nuclear plant and consequent release of radiation is not a political problem that traditional diplomats can solve. Nor is it a territorial problem, since released radiation recognizes no borders. It is an epistemic problem that can only be solved by those knowledgeable in the field.

Increasingly, transnational concerns ranging from the environment to economic development require solutions based on professional knowledge. Almost every aspect of life, national and international, has already been specialized to such an extent that at the policymaking level the involvement of relevant epistemic communities is inevitable. Experts rather than rhetoricians are needed to grow more food more efficiently, to cure diseases that know no national borders, to study the dynamics of economic forces in global markets, to understand the impact of development on the environment, and to examine the sociopsychological effects of racism, sexism, fanaticism and patriotism. Thus when professional knowledge is the driving paradigm, epistemic rather than rhetorical communities are more suitable for seriously seeking durable solutions to human problems.

Although knowledge-based communities can be coerced into working only for the benefit of a single nation-state, most epistemic communities are by their very nature universal. So epistemic communities devoted to specialized fields need not confine themselves to the boundaries of the nation-state. Nor must they fall into the trap of rhetorical communities that operate at a low, selfish level of moral development. National institutions and rhetorical communities may wish to regulate epistemic communities for the benefit of specific nation-states. But regional and global organizations emancipate epistemic communities, allowing them to pursue and use knowledge without nationalistic restrictions. When organizations collaborate with each other, epistemic communities can also come together to share their knowledge, research and goals. This universal coordination among epistemic communities may be the beginning of a new era in which human beings may rapidly evolve into a knowledge-based species. In this evolution, however, the nation-state may have to mutate to mitigate its citizens' irrational attachment to ethnicity or an artificially marked-out piece of territory. Although institutional enmeshment is crucial to the evolution of the state, the process would be incomplete without an additional factor: normative enmeshment.

2. Normative Enmeshment

Normative enmeshment is one of the most remarkable features of contemporary international law. The term refers to common legal values nation-states adopt in their respective legal systems. For example, if each state's criminal system outlaws official torture as a method of securing confessions from the accused, this common value is an example of normative enmeshment. The degree of enmeshment may vary from one area of law to another. States may embrace common values in the area of trade, but they may still have different legal values in the area of family law. Likewise, normative enmeshment may be more extensive regionally than globally. The two processes of enmeshment are almost always synergetic: institutional enmeshment directly affects the state's internal legal system as the state conforms its laws to the purposes of international organizations. Normative enmeshment results in the development of institutions to secure state compliance with international norms.

One concept is crucial to normative enmeshment: common values emanate from the authority of international law. In a major shift away from the Grotian theory, contemporary international law directly regulates the state's internal sovereignty, thereby causing normative enmeshment among national legal systems. Part of this enmeshment is caused by the forces of economic integration. Each state that is a member of the World Trade Organization, for example, enacts the common principles of free trade into domestic legislation. A similar process of enmeshment may also occur at the regional level. The North American Free Trade Agreement mandates that the parties conform their internal laws to the objectives of the Agreement, thereby causing normative enmeshment among the laws of Canada, Mexico and the United States. To facilitate transnational business transactions at both regional and global levels, a uniform contract law called the United Nations Convention on Contracts for the International Sale of Goods (1980) has been enacted, governing the formation and performance of agreements between nationals of different states. So, the process of normative enmeshment is increasingly harmonizing the states' trade laws.

The most significant, and somewhat controversial, normative enmeshment is taking place in the area of human rights and obligations. The human rights movement, which began with the establishment of the United Nations, has now matured into an indispensable part of the contemporary international legal system. An International Bill of Rights[6] has been codified, establishing a legal regime that compels governments to protect the basic dignity of the

---

6. The following documents collectively constitute the International Bill of Rights: (1) the Universal Declaration of Human Rights; (2) the International Covenant on Civil and Political Rights; (3) the International Covenant on Economic, Social and Cultural Rights; (4) the Optional Protocol to the International Covenant on Civil and Political Rights; and (5) the Second Optional Protocol to the International Covenant on Civil and Political Rights, aiming at the abolition of the death penalty.

human person and respect related rights without which no individual can develop into a productive and responsible member of global society. Under classical international law, governments were free to organize domestic social, civil and economic institutions as they saw fit, without legal scrutiny from the rest of the world. But under the law of human rights, governments must adhere to universally recognized norms when laying out their domestic legal orders. Classical international law conferred few rights and obligations on individuals, who thus had to seek protection from the same governments that violated their rights. Contemporary international law embraces the individual, compelling governments to comply with the International Bill of Rights. This shift from a national approach to an international law of rights has weakened the classic notion of internal sovereignty.

The impact of human rights law on internal sovereignty of the nation-state is twofold. First, human rights law reduces the *normative monopoly* of the nation-state over defining fundamental rights and obligations of the individual. Second, human rights law diminishes the nation-state's *institutional monopoly* over the protection of individual rights and obligations.

It is important to understand how contemporary international law digressed from classical international law and the Grotian theory, which recognized the state's primary authority to regulate the conduct of the individual. Before the emergence of the law of human rights, the relationship between individuals and the state was a matter within the domestic jurisdiction of the state. Whether individual rights were protected varied from state to state. Some states practiced slavery, some instituted a rigid caste system, some denied civil and political rights to women and minorities, some provided no rights at all. The state monopolized the legislative process determining which individual rights would be recognized and which groups within the community would be entitled to enjoy these rights.

The civil rights movements, including the one in the United States in 1960s, arose against domestic rulers and laws, often demanding rights from the same ruling class that set up the coercive systems. But legal help from international institutions was unavailable. The state was accountable to no external organizations for the treatment of its own citizens. Constitutionalism attempted to protect some fundamental rights and freedoms against shifting legislative priorities and political majorities. But even this attempt was an essentially national phenomenon. Whether a state adopted a constitution granting rights to its citizens was a matter within the domestic jurisdiction of the state, as an attribute of its internal sovereignty. So classical international law did not require states to adopt constitutions. It provided no legal relief to the individual.

Historical forces dictated this exclusion of the individual from the realm of classical international law. When it first emerged, international law was a body of norms created to regulate a predacious world driven by a constant state of war. Political philosophy, beginning with ancient Hindu and Greek mythologies, Hammurabic and Roman legal traditions, and the Middle Eastern religious doctrines of Judaism, Christianity and Islam, extensively examined and refined the rights and obligations of the individual with respect to the community, the church and the cosmic order. The process of civilizing the individual was thus well on its way in almost all communities of the world. Lacking was a process that would begin to civilize the behavior of nations toward each other. The two processes had not been systematically joined.[7] Consequently, a nation comprised of civilized individuals could act with crude brutality in its wars with other nations. The gap had to be filled. Dedicated to developing such a moral and legal process, the early writers initiated a "law of nations" that rightfully omitted the focus on the individual and instead dealt predominantly with matters of war and peace among nations.

Recall that one aim of classical international law was to repudiate the universal authority of the Roman Catholic Church. This was achieved by reorienting the individual, legally and psychologically, from church to state. The disengagement of individuals from universal religious institutions reduced them to mere subjects of specific nation-states. The formal subjection of the individual to the state and denial of recourse to supranational institutions, was an integral part the state's internal sovereignty. Individual rights and obligations arose from the state's internal laws and from no other source.

Such separation of the individual from all sources external to the state effectively minimized the authority of medieval institutions that claimed jurisdiction over all individuals regardless of their nationality. It also fortified the state's internal sovereignty, positing that the individual's first commitment ought be to the state and that the commitment should be total. In this doctrine of commitment lay the foundation of patriotism, the individual obligation to defend the state even at the cost of life, often sacrificed without compensation. Such a doctrine also justified harsh and broad laws against treason.

Reducing the authority of the church over individuals was justifiable in view of the religious diversity of the world. At a more fundamental level, however, the exclusion of individuals from all universal normative domains initiated a positivist process that compartmentalized the moral psyche of the human race. Patriotic attachment to the nation-state entrenched division among members of the human family. Physical borders created psychological barriers, and *vice versa*, obstructing the way to a gracious world in which human compassion knows no geographical boundaries. The individual was subordinated to the nation-state, sometimes without any rights at all, sometimes with some

---

7. Some elements of natural law, however, developed in all ancient civilizations to regulate inter-group behavior. The ancient Greeks protected the inviolability of envoys, freedom of trading and the sanctity of treaties. In ancient India, the rules of behavior among Hindu Rajahs bear some resemblance to modern international law. Humane treatment of prisoners of war was established to reduce the brutality of war. Similarly, in the seventh century Islamic countries began to develop a sophisticated sense of international law regarding the humane treatment of prisoners of war, and good faith observance of treaties, a command in the Koran. Despite these promising beginnings, international law as a separate discipline took centuries to develop.

protection but always expendable in war. The subjection of the individual to the state advanced the interests of the ruling elites, but it was neither good for the world as a whole nor for individuals. It impeded the political and moral development of individuals as responsible members of global society

Human rights law rehabilitates the individual as the proper subject of international law. A body of individual rights and obligations has developed, diminishing the internal sovereignty of the nation-state to the extent that no state can lawfully deny the rights or waive the obligations sanctioned by contemporary international law. The law of human rights dismantles the state's unlimited authority over the individual. It defines the universal rights and obligations to which each individual is entitled in any state without discrimination on such dubious bases as race, religion or gender. It also obligates states to incorporate these fundamental rights and obligations into their domestic laws and constitutions.

Thus human rights law may be distinguished from state constitutionalism. State constitutionalism, though an important phenomenon in the evolutionary history of civil and political liberties, is essentially a political process favoring stronger groups within the nation-state. Rarely is it founded on the inherent dignity of the human person. For example, the United States constitution, a document many Americans revere with religious conviction, is an exceptional experiment in the development of individual rights and freedoms and creation of a system that many nations have borrowed. Yet the inherent dignity of the human person is not a fundamental assumption of constitutional jurisprudence in the United States. Originally, the constitution and its judicial interpretations tolerated slavery, instituted racial segregation and denied universal suffrage. The amendment procedure and judicial review, corrective mechanisms built into the constitution, have worked over time to extend liberties to previously excluded groups. But even today, the constitution offers little protection to groups disfavored on the bases of sexual orientation, language and alienage. Furthermore, it protects a limited number of rights, some of which are predacious in nature such as the right to own guns and engage in hate speech. And even though a statutory welfare regime has been established, the constitution itself preserves no social, cultural or economic rights, such as the rights to an adequate standard of living, shelter and health. And the United States constitution is not alone in its normative shortcomings. Many national constitutions have highly decorative language, but fail to protect even basic rights against the state's coercive machinery.

Based on the inherent dignity of the human person, human rights law has developed a set of rights and obligations that cut across national, racial, cultural, linguistic and religious borders. The law refuses to artificially separate civil and political rights from social, cultural and economic rights. Nor are these rights and obligations dependent upon formal citizenship. They flow from the dignity of the human person and, as such, cannot be denied based on such questionable criteria as race, color, gender, language, religion, political or other opinion, national or social origin, property, birth or other status. Nor are they dismissed as the creation of idealist rhetoricians, which may be compromised in the real world. They challenge the normative monopoly of the nation-state that has, historically, conferred rights only upon political and social elites. The law of human rights strives to create and preserve a gracious world in which all human beings are born free and equal in dignity and rights.

Universal in nature, human rights law counters the exaggerated claims of cultural diversity some ruling elites make to retain their normative monopolies over rights and obligations. Although states with diverse backgrounds are signatories to the International Bill of Rights and other important human rights treaties, some ruling elites insist the human rights law is a product of Western culture that, in their view, overly emphasizes the rights and not the obligations of the individual. Before the collapse of the Soviet Union, communists states were particularly critical of civil and political rights, whereas capitalist states showed reluctance to accept social, economic and cultural rights. This dichotomy of rights is now less common, as most states have begun to recognize the integrity and wholeness of the law of human rights.

The cultural diversity argument is also losing ground because human rights law itself is sensitive to cultural diversity and strives to protect the rights of linguistic, cultural and religious minorities and other unique groups including indigenous populations. However, the law rejects the frivolous "cultural" arguments that a state may make to defend the commission of torture, suppression of women, exploitation of children or denial of the right to religion or education. No longer may a state lawfully invoke its internal sovereignty to deviate from the regime of universal rights.

This does not imply that the existing human rights law is carved in stone or that perfect standards have now been achieved. The law will continue to evolve as rights and duties are refined to accommodate cultural diversity and global imperatives. Already, the concept of individual duties and the people's collective rights has tempered the discourse of individual rights. The African Charter on Human and Peoples' Rights, for example, sets out individual rights in relation to duties that the individual owes to the family, society, the state and the world. This balance between rights and duties is consistent with the teachings of the Universal Declaration of Human Rights, which states, "Everyone has duties to the community in which alone the free and full development of his (her) personality is possible." Moreover, such balance informs the individual that he or she is not simply a consumer of rights but also a producer of goodwill, intelligence and compassion, a conscientious citizen of the gracious world.

Furthermore, the law of human rights protects the people's collective right to a democratic government, thus changing the principle of political independence, an important tenet of international law. This principle, codified in the United Nations Charter, has previously been interpreted to allow states to institute almost any form of government. Classical international law requires the state to have an effective government, a standard that many forms of government ranging from monarchy to military can satisfy. Recall that even Grotius had argued that no single form of government was superior.

But almost every era favors a particular form of government over all others. The middle ages viewed monarchy as the most preferred form of government since it supposedly reflected the divine order under One God. More recently, however, the world has begun to embrace democracy as a universal normative principle. As a result, the principle of political independence has acquired a new, democratic meaning.

Several influences affect the new linkage between political independence and democracy. First, the collapse of communism in Eastern Europe undermined the authoritarian form of government, a model that for decades competed with democracy by promising efficient and egalitarian social and economic development. Authoritarian governments rejected human rights law, calling it a construct of capitalist powers designed to undermine collective modes of production and the equitable distribution of social goods among the people. They invoked the principle of political independence to defend their internal social, economic and political institutions. However, the breakup of the Soviet Union, which had been a formidable superpower and a nation that refined communist theories and put them into use at home and abroad, exposed the fragility of authoritarian assumptions, especially the notion that the state and not the people have the right to political independence and that people prefer security over liberty. When Russia, the mainstay of the former Soviet Union, embraced democracy, however imperfectly, the authoritarian model as a legitimate expression of political independence began to lose respect and credibility.

Second, the successes of leading democracies such as the United States, Germany and Japan demonstrate that the political independence of the people, expressed through periodic, free and fair elections, is not detrimental to economic prosperity but in fact provides a solid foundation to involve people in building stable social and economic institutions. The success of democratic institutions in Germany and Japan is an even more dramatic reminder that authoritarian states, as Germany and Japan were until after World War II, benefit immensely if they join the community of democratic states. Democracy in India, a heavily populated and poor country, is an additional source of inspiration for the developing nations of the world, many of which once believed that the authoritarian model was more conducive to rapid socioeconomic development.

The third and perhaps most important reason for the emergence of democracy as a preferred form of government is rooted in an emerging normative enmeshment. The Universal Declaration of Human Rights, adopted as early as 1948, maintains that the will of the people shall be the basis of the authority of government and accordingly requires periodic and genuine elections by universal and equal suffrage. Since the Declaration has been treated as a moral rather than legal document, the principle of democracy has remained controversial in character. The International Covenant on Civil and Political Rights, concluded in 1966, codified the democratic principle into positive law.

But the acceptance of the democratic principle has been problematic. Initially, many states refused to sign the Covenant. Moreover, the rise of one-party political systems, in which elections are held but the candidates running for political office all belong to the same official party and espouse the same political agendas, added confusion to the democratic principle. And some states continue to insist on the validity of classical international law, and its principle of political independence of nations rather than peoples.

In this normative transition from classical to contemporary international law, the democratic principle still competes with the old interpretation of political independence. The democratic principle requires governments to seek legitimacy through periodic and genuine elections. The classic interpretation of political independence mandates no one form of government. Between the two competing principles, the concept of internal sovereignty is more compatible with the classic interpretation of political independence. This is so because a state, by virtue of its sovereignty, ought to be able to freely choose its own form of government without legal or moral scrutiny from the rest of the world. The democratic principle, on the other hand, diminishes the scope of internal sovereignty, requiring every state to adopt a form of government in which the people have the right to elect and remove political officials.

To reconcile the two principles, a major analytical shift is in the making. If the principle of political independence belongs to the state and is superior to the democratic principle, then the people have no right to assert their will against the state's coercive might, a rule supported by both Grotius and Hans Kelsen. If the people and not the state have the right of political independence, then the two principles merge in harmony. The democratic principle safeguards the political independence of the people from all forms of authoritarianism by giving them the right to periodically review and remove unacceptable governments. Thus the democratic principle is likely to triumph if the principle of political independence is untied from the state and tied to the people. Then, the people and not the state would be the custodians of political independence. They and not the state would determine the form of government.

The democratic principle as a rule of normative enmeshment should not be confused with the state's domestic democracy. If the democratic principle is imposed from within the state by a domestic constitution without the broader impetus of international law, the state's internal sovereignty in the classical sense remains intact. The state then remains free to dismantle democracy and institute a different form of government. However, when the democratic principle is imposed by international law, the state is disabled from invoking its internal sovereignty to choose a contrary form of government. Thus, an international democratic principle is no longer simply a product of state constitutions. It is a principle of normative enmeshment that no state or people may ordinarily reject.

Although the democratic principle is more widely accepted now than it was a few decades ago, the old view of political independence still persists. China, a permanent member of the United Nations Security Council, has not yet embraced the democratic principle. Russia, another permanent member, has a fragile democracy and could revert to authoritarianism. Most Arab states, the principal custodians of Islamic traditions, embraced by close to a billion people around the world, have non-democratic systems. Many states around the world have instituted fragile democracies only after coming under pressures from international organizations. Thus the normative tension between the old interpretation of political independence and the human-rights-based democratic principle is not yet fully resolved. Whether the two principles will indeed merge in the future is unclear, though the democratic momentum prevailing among the communities of the world suggest that they will. This merger, if elevated to a universal normative enmeshment, will weaken the state's traditional authority, that is, its internal sovereignty to choose a non-democratic form of government. Accordingly, the principles of political independence and the exclusion of the individual from the realm of international law will undergo qualitative transformation, providing a new legal basis for interstate and private international organizations to hold governments accountable for what they do to their people.

The law of human rights and obligations has established machinery to monitor state compliance, thus weakening the state's traditional monopoly on enforcement. Since the emergence of the nation-state, individual rights and obligations have not only been created through domestic procedures but also exclusively enforced through internal state institutions such as administrative and judicial tribunals. State institutions, in their interpretation and enforcement of individual rights and obligations, were accountable to no international bodies. In fact, no international institutions were available to complain against the state's human rights violations. As a result, individuals or groups that failed to procure or safeguard rights through domestic channels had no further recourse to challenge the interpretative or enforcement decisions of state institutions. Thus the state enjoyed a legal monopoly over both the creation and enforcement of rights. This unshared dominion over the individual vested the nation-state with awesome authority to deny rights with impunity, practice arbitrary enforcement and conceal its human rights violations from the international community.

Interstate and private human rights organizations have significantly reversed this national monopoly over the enforcement of human rights. Many interstate human rights institutions are created by nation-states. For example, the United Nations Commission on the Status of Women, founded in 1946, is an intergovernmental institution that studies women's rights in political, economic, civil, social and educational fields. Regional human rights institutions have also been founded to carry out both general and specific examinations of human rights violations and realization. In addition to these institutions, several treaty-based epistemic committees, composed of experts on human rights issues who act in their personal capacity and not as the representatives of states, have been established to study specific areas. The Committee on the Elimination of Racial Discrimination, established in 1970 in accordance with the provision of the International Convention on the Elimination of All Forms of Racial Discrimination, considers reports on member states' implementation of the norms of the Convention. It also receives communications from nationals whose states have accepted the competence of the Committee. These global and regional institutions together furnish a framework for the study of the conduct of governments as well as a way to encourage them to comply with obligations arising from human rights declarations, treaties and covenants.

Expert committees established to enforce specific treaties are likely to develop a human rights jurisprudence, clarifying the principles contained in such treaties. The Human Rights Committee, established in accordance with provisions of the International Covenant on Civil and Political Rights, studies the measures member states have adopted in compliance with the Covenant. Member states may also authorize the Committee to receive written communications from individuals who claim that any of their rights enumerated in the Covenant have been violated. Although the Committee has no enforcement authority, it considers communications in light of available evidence and forwards its views to the offending state and the complaining individual.

Private human rights organizations are non-governmental organizations that function as transnational actors to investigate and expose human rights violations. Diverse in origin, membership and scope of activity, these organizations cannot be delineated by a single formula. Large and small, global and regional, innumerable private organizations working for the protection of human rights often play a decisive role in dismantling the internal sovereignty many governments summon to defend and conceal atrocities against individuals and groups in violation of assumed international obligations.[8] A few examples may be noted. Founded at Oxford in 1942 to combat civilian famine in war-torn Europe, Oxfam has expanded its transnational commitment to relieve suffering caused by poverty. Launched in 1961 by a London barrister, Amnesty International has become a powerful institution that opposes detention of prisoners of conscience, imposition of the death penalty, and infliction of torture or other cruel, inhuman or degrading treatment. Formed in 1969 in the United States, Friends of the Earth is now an international organization that exposes governmental policies generating misuse and abuse of natural resources. Many such non-governmental organizations enjoy consultative status with the United Nations Commission on Human Rights to which they provide information regarding violations of human rights.

Interstate and private human rights organizations challenge the internal sovereignty of the nation-state. They investigate, discuss, debate and condemn human rights violations. Thus matters once exclusively within the domestic jurisdiction of the nation-state are now regularly exposed, criticized and condemned by interstate human rights institutions. Private human rights organizations also penetrate the boundaries of the nation-state to study prison conditions, police brutality, official corruption, arbitrary executions, persecution of political dissidents, subjection of women, suppression of minorities, forced assimilation of indigenous populations and a host of other violations govern-

---

8. Over one thousand non-governmental organizations attended the San Francisco conference called in 1945 to formulate the United Nations Charter. The number of non-governmental organizations with transnational interests is overwhelming.

ments previously committed and concealed from the world in the name of internal sovereignty and political independence. They gather evidence of human rights violations, then disseminate the information through global media to embarrass the government, and finally share this damaging information with global and regional intergovernmental institutions for a more formal hearing and condemnation. This exposure puts pressure on the offending state to comply with its human rights commitments.

Although the nation-state's normative and institutional monopoly over individual rights and obligations is under increasing pressure, it is still too early to assert that the human rights law has effectively nullified the internal sovereignty of the nation-state. The rhetoric of sovereignty is still employed in the discourse of human rights, and some governments, particularly those with bad human rights record, resist the intrusion of interstate and private human rights organization into their so-called "internal affairs" Powerful states still wish to retain their exclusive authority over individual rights and obligations. The United States, for example, subjects all treaties to its constitutional jurisprudence. Accordingly, any human right principle inconsistent with the text or interpretation of the federal constitution is *ipso facto* unenforceable within the United States borders. This internal constitutional superiority over the norms of human rights treaties preempts any substantial change in constitutional jurisprudence from without. Thus it deprives the individual of new human rights not provided in the federal constitution. However, many United States nationals are so emotionally tied to the federal constitution that many would resist, some even resorting to violence, if the federal constitution were to be subordinated to the human rights law. Moreover, the United States has thus far not accepted the competence of any human rights body to receive communications from individuals, thereby preserving its institutional hold over the interpretation and enforcement of individual rights.

The United States is not alone in its reluctance to accept the normative and institutional authority of human rights law. Many other states also grudge the creeping influence of human rights treaties and organizations. In fact, human rights law faces several hurdles in the process of diminishing the internal sovereignty of the nation-state. Most human rights treaties are written in ambiguous text specifically to accommodate diverse religious and cultural concerns. Even then, some states still refuse to sign these treaties to protect their inconsistent practices. Others attach reservations to these treaties. In many states human rights treaties cannot be enforced through domestic courts. And many states do not accept the competence of global or regional human rights institutions to receive complaints from other states or individuals, thus attempting to shield their internal sovereignty from direct external censure.

But despite their continuing resistance to normative and institutional aspects of the human rights law, nation-states can no longer effectively conceal human rights violations. Some human rights institutions, such as the United Nations Commission of Human Rights, have universal jurisdiction over almost all states. The United Nations organs, including the General

Assembly, the Economic and Social Council and the Security Council, have institutional competence to bring human rights violations before the international community and pressure the offending government to change its behavior. And non-governmental organizations are even more effective in gathering and disseminating damaging information. The impact of private human rights organizations is substantial on most governments. Democratic governments, which can be voted out in the next elections, care to maintain good human rights records. Thus they normally allow private organizations to gather and disseminate information, since denying access to such organizations in itself can damage the credibility of the government. Even most authoritarian governments fear exposure in the global media and consequently go out of their way to conceal human rights violations. Almost all offender states deny violating human rights, which suggests that states can no longer invoke their internal sovereignty to assert that they can do whatever they please within the confines of their territory. This authority is now unavailable.

Ironically, nation-states themselves have created the universal law of individual rights and obligations, a law that reduces their awesome authority over the individual. Although created over the past few decades through the treaty process, human rights law is now so deeply entrenched in customary law that no state can hide behind the frivolous argument that because it has signed no human rights treaties, it has no human rights obligations. If accused, most governments deny or lie that they have committed such violations. This is so because no government can now lawfully invoke the old arguments of state sovereignty or domestic jurisdiction to assert that it has complete authority over people within confines of the nation-state.

The nation-state is under tremendous pressure to adapt to the new realities of contemporary international law. Its external sovereignty, its independence to conduct an independent foreign policy, is now less relevant than its capacity to coordinate its foreign policy with regional and global interests. It still has the power to make international law through custom and treaty. But the fast-emerging formal and functional authority of regional and global organizations to form and execute international policy challenges the formerly exclusive law-making domain of nation-states. Since nation-states have little or no choice but to join international organizations, their capacity to function in isolation or in direct opposition to these organizations has significantly diminished. While the state must cooperate in the realm of foreign affairs or face ostracism and the loss of shared benefits, it is also under legal, moral and economic pressure to institute a domestic legal system that protects the basic rights and duties of all persons. The ruling elites may no longer hide behind excuses derived from culture, religion or ethnicity to seek exemption from a universally recognized normative enmeshment in many areas of law, including the regime of human rights. In view of these formidable challenges, many nation states have begun to pool their sovereignties, in part to compete more effectively in global markets and in part to recognize that sovereign borders have become dysfunctional. Among such communities, the European Union provides the most useful example of institutional and normative enmeshment.

Chapter Six

The Example of European Union

The European Union illustrates the process by which the nation-state may gradually lose its traditional attributes. It also indicates how normative and institutional enmeshment may weaken the state's internal and external sovereignty. Designed to promote economic and social progress, the Union dismantles its member states' internal borders, allowing the free flow of goods, services, capital, labor and persons. As socioeconomic enmeshment expands, the member states are likely to establish a monetary union, including the creation of a single currency. Furthermore, the member states vow to assert a common identity on the international scene, especially through the implementation of a common foreign and security policy. This process may lead to the eventual framing of a common defense policy. If the present momentum toward unification continues and new members are successfully recruited and integrated,[1] the process that began with six nations and limited economic cooperation may ultimately lead to a prosperous, human rights-oriented, unified Europe. As a Leibnizian monad, the European Union will gradually unfold its inner truth.

One Europe is an old medieval dream waiting to be realized, but it is a difficult if not unattainable goal. Whether the European Union will finally dissolve the separate legal status of member states is a question most difficult to answer. One result, however, seems certain: no member state within the European Union will be able to reassert the prime attributes of the classic state, an entity that emerged out of the Peace of Westphalia and was finally able to dismantle the era of empires. One might pontificate that Western Europe is attempting to resurrect another Holy Roman Empire in the cloak of the European Union, this time using the charisma of the markets. The rise of Germany as the Union's most powerful member may confuse the dynamics of the European Union, rekindling the old nationalistic feelings that unraveled the Holy Roman Empire. The European Union has few parallels with the defunct empire, however, particularly because medieval religionism seems to have lost its hold on the secular spirit of Western Europe. If the objectives of the European Union are successfully achieved, the extinction of the nation-state may occur first in Europe, the same continent that created the concept.

Inspired by the European cooperative experience, many economic communities have emerged in different regions and subregions of the world. They vary in size, in combined economic power and in the ability to affect or dominate regional and global markets. The idea of an interstate economic union is

---

1. Already three more states, Sweden, Austria and Finland, have been admitted into the communities, with several others waiting in line.

simple. Just as corporations merge in order to compete more effectively in markets, so nations pool their authorities and resources to enhance their combined economic power. The North American Free Trade Agreement, joining Canada, the United States and Mexico, has created a regional coalition with a large combined population and economic might. If economic integration continues in the Americas other states will be invited to join, thus further magnifying the region's united strength. And the process of economic enmeshment is no longer confined to rich states. Developing states in Western Africa and South Asia, some of which are very poor, have also established economic communities to promote free trade in their respective regions. The dynamics of global markets are such that no nation-state, rich or poor, can survive or thrive on its own without merging its economic interests with those of other states. That is why the traditional notion of economic autonomy faces the imperative of border-free regional markets. Each regional community will have to find its own way, since merely mimicking Europe will achieve few results. Nonetheless, the European Union offers a powerful example of interstate cooperation and its possible pitfalls.

The idea of an economic community was first developed by some of the same nations that for centuries decided the questions of war and peace on the European continent. In 1951, three hundred years after the Peace of Westphalia and only a few years after the unprecedented devastation of the Second World War, six nations, France, West Germany, Italy, the Netherlands, Belgium and Luxembourg, signed a treaty in Paris to institute the European Coal and Steel Community. In some ways, the community was a modest beginning in economic cooperation. But in an another way, it was a momentous step toward fusing France and parts of the former Holy Roman Empire into a new union. For centuries, Italian popes and German emperors strived to expand the Holy Roman Empire into a supranational union, an idea French nationalistic forces resisted with unshakable determination. In 1951, however, France itself led the initiative to begin a process of merger, laying the foundation of a unified and prosperous Europe – a unification now so successful that many other European nations, including Muslim Turkey, the successor to the defunct Ottoman empire, now petition to join.[2]

The success of the European economic community lay in a gradual but steady approach toward merging the economies of member states and expanding its membership. In 1957, a few years after the institution of the coal and steel community, the same six nations signed two separate treaties in the ancient city of Rome to establish two more communities: the European Atomic Energy Community and the European Economic Community. The European Economic Community, due to its more ambitious scope, became

---

2. If Muslim Turkey is excluded from the Union, as some in Europe wish, the European Union may acquire a Christian image, reviving once again the same harmful contradiction that defined the middle ages. The exclusion of Turkey, however, is not critical to the prosperity or solidarity of the European Union.

the crown jewel of the three communities. Initially, each community had its own separate institutional framework. But the 1965 Merger Treaty enmeshed the separate institutions of each community, creating a single Commission and a single Council. Despite this institutional enmeshment, however, the three communities continued to function as separate entities.

As these communities began to reap substantial economic benefits for the founding member states, other European nations sought to join the communities, popularly known as the common market. For fear of losing its sovereignty, the United Kingdom was at first reluctant to join. The economic success of the common market was too tempting, however, to safeguard the traditional notion of state sovereignty. In 1973, along with Denmark and the Republic of Ireland, the United Kingdom finally joined the communities.[3] In 1979 Greece and in 1986 Spain and Portugal, the relatively less developed European nations, entered the common market, bringing the total membership to twelve.

The twelve members later signed two additional treaties to further strengthen the existing legal regime of the communities and to achieve "an ever closer union among the peoples of Europe," a goal stated in the preamble to the 1957 European Economic Community Treaty. The Single European Act, signed in 1986, proposed a massive task of normative enmeshment: the harmonization of standards to remove physical and technical state barriers that impede the free flow of labor, capital, goods and services. The Act also introduced procedural changes to expedite the communities' decision-making process. Above all, the Act set up the deadline of December 31, 1992 to complete the proposed single market.

After successfully achieving the primary goals of normative enmeshment set out in the Single European Act, the member states signed the 1992 Maastricht treaty, officially known as the Treaty on European Union (Union Treaty). The Union Treaty entered into force on November 1, 1993, after the German Federal Constitutional Court dismissed domestic challenges to the Treaty. The Union Treaty is a future-oriented, executory agreement that seeks both institutional and normative enmeshment in diverse areas of internal and external cooperation among the member states. It marks a new stage in the process of creating an ever closer union among the peoples of Europe.

For understanding the institutional enmeshment of the European Union one must note the important distinction between two types of institutions: intergovernmental and communitarian. Both types of institutions are established to carry out the legislative and executive functions of the Union. Each type varies, however, in its orientation and purpose. The Council of Ministers is the Union's intergovernmental institution, in which each member state protects its national interests and policies. Although the Council facilitates cooperation among the member states for achieving the Union's objectives, it

3. France under General de Gaulle blocked the entry of the United Kingdom for some years.

is nonetheless an intergovernmental body in which the member states pool rather than sacrifice their individual sovereignty. Despite its intergovernmental character, however, the Council is no equalitarian institution. The member states are allocated unequal voting power in the Council, taking into account their respective fiscal might. In most economic matters, the decision-making process in the Council requires a qualified voting majority. Joint action in other matters, including the formulation of a common foreign policy, requires a unanimous vote.

In contrast to the Council, the Commission is a communitarian institution; it protects the shared interests and policies of the Union or Community. Thus the Commission is dedicated to the interests of no single member state. The members of the Commission, though nationals of the member states, theoretically must be independent beyond doubt. In the performance of their duties, the members of the Commission "neither seek nor take instructions from any government or any other body." Sensitive to but not dictated by national interests, the Commission works toward the integration of national economies and social policies. In fact, the Commission may arguably seek to enmesh the sovereignties of member states into the single authority of the Union.

The contrast between the two types of institutions represents the tension between nationalism and communitarianism. Intergovernmental institutions protect the prime attributes of the nation-state, whereas communitarian institutions strive to weaken them. Defenders of national sovereignty wish to lodge the primary decision-making authority in intergovernmental institutions. Moreover, they prefer unanimity over qualified voting majority as the rule of decision-making, because the principle of unanimity protects the sovereignty of even a small member state with low voting power, a state that can easily be compromised under the rule of qualified voting majority. The advocates of communitarianism prefer majoritarian voting procedures, since requirement of unanimity causes delay and inefficiency, granting even a micro member state, such as Luxembourg, the formidable power to veto an otherwise broadly supported decision. The European Union thus experiences the conflicting tendencies of its institutions. It is unlikely that communitarianism will completely replace intergovernmentalism in the near future. But communitarianism will play a critical role in the unfolding of the European Union, an intriguing experiment in a continent known for its tribalism, strife, unpredictability and the will to create innovative modes of social organization.

There is some confusion regarding the legal nature of the European Union, some real, some generated by mixing of titles. The confusion over titles is easy to sort out. It is unclear to many in legal circles, particularly outside Europe, whether the European Union has replaced the European Community. A superficial reading of the Union Treaty gives the misleading impression that the European Union is a new legal entity. But this is not so, at least not yet. The European Union has not succeeded or dissolved any of the three communities. The Union treaty has amended the founding treaties of the three communities, but each community continues to exist in its own right as a separate legal entity with differing responsibilities. Much confusion arises from the use of the title "Community." The title is used sometimes to specifically refer to one of the three European communities, sometimes to describe all the three communities together, and sometimes to simply allude to the member states. The label "Community" is also used to refer to the European Union. So confusion prevails when the same label is used to refer to different entities.

Confusion about the Union's legal status further complicates the matter, mystifying its nature. The European Union is neither a federation nor an international organization nor a new consolidated superstate. It is more than the existing three communities, more than a single economic market, more than a mere association of member states, but less than an autonomous entity. According to the Union Treaty, the member states shall assert the Union's identity on the international scene. The Union must nevertheless respect the national identities of its member states. Such tensions are perhaps inevitable to accommodate the differing visions of the member states. The reasons for the Union's current formlessness are also rooted in the classic evolutionary struggle when an existing form, in this case the nation-state, experiences the process of slow, grinding extinction. As a new creature, the European Union is in that ambiguous stage of transition when a caterpillar is no longer a caterpillar but not yet a butterfly.

1. Objectives of the European Union

To understand how traditional state sovereignty contends to survive in the Union's normative and institutional framework, one must examine the shared objectives the member states aspire to achieve. Conceptually, it is easy to understand that any interstate pursuit requires cooperation. It is also easy to understand that interstate cooperation will bear no fruit if the member states arbitrarily reassert their willful autonomy to protect their national interests. Sustainable interstate cooperation is possible only when cooperating states commit themselves to the common enterprise under all circumstances, particularly in times of adversity. No such profound commitment is yet apparent in the case of the European Union. Nonetheless, the Union has established an enmeshment process in which the traditional forces of nationalism compete and collide with the motif of shared objectives.

To begin with, the Union aims at promoting economic and social progress that is both balanced and sustainable. The addition of a social dimension to economic integration changes the original design of the common market, which was primarily concerned with removing barriers to the free flow of goods, services, capital and labor. Social cohesion is in many ways inevitable now that economic integration is intensified. The Union strives to develop a common policy in the spheres of commerce, agriculture, fisheries and transport. To safeguard the capitalist system from monopolies and price fixing, a common competition policy assures that the internal market is not distorted. To further strengthen the competitiveness of Community industries, the member states undertake to promote research and technological development.

They also undertake to make necessary changes in their laws to facilitate the functioning of the common market. If economic enmeshment is achieved as scheduled, the Union will establish economic and monetary union, ultimately including a single currency.

Free markets alone do not cause social cohesion. In fact, the free play of market forces without the constraints of distributional justice or concern for workers can lead to social fragmentation, widening the gap between social classes and resulting in the exploitation of labor and consumers. An obsessive focus on economic development is also detrimental to the environment. To safeguard against these and other excesses of capitalism, the Union adds an important social dimension to the system. Accordingly, the member states are committed to pursue a set of social policies, including the establishment of a social fund, the attainment of a high level of health protection, a contribution to education and the strengthening of consumer protection. The Union also promises to institute a policy in the sphere of the environment.

The Union is sensitive to the fact that uneven economic and social development can be particularly detrimental when diverse ethnic and national communities are joined into a common market. Right now, not all member states of the Union enjoy the same standard of living. Greece and Portugal are markedly less developed than Germany and the Netherlands. Moreover, not all regions within the territory of every member state are equally developed, nor do they reap equitable economic benefits from the merger of national economies. If the existing imbalance in the standard of living among diverse regions and subregions continues or worsens, economic integration will advance only the interests of manufacturers, bankers and traders. To avoid such economic and social disparity, a commitment is made to promote overall harmonious development. Equitable and wide-spread economic and social development may minimize divergence among various regions. It may also reduce the backwardness of rural areas.

To emphasize the multi-dimensional character of the European Union, the Maastricht Treaty makes symbolic but important linguistic changes. It shortens the name of the European Economic Community to simply the European Community. This change in the title of the most important of the three communities is designed to demonstrate that economic integration is no longer the sole focus of the Union. Article 2 of the Treaty of Rome, which established the European (Economic) Community, is also amended to underscore that the economic goals of the common market are to be achieved in the context of "social cohesion and solidarity among member states." The 1989 Social Charter that safeguards the rights of workers, such as improved living and working conditions, proper social protection and high employment, was included in the original draft of the Union Treaty. Due to the objection of the United Kingdom, the member state most attached to the concept of national sovereignty, the Social Charter was dropped from the final draft. The charter is incorporated in a separate agreement, called the Protocol on Social Policy, binding the remaining member states to a social policy that constitutes an integral part of the *acquis commununautaire*. When and if its current conservative government is voted out of power, the United Kingdom may reconsider the adoption of the Social Charter. Meanwhile, the United Kingdom remains under an obligation arising from other provisions of the Union Treaty to work in cooperation with other member states toward actualizing the legal goal of social cohesion.

Efforts toward creating social cohesion among the peoples of the Union constitute a pragmatic goal that, if successfully achieved, will strengthen the foundation of the Union. This goal minimizes the rhetoric and reality of national interests, the pursuit of which can turn any common market into a source of mutual exploitation, a predacious regional arrangement in which few benefit at the cost of many.[4] When joint economic resources are allocated to assist underdeveloped regions, the goal of social cohesion exacts a temporary cost from the more affluent members of the Union. Thus, if the member states' commitment to social cohesion is simply rhetorical or if the single common market results in the subordination of weak states, the doctrine of national sovereignty will most likely resurface. Less advantaged but equally proud member states of the Union will reassert their nationalism. In the worst case, the domination of a single member state, such as Germany, over the entire Union would resurrect bitter historical memories of mutual doubt, resistance and warfare.

Closely related to the peril of a single member domination is the pitfall of social uniformity. The establishment of a single economic market requires massive harmonization of standards, a goal the 1986 Single European Act has already achieved to a large extent, But standardization inevitably causes some social cohesion. And social cohesion also occurs when businesses, manufacturers and advertisers create common consumer preferences. If economic integration is subject to a well-defined social policy, such as equitable labor standards throughout the Union, it will too produce some social cohesion. Despite these inevitable effects, social cohesion should not be confused with social uniformity.

Social uniformity aims at diluting differing cultural practices. It subordinates minor languages and creates the hegemony of one dominant culture over the subtleties of diversity. No matter how high the standard of living the people may enjoy, most prefer not to sacrifice their culturally differentiated identities for the sake of a well-stocked market. To safeguard against such social standardization, Article F of the Union Treaty mandates respect for national identities. In fact, the amended version of Article 3 of the European Community treaty refers to "the flowering of the cultures" of the member states. These principle may be extended to protect even subnational identities, including those of non-European minorities. The ideal of social cohesion is

4. Unfortunately, the discourse of national interests is rampant among the member states of the North American Free Trade Agreement, particularly the United States. Such rhetoric will change as regional cooperation is further intensified.

therefore fully congruent with the protection of linguistic, ethnic and religious diversity.

The second objective of the Union is to assert its identity on the international scene by adopting common positions and taking joint actions in foreign affairs. The Union Treaty mandates that member states implement, in the name of the European Union, a common foreign and security policy, including the eventual framing of a common defense policy. Member states are required to inform and consult one another on foreign matters of general interest so that a common position may be defined in a mutually trustful and informed manner. Once a common policy has been formulated, it must be implemented in the name of the European Union. No member state is allowed to undermine the common position by negative comments. Nor is a member state permitted to take any action contrary to the Union's interests or likely to impair the Union's effectiveness as a cohesive force in international relations. In fact, the member states must support the Union's policy actively and unreservedly in a spirit of loyalty and mutual solidarity. Such a course of action ensures that the Union's combined influence is exerted as effectively as possible by means of concerted and convergent action. Furthermore, no member state may opt out of this regime of common foreign policy.

Under the principle of *acquis communautaire*, no member state is allowed to pick and choose the defining characteristics of the Union. Still, a few exemptions have been granted. Both the United Kingdom and Denmark, for example, have reserved the right to opt out of the third stage of economic integration, which requires the institution of a single currency. The United Kingdom has also opted out of the Social Charter. In matters of common foreign and security policy, however, no such exemption is allowed. Nor is any such exemption likely to be granted in the future to new member states. If an applicant state has a history of pursuing an independent foreign policy, the Union may demand "specific and binding assurances" with respect to its common foreign and security policy before the state is admitted into the Union. Because of its proximity to both Western Europe and the former Soviet Union, Finland traditionally pursued neutrality in foreign affairs. To ensure that Finland would abandon its neutrality and adhere to the Union's common foreign policy, specific assurances were sought from Finland at the time of its induction into the Union.

Despite commitment to a common foreign policy, however, the existing procedures to define and implement joint positions and actions are subject to intergovernmentalism. The Union Treaty mandates that the Commission, a communitarian institution, be fully associated with the work related to the common foreign and security policy. The Commission may even submit proposals. Yet the task of forging a common foreign policy is assigned to the Council, an intergovernmental body. To further reinforce the intergovernmental control of foreign policy, the decision-making process is subject to unanimity, thus allowing any one member state to veto joint action.

So far intergovernmentalism has failed to produce a vigorous common foreign policy, inviting the suggestion that the Commission should be given a more meaningful role in foreign policy. It has also been suggested that the unanimity requirement be relaxed. The Union Treaty already authorizes the Council to define those matters on which decisions are to be taken by a qualified majority. If effective procedures are instituted to assure the formation and execution of a common foreign policy, at least with respect to important international matters, the objective of asserting the Union's identity on the international scene will become more pragmatic and attainable. Regardless of the procedures, the Union Treaty envisions a future in which each member state will be disabled from pursuing an independent foreign policy.

So what are the legal consequences of the Union's objective of a common foreign policy? If this objective is fully accomplished, the member states' claim to separate statehood under international law becomes suspect. Since exclusive control over foreign policy has been a defining attribute of the sovereign state, one may argue that no entity lacking such competence may assert separate statehood. This argument, however, is flawed because voluntary disability is not synonymous with actual incompetence. No member state suffers from any actual incompetence to conduct foreign policy. It may therefore be argued that no member state loses its statehood by voluntarily transferring its foreign policy competence to the Union. This argument, however, makes sense only if each member state retains the right to withdraw its voluntary disability and reassert its foreign policy competence. But in the Union this right has not been retained. The Union Treaty forbids member states from opting out of the regime of common foreign policy. Of course, a member state could totally withdraw from the Union, but even this scenario is highly unlikely due to the complex enmeshment of the member states' economic and social policies. In addition, the Union Treaty is concluded for an indefinite period.

If intergovernmentalism is discarded and the communitarian institutions become mainly responsible for conducting the Union's common foreign policy, the Union will then be indistinguishable from a federation. A federation, such as the United States, disables its constituent units from pursuing independent foreign and security policy. This disability is often legally imposed since many constituent units otherwise continue to possess the means to conduct foreign policy. It is unlikely that the Union will progress toward a federation or that its constitutional provisions will formally disable the member states from conducting independent foreign policy. No member state is prepared to adopt such a clear legal path. Therefore, the interplay between intergovernmentalism and communitarianism will remain muddled, even kept deliberately unclear to some extent.

Moreover, the Union benefits from its institutional complexity and lack of clarity. If the Union is turned into a clear-cut federation, the member states will lose their separate votes in international organizations, like the United Nations Security Council. Both France and the United Kingdom are permanent members of the Council, each having a separate vote and veto. If the Union is turned into a federation, all its member states will be counted as a single state. The Union, as a single state, would certainly be granted a permanent seat in the Security Council and would also be able to obtain veto power.

But the trade-off is unprofitable. France and the United Kingdom would lose their separate votes and vetos. In addition, no other member state of the Union could be elected even as a non-permanent member of the Security Council. The notion that Germany should be admitted as a permanent member into the Security Council would lose its legal basis. Similarly, the Union as a federated entity would have just one vote, not its present fifteen votes, in the United Nations General Assembly. This dilution of voting power in the United Nations and hundreds of other international organizations is a heavy price to pay for turning the Union into a federation. To retain the individual voting power of its member states in international organizations, therefore, the Union is likely to retain its legally ambiguous character.

In its present status, however, the European Union has introduced a legal contradiction into the theory of international law: a nation-state can be independent to exercise its external sovereignty but simultaneously bound to pursue policies determined by a regional entity. To the external world, each member state of the Union is a sovereign state with separate voting power. By law, however, each member state is obligated to use its power to advance the identity of the European Union through joint positions and actions.

This legal contradiction serves several useful purposes. It maintains a transitional period in which member states are not yet prepared to relinquish their separate identities. It cultivates a legal and psychological environment in which the European identity may gradually emerge. It allows member states to use their separate votes to enhance the Union's power and prestige in international organizations. It is also quite likely that such a contradiction, if maintained over the next few decades, may in fact modify the traditional rule of international law that requires the capacity to conduct foreign policy as an essential ingredient of statehood.

The Union's third objective is to strengthen the protection of individual rights and freedoms. The Union Treaty incorporates the European Convention for the Protection of Human Rights and Fundamental Freedoms into the Community's legal regime. This normative enmeshment influences not only the constitutional jurisprudence of each state but also introduces fundamental human rights into the economic and social principles of Community law. Even before this incorporation, all member states of the Union already participated in the legal regime of human rights established by the European Convention. Yet for many years the European Convention was not a formal part of the Community law. The European Court of Justice, the judicial institution of the Union, began to incorporate the concept of fundamental rights into the Community law. In the famous case of *Internationale Handelsgesellschaft*, the Court stated that international treaties for the protection of human rights approved by the member states should be followed within the framework of Community law. The Union Treaty reaffirms the Court's jurisprudence by formally incorporating the European Convention into the Union's legal system, underscoring the point that social cohesion requires more than the mere circulation of goods and capital. Fair treatment of individuals is the key to the establishment of a just and well-ordered community.

In addition to the rights and freedoms mentioned in the European Convention, the Union Treaty introduces the concept of Union citizenship. Every national of a member state is a citizen of the Union, a title conferring two important rights. First, every citizen of the Union has the right to move and reside freely anywhere within the territory of the member states. Second, every citizen residing in a member state of which he is not a national has the right to political participation, including the right to vote and the related right to contest for political office under the same conditions as nationals of that state. Traditionally, the right to political participation is limited to nationals of the nation-state. In the United States, for example, the right to vote is unavailable to legal residents who retain a foreign nationality. Citizenship in the Union makes it unlawful to deny the right to vote on the basis of nationality, provided the nationality is of one of the member states. Thus an Italian who resides in the United Kingdom may vote and run for political office in the United Kingdom.

The right to freedom of movement within the Union and the right to political participation may minimize the extreme expressions of patriotism. The nation-state is not only a territorial entity but a psychological reality that binds the individual to the nation-state. Nation-states have been successful in waging wars against each other primarily because their nationals are willing to sacrifice their lives to preserve the geopsychological borders of their home state. If individuals can freely move across boundaries, establish their residences at places of their choosing, and participate in the political process at their places of residence, the dynamics of geopsychological borders change. Due to cultural and linguistic bonding, individuals will continue to cherish their home states, a natural inclination that must not be regulated. But aggressive patriotism stemming from rigidly-controlled borders, immobility and over-attachment to the political process of a single state is significantly weakened if individuals enjoy freedom of movement and possess the right to political participation where they reside. Individuals begin to develop feelings of affinity for a state where they can freely live, work, participate in the political process and even hold office.

The incorporation of the European Convention on Human Rights into the Community law further strengthens the Union's citizenship. The Community law now assures that the Union's citizens will enjoy the same fundamental rights in any member state in which they reside. Thus the right to freedom of movement within the Union will be even more meaningful. Contrary to the prediction that nationals of low-wage member states would move and establish residence in rich member states, no such *en masse* migration has taken place, This provides a rare insight into human behavior: despite open borders, most people choose to live in their own ethnic, cultural and religious communities.

Ordinarily, nation-states discriminate between nationals and non-nationals, offering fewer rights to foreigners. The Community law informed by the European Convention is likely to reverse such discrimination, forbidding member states from denying fundamental rights to migrants who are not their nationals. This shift from nationality-based rights to human rights is a major step toward the moral development of the Community law. A uniform regime of human rights in the entire territory of the Union may establish social cohesion based on the dignity of the human person rather than simply on the forces of the market. This respect for individual rights will nurture the roots of the Union.

The involvement of citizens in the affairs of the Union is further guaranteed by granting them the right to vote for the Union's political institution, the European Parliament. Previously known as the Assembly, the Parliament was created by the 1957 Treaty of Rome establishing the European Community. It was originally a non-elected body with few powers. The introduction of direct elections which occurred in 1979 transformed the Parliament into a democratic, communitarian institution, though at the time no uniform voting procedures were yet in place. The Union Treaty vests the Parliament with the authority to draw up proposals for elections by direct universal suffrage in accordance with a uniform procedure for all member states.

Taking its population and economic power into account, each member state is allocated a specified number of representatives in the Parliament.[5] Elected for five years, each representative is required to vote on an individual and personal basis. This requirement encourages representatives to think in unified European terms and not to use the Parliament as a vehicle to uncritically advance their national interests. Consequently the Parliament becomes a communitarian rather than an intergovernmental institution. To further promote integration within the Union, the Union Treaty encourages the formation of political parties at the European level. The first election of the Parliament by a direct, universal vote occurred in 1994.

Before its democratization, the Parliament was more or less a decorative institution designed to follow the executive and bureaucratic institutions of the Community, the Council and the Commission. This is no longer true. The Parliament is now vested with substantial powers, which are likely to expand further in the future. It plays a substantial role in the formulation of common positions proposed by the Commission and adopted by the Council. It can veto the entry of new states into the Union. The most notable power of the Parliament is its vote of approval for the Commission as a body. The Commission, the guardian of the Union, is vested with the authority to propose legislation, to assure compliance with Community law by the member states, and to enact secondary legislation to implement details of an approved policy. To provide a check on this awesome power, the Parliament can use a vote of no-confidence to force the Commission to resign as a body. One must note, however, that both the Commission and the Parliament are essentially

5. Currently, for example, the Parliament consists of fifteen member states and has a total of 626 representatives. Germany has 99, France, the United Kingdom and Italy each have 87, Luxembourg has 12. This allocation is likely to change when new states are added to the Union.

communitarian institutions, more devoted to the interests of the Union than those of individual member states.

To safeguard the Parliament, the Union Treaty allows the Parliament to protect its prerogatives through the Court of Justice, the Union's judicial institution. If the Council and the Commission act to restrict the Parliament's constitutional powers, the Court of Justice has jurisdiction to review the legality of such restrictions. Thus the Parliament can legally defend its authority against intergovernmentalism expressed through the Council as well as against the bureaucratic excesses of the Commission. The Parliament is also authorized to bring an action before the Court if either the Council or the Commission fails to act as required by law. Therefore, a vigorous Parliament will have both the popular will and legal authority to compel a reluctant Council or Commission to implement lawfully adopted policies. Presently the Parliament has no general right to challenge acts of the Council and the Commission. But the Parliament, as a democratic institution, is likely to guide both institutional and normative enmeshment since it can both mitigate intergovernmental retrenchment toward national sovereignty and slow an ambitious but unsustainable advance toward total fusion.

The evolution of the Parliament into a democratic and increasingly powerful communitarian institution is likely to transform the nature of the European Union. No longer will the Union be an elitist, market-driven, bureaucratic superstructure imposed upon the uninformed nationals of the member states. Ordinary people usually benefit from the dynamics of a single market, free trade and open borders. Still, they can easily be excluded from the decision-making process based on the assumption that supranational institutions ought to be controlled by well-intentioned politicians, knowledgeable bureaucrats and epistemic circles. Since this democratic deficit cannot be the basis of stable and reliable regional institutions, the European Union has rightfully injected popular will into the equation of markets. The participation of the people in periodic elections of the Parliament is likely to strengthen the Union, especially when candidates running for the Parliament publicly explain, defend and debate the Union's present and future goals. Thus, the people not only have a direct voice in shaping the Union's policies but also control the pace with which communitarian institutions proceed toward an ever-closer union.

The Union's fourth objective is to develop close cooperation on justice and home affairs, matters that traditionally fall under the internal sovereignty of the nation-state. Ordinarily, each nation-state develops its own laws and policies regarding crime, drug addiction, international fraud and terrorism; the state also controls legal and illegal immigration, visa requirements, conditions of alien residence, family reunion and access to employment. A federal nation-state often allocates legislative, judicial and enforcement jurisdiction between local and federal governments, identifying matters to be dealt with at the federal level. For the sake of convenience and efficiency, however, the authority to control immigration, refugees and political asylum is almost always allotted to federal agencies.

Due to the Union's ambiguous status as an entity, no effective formula for the allocation of jurisdiction between member states and communitarian institutions has yet been designed. The lingering notion of state sovereignty impedes the development of communitarian agencies vested with the authority to supervise matters affecting the entire Union. The Union's integration process, however, now requires that some domestic matters must be controlled at the Community level. For example, unless a common visa policy is adopted the Union's internal borders cannot be dissolved to allow the completely free circulation of persons because foreign nationals lawfully admitted by one member state may not be acceptable to others. Similarly, internal border check points cannot be withdrawn unless a communitarian system is established to apprehend criminals, who could otherwise freely move throughout the Union.

Just like the common foreign and security policy, justice and home affairs are currently subject to intergovernmentalism. Although the Commission is to be involved in developing common positions and joint action regarding home affairs, the primary authority to act rests with the Council. Moreover, the Council is required to act unanimously, a rule that vests each member state with a veto to block joint action. Critics of the existing procedures argue for a more vigorous involvement of communitarian institutions in the development of comprehensive and effective home affairs policies. They also wish to replace the unanimous voting procedure with a qualified majority, a proposal that would directly weaken the sovereignty of smaller member states with lower voting power in the Council.

Given current inefficiencies ensuing from intergovernmental cooperation, the Union procedures are likely to be modified. Whether intergovernmentalism lingers or communitarian institutions assume primary responsibility for the Union's internal affairs, the Union must establish effective enforcement agencies, such as the European Police Office, to counter terrorism, unlawful drug trafficking and other serious forms of international crime. It also seems inevitable that the member states will adopt a common immigration and visa policy to streamline immigration, asylum and tourism from the rest of the world. Since these policies directly infringe upon the notion of domestic jurisdiction over internal affairs, a notion deeply imbedded in the classic concept of the nation-state, the tension between intergovernmentalism and communitarianism will continue to exist until the role of national sovereignty in the normative discourse subsides. Meanwhile, the progressive involvement of communitarian institutions such as the Commission and the Parliament in justice and home affairs is likely to weaken intergovernmentalism. If the democratically-elected Parliament emerges as the Union's most powerful institution, it may assert the authority to initiate or demand binding legislation dealing with internal security and other domestic matters that can no longer be left to the discretion of individual member states.

The fields of justice and home affairs create serious questions about the Union's identity for both the Europeans and the rest of the world. The Union's identity can certainly be asserted through the implementation of a common foreign and security policy, a course of action specifically suggested by the Union Treaty. But its identity is just as tied to what the Union does at home as to what it does abroad, simply because one is inseparable from the other.

In this context, the presence of non-European immigrants poses the most serious challenge to the Union's identity. Even though non-European ethnic groups living in the Union come from all parts of the world, many large immigrant populations have arrived from territories that were once under colonial rule. In fact, the pattern of immigration has closely followed past colonization in that each former colonizer still has a substantial immigrant population from former colonies. So the presence of South Asians in the United Kingdom, Indonesians in the Netherlands and Algerians and sub-Saharan Africans in France is no mere coincidence. Former colonialism, however, may not fully explain the presence of all immigrants. Prosperous European economies and a vigorous culture of individual freedom continue to attract the people of poor and oppressive countries. Favorable economic opportunities in Germany, for example, have lured many immigrants from Eastern Europe, including a sizable population of Turks.

Some immigrant groups willingly adopt the language and culture of their new home state and participate in its sociopolitical life. Others wish to preserve their separate identities, distinctive cultures and religions; some cannot fully assimilate because of their immutable characteristics such as color and race. The reaction of the Union's native populations to immigrants is complex and diverse. Some native groups, such as Neo-Nazis, advocate racism and show little tolerance for any immigrants. Some are more culturally-bound and accordingly resent only those immigrant groups that wish to assert their separate cultural identities. National politicians are often equally divided. Some preach coexistence, others propose assimilation. Extremist political groups propose a collective expulsion of even those "immigrants" who are born and raised in European countries.

Among immigrant populations, Muslims pose the most serious challenge to the Union's identity. Even though Muslims residing in member states come from cultures and nations as far apart as Indonesia and Morocco, together they constitute a substantial minority group within the confines of the Union. Though almost always willing to adopt the language of their new home states, most Muslims tend to preserve their separate religious identity. By way of segregation, Muslims set up their own separate communities, build mosques, send their children to Islamic schools and nurture traditional families. Due to their high-profile identity and segregationist tendencies, Muslims more than other immigrant groups are likely to cause tension in relations with native populations. This tension is further aggravated when the presence of Muslims is seen though the colorful prism of history: the Muslim occupation of the Iberian peninsula, the Catholic crusades of the middle ages, the expulsion of Muslims from Spain or their forced conversion to Christianity, the Ottoman empire's conquest of Eastern Europe and the European colonization of most parts of the Islamic world highlight the see-saw struggle between Muslims and Europeans.

Although Europeans and Muslims are at peace with each other and no recent war has pitted them against each other, a cold apprehension nonetheless exists between the two and a peaceful cultural discourse between them has yet to begin. Mutual mistrust confuses the dynamics of dialogue. Terrorist activities by some extremist Muslim groups further complicates the equation. It remains to be seen whether Muslim Turkey will be allowed to join the Union. Thus, how the Union handles the justice and home affairs with respect to immigrants in general and Muslim immigrants in particular will do much to determine the Union's image. If the Union emerges as an exclusively European entity, Islamic and other minorities residing within Europe will face difficulty. If the 15th century Spanish solution of Moorish expulsion is used to eradicate minorities from Europe, the Union may achieve its social cohesiveness but the moral cost would be staggering. If the German solution of Jewish extermination is used to "cleanse" the Union, history will sadly repeat itself without remorse.

The European Convention of human rights is now an integral part of the Union's legal system, specifically mentioned in provisions dealing with justice and home affairs. The Convention specifically prohibits discrimination on the basis of race, color or religion. Moreover, it forbids mass expulsion of immigrants. If the Court of Justice and the European Court of Human Rights successfully safeguard racial and religious minorities, the definition of Europe itself is likely to change. The Union must still protect itself against criminals and terrorists, both domestic and foreign. Yet the imperative of internal security cannot be used as a legal pretext to extinguish justice, malign religions, practice discrimination or give private hate groups free reign to harass ethnic and religious minorities. Nor would it be legally defensible to adopt home policies that reduce minorities to a permanent underclass status or suppress their diverse cultures. The flowering of diverse cultures is an explicit goal of the Union, a goal that, if taken seriously, must protect the Asian and African cultures immigrant populations have brought to Europe. So the Union's identity, however it unfolds, is inextricably tied to its justice and home affairs, including its decision to offer or deny fundamental human rights to all.

In view of its overall objectives, the European Union is a unique social experiment in establishing institutional and normative enmeshment among member states. The tension between national sovereignty and communitarian goals muddles a clear vision of the Union's future. Yet how the Union itself unfolds will be a point of great interest. If the Union evolves into a classic federation, a highly unlikely outcome, such an evolution will add nothing new to the theory of international law. If, however, the member states retain their separate identities in a cooperative but border-free regional enmeshment, the classic structure of the nation-state would mutate into a new identity called Free State. This regional emergence of Free State may then provide insights useful for creating a similar phenomenon at the global level. However, one must examine how the Union preserves a crucial but potentially competing value, the idea of more intimate government at the local level.

2. SUBSIDIARITY PRINCIPLE: BLOSSOMING OF LOCAL COMMUNITIES

The Union Treaty introduces subsidiarity, an awkward and ugly word but nonetheless a useful concept, to impede the excessive and unnecessary centralization of power at the communitarian level.[6] It mandates that the Union's objective of economic harmonization, the institution of a common foreign and security policy, the protection of citizens' rights and interests, and the establishment of judicial cooperation and common home policies be achieved "while respecting the principle of subsidiarity." The subsidiarity principle allows communitarian institutions to take action only if and to the extent that the objectives of the proposed action cannot be sufficiently achieved by the member states. Thus subsidiarity repudiates the mindless desire to shift the decision-making authority from local and national governments to communitarian institutions.

In this regard, two important questions need to be answered. First, what is the purpose of introducing the subsidiarity principle into the Union's legal system? And second, how does the principle work to discourage excessive communitization of power?

To answer the first question one might simply assert that concentration of power is per se dangerous; the history of constitutionalism throughout the world teaches the simple lesson that power ought to be divided and diffused at many different levels of government to avoid dictatorship by the few and, most important, to preempt the self-righteous but serious mistakes of ruling elites disconnected from the people. The European history is particularly instructive: fascination with total power produced totalitarian ideologies such as fascism and communism and caused needless wars of mutual domination and destruction. In view of this history, the architects of the Union introduced the subsidiarity principle to preempt communitarian institutions from ever turning into authoritarian squads.

Another reason for introducing the subsidiarity principle is to preserve the nation-state as a sociopolitical unit. Some member states, such the United Kingdom, argue that the Union should be established without renouncing the concept of the nation-state. They are reluctant to concede too much authority to communitarian institutions. In fact, they demand that some of the authority already vested in the Union be repatriated to the member states. Even the most pro-Union member states, such as Germany, have not yet argued for a total extinction of the nation-state. The field of justice and home affairs has shown little progress toward integration because some member states resist the

---

6. In 1931 Pope Pius XI issued an encyclical articulating the concept of subsidiarity in following words: "Just as it is wrong to withdraw from the individual and commit to a group what private enterprise and industry can accomplish, so too it is an injustice, a grave evil and a disturbance of the right order, for a larger and a higher association to arrogate to itself functions which can be performed efficiently by smaller and lower societies."

idea of Union agencies looking into nooks and crannies of their day-to-day lives. The subsidiarity principle is designed to alleviate the concerns of those who wish to preserve at least some vestiges of the nation-state. It provides a conceptual tool to safeguard against unnecessary, inefficient or harmful accumulation of power at the center. In fact, it sets in motion a dialectical struggle between integration and localism, two powerful competing forces likely to moderate each other in the evolution of the Union. It also paves the way for a slow but stable enmeshment of political wills, social norms and national sentiments.

In addition to protecting national institutions, the subsidiarity principle may also be invoked to preserve subnational strata of authority. The principle mandates that decision-making authority ought to be as close to the people as possible. Only where the exercise of authority at the local level is inefficient or impractical should power be transferred upward. Thus the subsidiarity principle can serve to preserve local governments and subregional communities within the territory of a member state. In fact, the establishment of the Union is likely to sharpen the identities of subregions and subnationalities that previously remained suppressed within the confines of the nation-state. Scotland and Wales have already begun to assert their national identities by making separate though informal representations at the Union institutions. Many other regions are likely to become more protective of their separate identities, a development that can lawfully be accommodated, even encouraged, by the subsidiarity principle. Regions and local governments may become more active, demanding more decision-making authority closer to the people. Already the little-known European Union Committee for the Regions represents more than two hundred regional and local authorities in the member states. This Committee may play a useful role in implementing the concept of subsidiarity at the local level. If local authority is strengthened within the dynamics of communitarian institutions, the nation-state's authority may begin to dissipate in both directions, upward to the Union and downward to regions.

If invoked at the local level, the subsidiarity principle can resurrect local cultures that have previously been suppressed to maintain artificial solidarity of the nation-state. The blossoming of cultures is now an explicit goal of the Union. Though most European nations share the same basic traditions, a luxuriant diversity exists among the peoples of Europe. The fear that localism would cause the demise of the nation-state has been the driving paradigm to promote uniformity and suppress diversity. In Italy, for example, the Venetian culture has its own historical mystique, different from that of Rome or Florence. The subsidiarity principle prevents such rich regional diversity from being suppressed in order to buttress Italy as a nation-state or reinforce the European Union.

Localism when confined to immobile, rigid boundaries may be unhealthy. But when borders are fluid and the people benefit from a shared regional economy, no one should fear the nuances of language, art and music freely varying from region to region or nation to nation. Any forced standardization of human life can lead to existential suffocation, sadism and paranoia, a lesson that the whole humanity should have learned from the failed experiment of communist social engineering. To counter such standardization, the subsidiarity principle is designed to preserve national and local life, without threatening the integrity of communitarian structures that can be defended by the supremacy doctrine.

In many ways, the subsidiarity principle is the antipode of the supremacy doctrine. Whereas the supremacy doctrine preempts national and local laws in favor of the community law, the subsidiarity principle preempts the community law in favor of national and local laws. The supremacy doctrine empowers communitarian institutions; the subsidiarity principle empowers national and local governments. The supremacy doctrine aims to unify power for the purpose of efficiency, uniformity, convenience and cost-effectiveness; the subsidiarity principle aims to diffuse power for the purpose of diversity, self-determination and proximity. Although in tension, subsidiarity and supremacy are not mutually exclusive concepts. They are competing paradigms that allocate authority at different levels of government. They also assure that centralization is achieved without regional alienation.

To further understand the operation of the subsidiarity principle, goal-subsidiarity should be distinguished from means-subsidiarity. Goal-subsidiarity allows national and local governments to set their own goals in those areas of economic, social, political and cultural life in which diversity rather than uniformity is the superior value. Accordingly, communitarian institutions refrain from interfering in the specified areas of national and local life. But even when all member states are obligated to achieve the same communitarian goal, means-subsidiarity allows them the choice of methods. Assuming that the same goal is attainable through different means, an assumption valid in many areas of policy implementation, means-subsidiarity empowers national and local governments to design their own systems to achieve the proposed objective. Means-subsidiarity may indeed be needed to respect the diverse social conditions of member states. If communitarian law specifies both the goal and the means, it invokes the supremacy doctrine in its full sweep, thereby preempting the subsidiarity principle.

Even though the distinction between goals and means is a useful analytical tool, goals are sometimes inseverable from means, since control over means may alter outcomes, and goals themselves may restrict the choice of means. A Community directive, for example, allows each member state to refuse entry to some citizens of the Union, who would otherwise be eligible, on the basis of its public policy. Theoretically, the directive allows each member state the discretion to define its own public policy for the purpose of excluding non-nationals from its territory. Yet in practice the authority to define public policy may conflict with recognized communitarian goals. If no restrictions are placed on the definition of public policy, a member state might exclude citizens of the Union in order to protect its own job market, a facially legitimate public policy that nonetheless directly conflicts with the Union's objective of economic integration. If the state is bound to define public policy within the constraints of communitarian goals, it is left with little or no meaningful discretion.[7] Thus goal-subsidiarity is indeed a more powerful version of the overall principle since it allows member states to both set goals and choose the means to achieve them.

Goal-subsidiarity is implemented by allocating powers or competences at different levels of government. Some enumerated powers are specifically allocated to central institutions. Given the fluidity and complexity of life, however, policymaking authority cannot precisely be divided into mutually exclusive spheres. Many policymaking spheres occupy concentric circles in which all levels of government may have concurrent interests. The subsidiarity principle is most useful in dealing with such concentric spheres of authority because it offers a strong working presumption that the decision-making authority ought to be exercised at the lowest level of government. Policymaking authority may not be arrogated to the center just to strengthen the Union since the Union's strength does not simply depend upon the centralization of power. Indeed any centralization without a corresponding democratic consent at the popular level will weaken rather than strengthen the Union and its institutions. Thus the subsidiarity principle provides a rudder to steer the Union.

Goal-subsidiarity is a useful concept to repatriate power from the center to national and local governments. Just because the center has previously exercised authority in a concurrent area is not *ipso facto* a good reason for it to continue to do so. If circumstances change or results prove unsatisfactory, or national or local governments experience alienation, communitarian institutions are under a legal obligation, arising from the subsidiarity principle, to reconsider the exercise of their relevant powers. If power is expatriated to national or local governments, such a devolution poses no threat to the Union or its institutional supremacy. Stability and even the very survival of the Union would be jeopardized if communitarian institutions suppressed the forces of localism. Democratization of the decision-making process at grass roots is, after all, the ultimate aim of the subsidiarity principle. In fact, once the Union has successfully cultivated its socio-psychological roots among citizens, repatriation of some authority to local governments may indeed further secure its power.

Means-subsidiarity furnishes additional freedom to national and subnational entities. The Union's jurisprudence has already devised two important tools to assure effective means-subsidiarity, one in the area of legislation and the other in adjudication. Communitarian legislation can be made in several different ways, including the promulgation of regulations and directives. Regulations bind the member states to enforce the communitarian law as it is and in its entirety, leaving little room for variation. In contrast, a directive is binding as to the result to be achieved but leaves the choice of form and methods to national authorities. Thus, whereas regulations serve to standardize both outcomes and means, directives focus only on outcomes. Although

---

7. The Court of Justice, for example, held that Belgium could not lawfully invoke public policy to exclude two non-national prostitutes who sought to practice their arts.

regulations are sometimes necessary to harmonize the critical areas of cooperation, directives are more compatible with the subsidiarity principle.

The jurisprudence of directives presupposes that some outcomes are best achieved when national governments possess the flexibility of means to enforce them. In 1989, the Television Without Frontiers Directive was introduced to encourage a single audiovisual and broadcasting market. The Directive is based on the controversial assumption that stable and legitimate political structures ought to be congruent with cultural communities. It sets a normative goal of achieving a single cultural identity and a logistical aim of time allocation. The normative goal promotes a unified European culture by encouraging the free circulation of audiovisual programs made in the member states. The logistical goal requires that member states ensure where practicable that a majority of transmission time is allocated to European works. The means to enforce these goals are left to the discretion of member states. Each member state may thus allocate different parts of the day and different days of the week to non-European programs. Each member state is also free to individually select foreign programs, mostly American productions, for broadcasting.

Although the Directive respects the principle of means-subsidiarity, the institution of a single audiovisual market excluding non-European programs is arguably not a legitimate goal the Union may impose upon member nations and subnational regions. Critics of the Directive are not content with mere means-subsidiarity that it offers; they call for goal-subsidiarity, pointing out that such central regulation of the audiovisual market is unnecessary, even irrational. In view of linguistic diversity within the Union, the discourse of a single culture is frightening, invoking the agonizing specter of the Third Reich. Moreover, peoples whose languages are not widely spoken in the Union, including Asian and African minorities, have little leeway to preserve their language-bound cultures in a unified audiovisual market. Whether the Directive will be modified to return more decision-making authority to national or subnational regions remains to be seen. This example, however, underscores the significance of subsidiarity, a principle most useful to weigh and allocate authority at different levels of policymaking. More important, the principle may be invoked to repatriate authority closer to the people when such authority exercised at a higher level, national or communitarian, produces unacceptable results.

Although the subsidiarity principle is addressed to the political and legislative institutions of the Union, it is equally meaningful in judicial administration. The Court of Justice, located in Luxembourg, and the Court of First Instance attached to the Court of Justice are the Union's judicial institutions. These courts enforce the Union's constitutional and communitarian law derived from founding treaties, communitarian legislation and the common principles and traditions of the member states. Allocation of judicial authority at the center is inevitable for resolving interstate disputes and creating a normative framework within which life throughout the Union can be made more predictable and subject to the rule of law. However, if judicial institutions are removed from the people they may assume a discomforting aura of remoteness, particularly in a highly diverse and multilingual society like the Union. To bring communitarian law and its judicial administration closer to the people, the Court of Justice has developed important legal doctrines that may collectively be called "subsidiarity jurisprudence."

Presently, citizens of the Union have no individual standing to bring suit directly in the Court of Justice. The doctrine of direct effects, however, allows individuals to invoke any communitarian law bearing directly upon the case in their national courts. The Court of Justice has held that treaties establishing the communitarian regime cannot be confined to mutual obligations between the contracting parties. They also impose obligations on individuals and confer legal rights on them as well. To assert such rights, however, individuals need not go to faraway courts; they may go directly to their own national courts. Moreover, private action derived from communitarian law is available both against states as well as other individuals. Article 189 of the Treaty establishing the European Community states that only regulations are directly applicable in all member states. The Court of Justice, however, has expanded the scope of communitarian law directly applicable in domestic cases. Accordingly, litigants may lawfully invoke the jurisdiction of national courts, based on the doctrine of direct effects, to prosecute causes of action flowing from almost any communitarian law, including founding treaties and secondary legislation such as regulations, directives and decisions. Courts and individuals may even invoke international agreements to which the European Community is a party. These doctrines expedite the flow of communitarian law into the national legal systems of member states.

If any communitarian law is directly effective to the case at hand, national courts are obligated under the supremacy doctrine to apply it, notwithstanding any contrary domestic legislation. However, whether a communitarian law is directly effective may be judged differently in different national courts. Such variation of interpretation may cause uncertainty in the law. To avoid varying national interpretations, the communitarian law provides a judicial mechanism, called a preliminary ruling, which allows a national court to refer to the Court of Justice any matter involving the interpretation of the treaty establishing the European Community, a treaty that generates a good deal of communitarian law. These preliminary hearings facilitate a more uniform application of communitarian law. However, varying national interpretations may also be beneficial since they provide transjudicial communications among diverse national courts within the Union, particularly when these courts criticize or rely on each other's legal analysis in articulating the norms of communitarian law. Such transjudicial communication enriches the discourse of communitarian law.

This availability of private action in national courts distinguishes communitarian law from international law even though the treaties establishing the fundamental law of the Union possess all the traditional characteristics of international law. Many nation-states, including the members of the Union, place internal jurisprudential barriers against invoking international law in private cases. These barriers originate from the classic assumption that international law deals with interstate claims that do not directly involve individuals. One such barrier is the distinction between self-executing and non self-executing treaties, which curtails the discretion of national courts to provide relief on the basis of treaties. Only self-executing treaties may directly be relied upon in national courts. Non self-executing treaties with no implementing legislation are rarely invoked as the basis for remedy, even if they are most relevant to the resolution of a case. A human rights convention that directly confers individual rights, for example, may not be invoked in national courts unless an implementing legislation accompanies it. Thus international law must first be nationalized before it can become part of a national legal order. Otherwise it stands apart from the national legal system and at best remains a basis for interstate rights and obligations.

Removing such doctrinal impediments with respect to communitarian law, the European Court of Justice has laid the foundation of a monistic legal order under which communitarian law is interwoven with national legal systems. International law remains a separate legal system. But communitarian law becomes an integral part of national legal systems of member states. National courts face fewer legal impediments when relying upon communitarian law to help decide cases before them. This institutional enmeshment strengthens the bond between national courts and the Union. Likewise, when individuals can directly benefit from the communitarian legal system and may on its basis seek remedies in their own local courts, they begin to develop a greater familiarity with what would otherwise be a remote legal system confined to the upper echelons and high-powered bureaucrats.

Most important, this diffusion of communitarian norms into national legal systems is consistent with the principle of subsidiarity. Excessive centralization of legislative, executive or judicial authority will inevitably move the Union toward a single entity, potentially producing strong central institutions. But a strong European Union achieved at the cost of demolishing more intimate governments at national and local levels would be inherently unstable, contributing little to international legal theory. At best, Europe would become a large, unified superstate. Thus the Union must strive to become neither a federation nor an overly centralized entity. Toward this end, the principle of subsidiarity will continue to remind policymakers that open borders should not be equated with centralization. Nor does socioeconomic integration at the regional level require cultural uniformity. Often, though not always, the best and the most effective allocation of authority is at levels closest to the people.

3. LESSONS FROM THE EUROPEAN UNION

Regional economic communities in other parts of the world can learn important lessons from the example and experience of the European Union. The most obvious lesson involves the economic success of the enterprise. The dynamics of the global economy dictate the merging of national economies into regional coalitions, because no national economy can be self-sufficient, nor can it thrive on its own, nor can it by itself effectively compete in the global market. Driven by these assumptions, the European nations have joined their economic assets, establishing an interlocked regional economy in order to raise their respective standards of living, acquire competitive advantages for their products in the world market and create more jobs in the region. These assumptions and goals are interwoven through the medium of law. Thus the European Union demonstrates that economic cooperation, if done for mutual benefit and under the rule of law, can lead to regional prosperity.

The institution of a single regional market, however, is not an event; it is a process that unfolds gradually, sometimes painfully, requiring a fundamental disavowal of nationalistic thinking. The joining of France and Germany, two countries with a long history of conflict, shows that a shared economic destiny can help minimize mutual suspicion and hostility. Alsace and Lorraine, a region over which France and Germany have shed much blood, now houses the European Parliament and the European Court of Human Rights, marking a fundamental shift in the sociology of the area and the aspirations of former enemies. Other regional communities such as the South Asian Association of Regional Cooperation, can learn from this example, by turning Kashmir, a source of constant friction between India and Pakistan, into an area of economic cooperation and implementation of human rights. Likewise, a new Palestinian state could house regional institutions of peace, economic coordination and human rights. Though the process of building peace in the Middle East seems difficult, the first steps appear to have been taken.

The dire predictions of the critics of the European Union have for the most part failed to materialize. The Union dispels the popular fear that dismantling economic borders invites massive population shifts from low-wage states to prosperous states. There is no evidence that Portuguese and Greeks have occupied Paris, London or Bonn. Other popular fears have also proven groundless. Dismantling of economic borders brings inevitable changes: some domestic producers lose in competition, and some businesses move capital and production facilities to low-wage areas. But these changes are not catastrophic. They are part of the essential dynamics of a single regional market. Thus what some people fear and what some politicians oppose must happen if economic forces are to be joined. For if no movement of capital, labor, goods and services occurs, no regional market will come into existence. In opposing the North American Free Trade Agreement, many in the United States painted a bleak picture of businesses from the North stampeding toward the South, leaving behind in the North a lower standard of living. Many in the United States bitterly oppose opening the borders to allow for free movement of labor. They fear that people from the South will rush into the United States. This fear is not totally unfounded. Unless the general standard of living improves in Mexico, free borders in North America would remain a distant dream. But unless the member states move toward relaxing their national borders, a vigorous North American market cannot be established.

The people in the European Union seem to have overcome many of the fears associated with open borders. But the rhetoric of national sovereignty or statism is nonetheless alive and well. This shows that the process of dismantling statism is neither easy nor rapid. But a vigorous dialogue about the merits and demerits of national sovereignty plays a critical role in reorienting the people toward regional or global solidarity. The geopsychological borders of the nation-state are so deeply ingrained in the minds of many citizens that they regard these borders as immutable realities. But when the usefulness of borders is challenged in a rational discourse, the people's sentimental attachment to the nation-state and its symbols, such as a flag or national anthem, assumes a more deliberate character. Just like unexamined racism, unexamined statism is hard to overcome. But its severity can be reduced by intelligent and honest exposure and dialogue. In a rational discourse, the proponents of national sovereignty tend to expose the artificiality of borders. Often unable to make rational arguments to defend sovereignty, they rouse patriotic coarse sentiments among people that more informed citizens refuse to take seriously. The history of the European Union highlights the failure of those who advocate statism and xenophobia.

When national borders are relaxed, any subsequent discourse on national sovereignty brings about an important linguistic transformation: The word "sovereignty" acquires a new meaning. It is no longer associated with complete independence, legal autonomy or national isolation. Rather, it simply expresses the sentiments of national identity. Derived from a common culture and shared historical memories, national identity supplies a sense of bonding; it is a human need that no economic market can fulfil. Moreover, no people will surrender their national identities for mere free flow of goods, services, capital, labor and tourists across their national borders. Most people understand that economic prosperity is not an inherent enemy of national identity. They also know that while poverty and oppression may diminish national pride, free markets and open borders may in fact reinforce national identities. Within the open borders of the Union, for example, the Italians and Greeks continue to cherish their unique linguistic, historical and cultural identities. Their national sovereignty in its cultural and linguistic sense is in no danger of dissolution regardless whether or not the Union establishes a common currency. So the fear of open borders is irrational to the extent that walls need not be built around a nation to protect its cultural identity.

Another important lesson the European Union teaches is the inevitable inclusion of a social dimension into the dynamics of an integrated economy. The fusion of national economies must serve the interests of producers so that they can compete more effectively. But a regional economy cannot be limited to the free circulation of commodities, nor can it be allowed to damage the environment or exploit the workers. The Social Charter introduced into the Union's legal system assures the protection of labor, as it places important constraints on otherwise exploitative forces of the market. Thus, in addition to serving the interests of regional manufacturers, investment bankers and traders, the benefits of an integrated economy must reach the ordinary people of the entire region. No single nation in the region ought to benefit at the expense of others.

To further humanize the single market, the regime of human rights, which previously stood apart from the common economic market, has been incorporated into the communitarian legal system. Market mechanisms will bring durable prosperity only if important fundamental rights are not sacrificed in the process. An organic approach toward regional development refuses to cut social life into separate economic, civil and political spheres. It joins them together so that no one sector is developed at the expense of another. A totalitarian regime that promises prosperity at the expense of civil and political rights is as unacceptable as a single economic market that promises unlimited consumerism at the expense of cultural and spiritual liberty. A market, for example, that flourishes by discriminating on the basis of race, religion or gender is inherently unstable even if it provides for everyone. Human needs are complex, and a meaningful life demands more than economic prosperity. This simple principle mandates that social life be so constructed that economic development is achieved without trading off basic human dignity. Accordingly, the law of human rights must be fused with the law of economics.

If the establishment of the European Union is a useful example for other regional economic communities, such as the North American Free Trade Agreement, the integration of a social dimension into the dynamics of regional markets must be carefully planned. The North American regime seems to have begun well. Still, there are obvious pitfalls. Due to its size and economic power, the United States possesses a dominating position in the hemisphere, a factor likely to breed suspicions of hegemony among other member states. And in the United States the political rhetoric of national interests has been elevated to a defining moral principle in the United States, a paradigm that policymakers and even legal scholars often invoke when analyzing the complex domain of regional integration – a rhetoric that confuses and scares other member states. The North American regime would fail to develop a powerful regional market if any member state attempts to impose its will on others. Nor would a single market thrive if it discriminates on the basis of race, gender or national origin or if it fails to raise the standard of living of ordinary people, including disadvantaged groups in the United States. Although the North American regime is in the early stages of economic integration, the social dimension dealing with labor and the environment has already been incorporated into the founding treaties. As the regional market expands in both scope and membership, a more explicit commitment to protecting diverse cultures, languages and peoples of the region may have to be made in order to lay a durable foundation for economic and social cooperation.

The American Convention on Human Rights, which protects civil and political rights, stands apart from the regional economic markets. And the United States is not yet a party to the Convention. The Convention's incorporation into the regional economic system must be an explicit goal, particularly when the membership in the North American Free Trade Agreement is expanded. Such an integrated approach may reduce the negative social impact of regional economic development unaccompanied by concern for fundamental civil and political rights. Without a commitment to the principles of non-discrimination and civil and political liberty, the North American market is likely to establish a predacious system that may thrive for a while but in the long run will benefit few and thus may sow the seeds of disintegration, even rebellion.

Yet another important lesson that other regional communities can learn from the European Union is wrapped in the subsidiarity principle, which mandates that as a rule the decision-making authority be exercised at the lowest level of sociopolitical organization unless such a course of action would demonstrably be imprudent or ineffective. Subsidiarity is a principle of self-determination that protects popular will at each level of society. It is designed to discourage concentration of power at any one level of policymaking. Compatible with open borders and human rights, the principle protects regional and subregional cultures, languages and ways of living. It allows supranational and global institutions to participate in the evolution of a grand human civilization that ties together all communities and nationalities into regional and global networks. But the subsidiarity principle permits no supranational institution to accumulate decision-making authority at the expense of suffocating life at national and subnational levels.

The most important lesson that the European Union teaches belongs to the realm of international legal theory. Regional states should not seek to establish a new superstate or a grand federation. They should form a union of diverse nations, in which each national and subnational unit is internally democratic, externally connected with other units in a free association. Despite institutional and normative enmeshment at the national and regional levels, each national or subnational unit remains free and autonomous. Such a unit, called Free State, shares few characteristics with the nation-state. The borders of a national or subnational unit are open to the free flow of goods, services, capital, labor and persons. The national or subnational unit celebrates its local identity, language, culture, traditions and religion. But its relationship with other units in the region is informed by the shared goals of economic prosperity, human rights and the building of a gracious world. When such unit opens its borders to the rest of the world, it becomes Free State. Each member state within the European Union is evolving into Free State. As Free State evolves at regional and global levels, the legal construct of the nation-state, which Grotius developed with keen intelligence, faces gradual but unavoidable extinction.

Part III:

The Emergence of Free-State

Chapter Seven

The Concept of Free State

The concept of Free State offers a new mode of sociopolitical organization. It replaces the nation-state that, due to its structural and normative defects, would be unable to effectively function in the changing global milieu. Just as the widespread reptile extinctions coincided with the rise of mammals, so the universal degeneration of nation-states would provide an environment for Free States to flourish. Analogous to any dying species, the nation-state may seek to extend its life and refuse to relinquish its prime attributes. Nonetheless the forces of evolution are resolved to bring about the extinction of nation-states.

Free State is no ideological entity waiting to be established by an army of revolutionaries. Rather, it is an evolutionary human construct that comes into existence through a gradual process. As a butterfly emerges from a cocoon, so Free State would arise from the shattered shell of the nation-state. But Free State survives and matures only when regional or global conditions are gracious and hospitable. So as legal and moral conditions change in the world, the nation-state would be forced to relinquish its traditional sovereignty and closed borders. And as the nation-state adapts to new global realities, it begins to mutate into Free State. This process of mutation is not linear, assured or free of setbacks.

Free State is an evolutionary entity in yet another way. Even though Free State is still in the process of becoming, it would inherit some features of the nation-state. Just like the nation-state, Free State is a human construct, a sociopolitical unit in which people organize their social, economic, cultural and religious life. Thus, Free State preserves cultural, religious or linguistic identities that people need to enjoy meaningful lives. In fact, Free State is more responsive to the practical and normative needs of communities in which diverse cultures blossom. Moreover, Free State retains at least three elements essential for the formation of the nation-state: distinct territory, population and government. Yet the role of Free State in communal and global contexts is markedly different. Free State does not enclose itself into a geopsychological box. Nor is every Free State required to demonstrate independent competence to conduct foreign policy. Amidst normative and institutional enmeshment Free State acts as an interdependent entity, often joining with other Free States to participate in regional and global networks.

Free State is no utopia beyond the realm of reality. It is an entity that must emerge from the norms of contemporary international law. If the principles of economic cooperation, environmental concerns, peaceful methods of dispute resolution and fundamental human rights are taken seriously and if nation-states protect and advance the stated purposes of the United Nations Charter and other eminent international agreements, which they are obligated to do, the nation-state will have little choice but to develop into Free State. One must not underestimate serious impediments in implementing the stated goals of contemporary international law. It is quite possible that the ideal Free State would never come into existence. Nonetheless, the evidence of normative and institutional enmeshment in global economic markets and universal human rights, as well as the example of the European Union, point toward the emergence of Free State.

It is unclear where in the world Free State will first appear. Nor is it clear whether the appearance of Free State would follow a single, uniform pattern throughout the world. Since Free State is a mutational entity, its emergence is likely to vary from region to region, even nation to nation. Some nation-states might influence the pace of their evolution, yet the changing conditions of global life would permit no nation-state to defy its eventual transformation to Free State. One need not assume that weaker nation-states would mutate first or that stronger nation-states would be better able to resist conversion. The process of mutation is determined by a complex set of forces over which no single nation-state has full control.

If the European Union remains intact, Free State may first emerge in its regional setting. The member states within the fold of the European Union have already mutated into the first stages of Free State, as they have begun to relinquish many traditional attributes of the nation-state. The Union, for example, requires the free flow of goods, services, capital, labor and persons among member states. Moreover, the member states have embraced interdependence and cooperation in various aspects of sociopolitical organization. They have instituted a common regime of human rights. Moreover, they are committed to peaceful settlement of disputes within the Union. All these developments are consistent with the character of Free State. If the European Union continues to develop in accordance with its normative plan the member states may further evolve into Free States. The example of the European Union has inspired many nation-states in other parts of the world to relinquish their traditional attributes and join in regional frameworks.

One important feature of Free State may be noted at the outset. Free State comes into existence when the nation-state completely relaxes its borders to allow the free circulation of goods, services, capital, labor and persons. When borders are opened at the regional level, such as in the European Union, regional Free States are born. When all nations of the world open their borders to each other, global Free States are born. Although a completely free and open world of Free States is a distant dream, regional Free States may soon appear in some parts of the world. At both regional and global levels, Free State will share the same three elements: territory, people and government. The fourth element, foreign policy competence, is optional. The relationship between these four elements in Free State, however, is much different than it is in the nation-state.

1. Elements of Free State

Just like the nation-state, Free State is a defined portion of the earth inhabited by the people. It may contain within its territory uninhabited or unhabitable lands, such as forests, lakes, canyons and mountains. No uninhabited portion of earth, however, can by itself stand as Free State. Even though Free States will most probably be situated on the earth, no theoretical reason precludes their establishment on other planets. Moreover, one need not restrict the definition of territory to any one type of surface, such as ground or water. Such restrictions are unnecessary. The concept of Free State articulated here relates primarily to human populations inhabiting the surface of the earth.

The significance of Free State's territory is different from that of the nation-state. The major distinction lies in the concept of borders. The nation-state's borders are sovereign, whereas Free State's borders are administrative. Sovereign borders may lawfully be closed to foreign elements, such as goods, services, labor, capital and persons. The nation-state has exclusive authority to regulate its sovereign borders, establishing rules and conditions under which foreign elements may or may not enter its territory. In view of economic or other benefits, the nation-state may, on its own or through reciprocal agreements with other states, relax restrictions on the inflow of foreign elements. Theoretically, however, the nation-state is under no obligation to open its sovereign borders to foreign objects or persons. Moreover, sovereign borders may also be closed against the state's own nationals who wish to leave the state either temporarily or permanently. Since classical international law recognized no right to freedom of movement, individuals could not lawfully compel their government to let them leave the state.

In contrast, administrative borders are essentially open for both inflow and outflow of goods, services, capital, labor and persons. They primarily define the territory of a Free State for purposes of legislative, administrative and judicial jurisdictions. One way to understand the legal meaning of administrative borders is to consider the borders of a province or a political subdivision in a federated nation-state. For example, Kansas, a constituent state in the United States, has administrative borders. Inside the federation, Kansas is a free state; its borders are almost completely open for objects and persons arriving from other constituent states as well as for those leaving the state. Despite open borders, Kansas is comprised of a well-defined territory that provides a useful legal basis for determining the scope of Kansas's authority over persons who reside within its territorial jurisdiction and over events that occur there. If the administrative borders of Kansas are open to the entire world, Kansas will become a global Free State.

Similarly, in the European Union the member states have converted their sovereign borders into administrative borders. When the objectives of the Union are fully achieved, the member states would probably become regional Free States. They still cannot claim to be global Free States unless the outer borders of the Union are opened to the rest of the world. A World Community of Free States would emerge when all nation-states convert their sovereign borders into administrative borders. Given the present trend toward regional consolidation, however, nation-states seem more willing to transform themselves into regional Free States. It is conceivable, though unlikely in the near future, that a world without sovereign borders would come into existence. At that time, the peoples of the world will embrace a new concept of freedom, leaving behind the era of nation-states.

The mutation of sovereign borders into administrative borders is a pragmatic adjustment to the new realties of global life. In some cases, sovereign borders bring no benefits but may inflict harm. No national economy, for example, is self-sufficient; therefore, almost every nation-state is forced to open its borders and allow some exchange of goods and services with other states. Nation-states have also learned from past experiences, including the early twentieth century global depression, that no one benefits when the sovereignty of borders is universally invoked to protect domestic industry and discourage the inflow of foreign products.

In some cases, sovereign borders cannot be maintained. The radiation from a nuclear accident, such as the one in Chernobyl, crosses the sovereign borders of many nation-states, driving home a simple point: some effects of global life can no longer be confined to the boundaries of any single nation-state. In some cases, however, nation-states are still able to maintain sovereign borders. Even when they allow free trade, most nation-states continue to resist free circulation of persons across state borders, often on the assumption that open borders would lure nationals of low-wage states. Although the assumption is not baseless, the fear it generates is somewhat exaggerated. In the light of the experience of European Union, states with more or less equal standards of living have little reason to maintain sovereign borders with respect to each other.

It appears that the gradual conversion of sovereign borders into administrative borders will begin with a free flow of goods, as it did in the European Union. Once a common market comes into existence, it facilitates further loosening of sovereign borders. Regional economic markets may thus provide the initial impetus for the conversion from sovereign into administrative borders. The more vigorous a regional market is, the more open its internal borders are likely to become. However, one need not overemphasize regional economic markets as an inevitable dialectical step in the process of achieving a world without sovereign borders. Seeing the benefits of Free State, nation-states may unilaterally choose to adopt administrative borders. Even a dramatic world-wide repudiation of sovereign borders cannot be ruled out. Due to the fear of international crime and lack of mutual familiarity among cultures and peoples of the world, however, a regional approach toward creating Free States seems more pragmatic and achievable.

Corresponding to the nation-state, Free State comes in no one size. As nation-states mutate into Free States, they may retain their existing territorial size. However, Free State is a more unified territorial unit. Therefore, Free State may or may not fully conform to the size of an existing nation-state. If a nation-state is too large, as Canada is, it may evolve into two or more Free States, simply because small territorial units establish a closer relationship between people and government. If a territorial unit is too small, maintaining a separate government may be too expensive. In such cases, territorial units may combine to constitute a more viable Free State. The process of territorial consolidation may continue to exist even after Free States have fully evolved. A large Free State may repatriate authority to its provinces for the establishment of separate Free States. Small Free States may reunite to establish one government.

A naturally coherent territorial unit, such as an island, is a flawless basis for establishing a single Free State. Likewise a historically constituted territorial unit, such as Chechnya, which contains a distinct ethnic, linguistic or religious group, may be an equally valid basis for establishing Free State. This is not to say, however, that the territory of Free State must be naturally defined or ethnically pure. Free State may contain multiple ethnic groups, and its territory may be a totally artificial subdivision of a continent in geological and geographical terms. Since Free State is a human creation, its territory, however defined, is a human construct too. And so even an island, such as Ireland, can accommodate more than one Free State.

Many nation-states, such as India, are composed of several historically distinct territorial units. Many such units would probably prefer not only to stay together but also collectively evolve into a single Free State. In the European Union, for example, the United Kingdom may retain its present size and constituent units. On the other hand, it is equally possible that some historically distinct units, such as Scotland, may wish to evolve into separate Free States. The rather peaceful breakup of the Soviet Union into fifteen independent republics was consistent with the evolution of Free States. If the Soviet Union had used force to maintain its imperialistic unity of these republics, the evolution of this region toward Free States would have been greatly impeded.

Consistent with the norms of contemporary international law, no Free State may acquire territory by war, threat or use of force, fraud and, more important, without the consent of the people inhabiting the territory. Colonial empires acquired substantial portions of the earth by cession, bargain, occupation and war, almost always without the consent of the people. Even nation-states have occupied territories without the consent of local populations. Free State refrains from any forcible territorial transaction. In this respect, even the traditional distinction between just and unjust war has no bearing. A just war with the explicit approval of the international community may be conducted to remove a threat to regional or global peace, as the Gulf War dislodged the Iraqi occupation of Kuwait. But not even a just war can be a lawful basis of territorial transfer from one state to another. Therefore the people, such as the Palestinians, whose territories Israel has occupied, in what it calls a war of self-defense, have the right to re-acquire their territories and establish Free State.

Under the evolving standards of self-determination, even peaceful territorial transfers made without the consent of inhabitants are illegal. No territorial claim derived from any source can override the principle of self-determination. Accordingly, any territorial dispute between two or more Free States must be resolved in accordance with the will of local inhabitants. Many territorial disputes between nation-states arise from conflicting legal claims. Kashmir is a disputed territory between India and Pakistan; the Kurile Islands seized by the Soviet Union at the end of the Second World War remain in dispute between Russia and Japan; the islands of Abu Musa and Tnub located near the Strait of Hormuz in the Persian Gulf are claimed by both Iran and the United Arab Emirates. According to the law of Free States, these disputes ought to be resolved in accordance with the free will of the people inhabiting these territories. If territory is the mainstay of the nation-state, people are the defining element of Free State. This critical distinction informs the enterprise of Free States.

People are the second and most important structural element of Free State. Just like the nation-state, no Free State comes into existence without a permanent population. In contrast to the nation-state, however, Free State attaches a different meaning to the notion of permanent population. But first it is important to understand that the notion of permanent population has several different meanings. For example, permanent population may refer to a state's present inhabitants who are born and raised there. This meaning distinguishes native-born inhabitants from foreign-born immigrants. Permanent population may also refer to a specific ethnic population that has lived and bred in a defined territory for several generations. This definition sees the population in an intergenerational context and distinguishes one ethnic group from the other. In yet another sense, the notion of permanent population may be used to distinguish stationary populations from gypsies, nomads and bedouins. This distinction is important because under the norms of international law, gypsies, nomadic peoples cannot institute a state since they do not qualify as a permanent population.

Sometimes the notion of permanent population is used interchangeably with the notion of a people. In contemporary sense, "a people" is analogous to an ethnic group. In classical literature, including the works of Grotius, people are defined in terms of a natural body made up of separate members but having a single essential character or a single spirit. Grotius compares a people with a river that carries the same characteristics, century after century, even though the water flowing through the river is not the same. This comparison is helpful in understanding how a population in the intergenerational process of transmitting language, culture and historical memories may acquire distinct identity as a people. "A people," therefore, is a historical metaphor, a figure of speech, to distinguish one ethnic or national group from another, such as the Serbs from the Croats.

Free State refuses to embrace the Grotian notion of a people as its definition of permanent population. Nor does it embrace the concept of permanent population in any other sense. Therefore, it discards the distinction between nationals and non-nationals, natives and immigrants, citizens and aliens. To accommodate the realities of new global life, including migrations and freedom of movement, Free State defines the requirement of people more broadly. All permanent residents who live in Free State constitute its people. In many cases, most permanent residents will indeed be the people born and raised in the state. This is so because most populations tend to be stationary since they wish to maintain their family ties, jobs and businesses, and develop special affection for the land where their ancestors lived. Since Free State is a dynamic entity with open borders, it cannot confine itself to any static concept of permanent population or a people. Accordingly, all permanent residents, wherever they come from and whoever they are, collectively constitute the people of Free State. In advancing his concept of "open republic," Jost Delbruck proposes that such a state must commit itself to equal citizenship for all people. In an open republic, ethnic, racial, and religious criteria cannot determine who may be a citizen.

Thus the permanent population of Free State may or may not consist of a single people or ethnic group. An ethnic group occupying a distinct territory may of course institute Free State. However, no Free State may lawfully exclude persons in order to maintain its ethnic purity on the basis of race, religion or culture. This constraint provides a direct contrast to discriminatory policies of the nation-state, such as those of Canada in the past, under which only white populations were allowed to immigrate for permanent residence. Any such exclusionary policies are incompatible with the all-inclusive nature of Free State.

To distinguish permanent residents from mere visitors, Free State may provide legal criteria. Persons born and raised in a Free State who have established residence for a length of time face no legal impediment to establish permanent residence. Persons born elsewhere may establish permanent residence by a present and fixed residence in Free State where they intend to remain for an indefinite period and to which they intend to return following any absence. Free State may prescribe a period of months before accepting such domiciliary residence. This is no novel idea. Even nation-states allow foreign nationals to become their citizens after a certain period of permanent residence. Free State, however, imposes far fewer residency requirements. Personal character, criminal record or lack of employment are not valid bases to exclude persons from becoming the permanent residents of a Free State. Needless to say, persons may freely change their permanent residence from one Free State to another.

Ordinarily, most persons are permanent residents of only one Free State. Under certain circumstances, however, a person may simultaneously be a permanent resident of two or more Free States. For example, a person who operates businesses in two Free States and accordingly has established residence in each state may be considered the permanent resident of both states. This dual residency is further reinforced if such a person pays taxes in both Free States.

Just like the nation-state, Free State is a political-legal entity managed by a government in accordance with the rule of law. The administrative borders of Free State permit free circulation of goods, services, capital, labor or persons. That does not mean, however, that a territory without sovereign borders cannot establish a government. A constituent unit within a federation has free borders, and yet free borders do not prevent the unit from instituting a separate government. Similarly, in a regional setting such as in the European

Union, the member states may dismantle their sovereign borders but still have national governments. Just like a political subdivision in a federation or a member state in a regional union, Free State functions in a complex normative and institutional framework. Nonetheless, Free State has its own government. Within the confines of its territory, Free State establishes its own separate legislature, courts and enforcement agencies. The highly developed concept of territorial jurisdiction furnishes a useful basis for defining the scope of Free State's governmental authority. It also provides legal criteria to resolve jurisdictional conflicts involving two or more Free States.

As a political-legal entity, Free State is anchored in a modified version of popular sovereignty, a notion Grotius discussed at length but declined to accept as a binding norm of international legal theory. By rehabilitating popular sovereignty, Free State rejects the Grotian concept of territorial sovereignty. Although territory is an essential element of Free State, people and not the territory are the heart and soul of Free State. Accordingly, no government may invoke its coercive power over the territory as its sole legitimate basis. Forced occupation of a territory, territorial conquest or even a domestic coup d'etat perpetrated against the will of the people cannot constitute a lawful basis to govern a Free State.

Grotius explains many faces of popular sovereignty. Democracy, under which the government is periodically elected by universal and equal suffrage, is the clearest example of popular sovereignty. However, conceptually, as Grotius points out, popular sovereignty may yield many other forms of government. A people may decide to institute aristocracy or kingship. They may without coercion renounce the right to choose a government and settle instead for a hereditary form of government under which the succession rules seek no further approval from the people. If the logic of popular sovereignty is taken to its extreme, a people could willingly embrace subjugation, foreign rule, even slavery. So if the people are sovereign in the Grotian sense, they may have a logical right to embrace oppressive forms of government.

Free State repudiates the Grotian logic and its concomitant oppressive versions of popular sovereignty. The Grotian logic that a people may exercise their free will to renounce popular sovereignty is derived from the notion of "a people" who continue to exist forever as a timeless body. Since Free State is not based on this notion, it views the concept of popular sovereignty in a different light. Free State asserts in a more realistic way that the right to popular sovereignty belongs to the living, not the dead. Therefore each living generation, not the timeless people, has the right to choose a government. When this analytical shift is made, it becomes easier to understand why no generation has a moral or legal right to bind subsequent generations into subjugation, occupation or slavery. Moreover, Free State places an intergenerational obligation on the present generation to reject all political theories that lead to any voluntary renunciation of popular sovereignty for future generations.

To further repudiate the Grotian logic of voluntary oppression, Free State distinguishes even between a living generation and an electorate. Accordingly, it adopts a specific conception of popular sovereignty under which the right to choose a government is granted to the electorate, not any one generation. Thus Free State embraces a version of popular sovereignty under which the government derives its authority from the will of an electorate freely expressed in periodic and genuine elections. In extreme circumstances, such as famine or war, under which free elections cannot be held, the democratic process may be temporarily suspended. But no electorate has any authority to embrace a concept of freedom that renounces the right to popular sovereignty for future electorates.

Even the concept of the electorate is more expansive in Free State. Unlike the nation-state, which confines political rights of voting and office-holding to its citizens, Free State extends these rights to all permanent residents. In a nation-state like the United States, no permanent residents of any foreign nationality can vote or contest political office in local or federal elections. But in the European Union, permanent residents who are nationals of other member states may vote in the state of their permanent residence. They may also run for local political offices at the place of their residence. However, no permanent residents who hold the nationality of non-member states are entitled to such political participation. In a world community of Free States, the right to political participation is extended to all permanent residents in each Free State without discrimination on the basis of national origin. Free State may lawfully require voters and candidates to meet reasonable residency requirements. A total denial of political participation to permanent residents, however, is part of the flawed logic of the nation-state that Free State declines to accept. The example of the European Union demonstrates that the distinction between nationals and non-nationals, at least in a regional setting, serves no useful purpose in denying the right to political participation to permanent residents who obey the laws, pay taxes and aspire to participate in the political process. As the world evolves into Free States, the notion of citizenship used by nation-states may either be discarded or modified to protect permanent residents' right to full political participation.

To bring government closer to the people, Free State views with suspicion any constitutional order that allocates the entire governmental authority to a center remote from the people. Consistent with the norm known as the subsidiarity principle in the European Union, Free State mandates that no decision be made at a higher level than necessary. Accordingly, if a Free State consists of several provinces or political subdivisions, governmental authority is distributed in a manner that vests provincial governments with a substantial degree of autonomy. Even within a large province or political subdivision, governmental authority is further decentralized to the county or city level to encourage vigorous and meaningful political participation. When a government is remote and the policymaking authority is highly centralized, the people may lose interest in the political process. Moreover, a remote government may also lose touch with the people and institute policies without any intimate knowledge of local conditions. To avoid such remote forms of government and ensuing consequences, Free State embraces the subsidiarity principle with the fewest possible reservations.

Despite decentralizing governmental authority at the local level, Free State is no atomistic entity cut off from the rest of the world. Rather, it is an integral part of regional and global networks. Its open borders are interwoven into the seamless unity of the entire region and the world. This raises another question: must Free State possess the capacity to conduct foreign policy?

Unlike the nation-state, no Free State is required to possess foreign policy competence as a prerequisite to claim statehood or enter the regime of international rights and obligations. Free State repudiates the notion of an "independent" foreign policy – an anachronistic concept belonging to a world in which nation-states had fewer contacts with each other and thus were highly independent in their internal and external affairs. Due to contemporary normative and institutional enmeshment, not even a powerful nation-state can pretend to conduct a truly independent foreign policy. Almost all nation-states, large and small, are members of regional and global organizations that limit the state's authority in multiple spheres of international activity. In addition they have contracted hundreds of international agreements, some indefinite in duration, that bind them in complex, inseverable and reciprocal networks of benefits and burdens. Louis Henkin states that a major purpose of foreign policy is to maintain international order that depends on a legal regime "of agreed assumptions, practices, commitments, expectations, reliances." He further points out that in order to obtain "the confidence bred by law, one pays the price of not being free to frustrate the expectations of others." Consequently, the notion of independent foreign policy has little meaning, even in the present era of nation-states.

The question then arises whether Free State must possess the capacity and the means to conduct an interdependent foreign policy. The capacity to conduct an interdependent foreign policy includes the state's legal standing to enter into international agreements. Just like the nation-state, each Free State is entitled to assume international rights and obligations and may become a party to regional and global treaties. To assume these rights and obligations, however, Free State may or may not have its own financial or technical resources. If a Free State lacks the resources to directly conduct its own foreign policy, it may lawfully delegate its authority to another Free State. In another case, several Free States may combine their resources to participate in international conferences. Likewise, to avoid unnecessary duplication or to save resources, Free States may pool their resources to send and receive common envoys, establish joint embassies and share diplomatic staff. They may even legally bind themselves to adopt a common foreign policy. Any delegation, cooperation or legal merger in conducting foreign policy does not diminish or terminate a Free State's statehood. Nor does any such course of action lessen a Free State's rights and obligations in the global legal system.

Just like nation-states, moreover, Free States are free to join international organizations as independent members. But nothing prevents Free States from pooling their resources or merging their legal identities for the purpose of claiming a single membership in an international organization. The European

Union, for example, claims fifteen separate memberships in the United Nations. On the other hand, the United States claims only one. The United States may continue to claim single membership even after evolving into Free State. However, no legal impediment prevents the United States from evolving into fifty separate Free States, with each Free State accordingly claiming separate membership in the United Nations. The fifty Free States of the United States would still be able pursue a common foreign policy. The breakup of the Soviet Union has added fifteen new states to almost all international organizations. Nothing prevents these former republics of the Soviet Union from pursuing a common foreign policy.

If each nation-state has a right to divide itself into several Free States and thus claim several votes in international organizations, such a right could potentially spawn countless Free States. It remains to be seen whether the incentive to have more votes in international organization will in itself be a powerful reason to break up nation-states. Even if this occurs, international organizations might respond by developing a more rational basis to allocate voting power to Free States. Even today, many international economic organizations, such as the International Monetary Fund, reject the principle of "one state, one vote" and instead allocate differing voting power on the basis of each state's economic strength. Similar criteria may be taken into account for allocating voting power to Free States. Even the principle of "one state, one vote" may assume a more realistic basis if Free States become more or less equal in the size of their territory, population or economic strength.

Whichever way the future map of the world unfolds, Free State modifies the fourth element of the nation-state. No longer will the competence to conduct foreign policy be an essential ingredient for the establishment of independent statehood. In fact, the state's competence to conduct foreign policy may become inconsequential if international organizations assume the primary responsibility for harmonizing and facilitating interstate affairs. If the normative and institutional enmeshment of regions and the world continues to deepen, Free States may delegate even more authority to international organizations. Epistemic bodies within these organizations may develop even more expertise for coordinating the efforts and resources of the world. They may be authorized to formulate and implement rational and morally defensible policies in diverse spheres of interstate activity. Such a knowledge-based management of interstate affairs would strengthen the moral objectives of Free State.

2. OBJECTIVES OF FREE STATE

Even though Free State shares important structural similarities with the sovereign state, its moral objectives are markedly different. The sovereign state is bound by international law in its external relations with other states. Yet within its own sovereign borders, it is an empty shell the ruling elite may fill with any values. The Grotian theory imposes no rules on the sovereign state with respect to the form of government or the state's responsibility toward the people. As the sole subject of international law, moreover, the sovereign state severs the individual's direct relationship with the international community. So individual rights and obligations, benefits and burdens, flow from the sovereign state's own internal constitution or laws.

In order to carry out the purposes of contemporary international law laid out in the United Nations Charter and other eminent international agreements, Free State is a moral entity that imposes direct duties on its government to work for the welfare of the people. Accordingly, the government is not only accountable to the people, it must serve them also. The government exists not for its own sake but to organize social life in accordance with the values and aspirations of the community. Moreover, the government is obligated to conduct its internal and external affairs within the constraints of international law. Unlike the sovereign state, Free State erects no barriers between individuals and international law. Instead, it acts as a legal medium to connect its people to the rest of the world. So the peoples of the world, not abstract state entities or ruling elites, become the primary custodians of mutual rights and obligations. The emergence of such a gracious world is inextricably tied to several specific objectives of Free State.

The first objective of Free State is to change the moral foundation of law. Legal positivism presents the state as a coercive entity that dictates legal behavior backed by sanctions. It further assumes that both states and individuals obey laws not for good moral reasons but to avoid assured penalties. Thus the fear of sanctions, a morally bankrupt vehicle for behavior modification, becomes the ultimate basis of law. Free State repudiates such a theory of human behavior. It may use force to prevent and punish criminal behavior; it may even impose pecuniary sanctions in civil matters. Despite the coercive authority at its disposal, Free State does not adopt the traditional model of the *pater familia* who maintains law and order in the household by the threat or use of his wrath.

To counter such paternalism, Free State adopts the principle of *mater familia.* Rejecting the male principle of sociopolitical organization rooted in egotism, superiority, hierarchy and domination, Free State adopts the female principle under which compassion, equality, interdependence and shared authority inform the enterprise of law. Accordingly, law is no longer viewed as a set of rules of behavior given by a superior sovereign who commands the coercive power to enforce them – a view advanced in the works of Thomas Hobbes, John Austin and Hans Kelsen. Instead, Free State is made in the image of a compassionate mother who uses her authority for the well-being of all members of the household. The legal order of Free State is designed to inculcate among citizens a positive consciousness, a higher moral reasoning. Individuals are taught to obey laws not merely to avoid sanctions or maximize self-interest, but out of appreciation for a system that benefits the people without discrimination on the basis of race, color, social status, sex or any other unlawful basis. The fear of sanctions remains in place only for those individuals who, despite concerted effort, are unable to reach a higher level of moral reasoning.

The principle of *mater familia* mandates the involvement of both women and men in the development of Free State. No legal, political, social or economic system can achieve sustainable development if women are systematically excluded from full participation. The involvement of women at all levels of policymaking alters the dynamics of society since women, more than men, foster compassion and inclusion rather than individuation and exclusion. In fact, women may be more suited to guide the creation and maintenance of Free State in which the principle of compassion protects the weak and the vulnerable and the principle of inclusion prohibits discrimination on the basis of race, religion or other unacceptable factors. Free state rejects the egotistical world associated with warfare, enslavement, colonialism and other spectacles of domination. It offers to create a gracious world in which the virtues of compassion and interdependence are recognized, encouraging individuals to exercise empathy and moral intelligence.

Consistent with the principle of *mater familia*, Free State repudiates all paternalistic forms of government such as personal dictatorship, communism, theocracy and military rule, indeed any legal system based on morally dubious assumptions that the people are ignorant, incompetent or untrustable. Personal dictatorship founded on the charisma, wisdom or superior intelligence of any one man is particularly incompatible with Free State, because no one person can know all the complex facets of government. Even if such a mythical figure did exist, Free State would still allow no personal rule. The mythification of personal rule often invites uncritical obedience, chilling rational and reflective social discourse. One party authoritarianism, whether it is communism or theocracy, shares the assumptions and goals of *pater familia* and, therefore, is equally incompatible with Free State. In fact, no system that outlaws criticism of government or a ruling party can be the lawful basis of Free State. Free state is a rational and moral enterprise in which the decision-making authority is vested in no single person, party or god.

Moreover, Free State is particularly incongruent with the concept of divine rule derived from the mythology of Middle Eastern religions. No one person, family or people may lawfully invoke any divine authority to govern a Free State, much less the world. Two modes of divine rule are extolled in the theocratic literature. The first mode is process-oriented, supporting the hereditary source of divine rule under which God chooses a particular person, family or people to rule a community, a nation or the entire world. The chosen elite retains the ruling authority generation after generation through a set of formal or informal succession rules. The second mode is result-oriented, holding that whoever successfully gains the authority to rule is considered to have divine support. Its justification lies in the simple assumption that no one person, family or people can obtain power without God's consent. Whereas the first mode imposes, defends and justifies the entrenchment of power in one specific person, family, tribe or race, the second mode anoints revolutionaries who overthrow existing systems. The two modes may come into direct conflict when a hereditary system believed to be anchored in divine rule is overthrown by revolutionaries claiming God's approval. Much bloodshed and oppression in history are directly attributable to the excesses of divine rule.

Repudiating all forms of paternalistic domination, Free State institutes the concept of shared responsibility in which the ordinary people are directly empowered to elect their rulers. Thomas Franck argues that democracy is on the way to becoming a global entitlement, and rulers will have to seek the validation of their empowerment in the consent of the governed. The peoples' right to democracy "increasingly will be promoted and protected by collective international processes."

Free State's elected rulers, whether women or men, serve the community for a pre-determined tenure of few years at the expiration of which they are obligated to seek renewal of their tenure from the people. Even during their lawful tenure, the rulers remain subject to recall. A democratic system under which the government is periodically elected in free and genuine elections is fully congruent with the principle of *mater familia.* However, the people may choose other forms of government, including constitutional monarchy, if the succession rules for choosing the monarch are periodically subject to the people's approval. A government irremovable through a peaceful legal method is inherently offensive to the nature of Free State.

Consistent with the principle of *mater familia*, Free State transforms the nature of politics. Free State politics may be defined as the means of persuading people to act or not to act in a certain way. This definition is the opposite of one available under the principle of *pater familia*, which characterizes politics as the art of acquiring and maintaining power, a definition that can reduce politics to a mere manipulative and deceptive enterprise. Since Free State government is based on the will of the people, the concept of politics as persuasive discourse becomes even more important. This is so because the candidates contesting for political office must persuade the people to vote for them. Even elected officials cannot stay in power for long if the policies and laws they institute fail to impress the people. Thus, Free State politics is the persuasive means by which the people establish political relationships with political parties and elected officials.

The transformation of politics from mere acquisition of power to candid persuasion brings about a parallel evolutionary change in the nature of political discourse. In a transparent democracy, political discourse is often vigorous, honest and consequential as it empowers the people to review, approve or condemn the behavior of elected officials and of those seeking political office. Consistent with the norms of free speech, Free State places the fewest possible restrictions on political discourse.

Yet as a general principle, Free State replaces rhetorical politics with epistemic discourse. Rhetorical politics is often manipulative and deceptive. It panders to the people's sentiments rooted in the lower levels of moral intelligence. For example, a leader who evokes racial or religious hatred among the people engages in rhetorical politics. Similarly, rhetorical politics may invoke fear, greed or selfishness. In contrast, epistemic discourse is informed by knowledge including scientific, legal and moral reasoning. Most important, it respects moral intelligence and the associated virtues of compassion, generosity and sharing. Epistemic discourse, most suited to the nature of Free State, can be contentious in content and style, but it operates within rational, moral and spiritual constraints. While personal charisma, egotism and demagoguery steer rhetorical politics, virtue, wisdom and moral intelligence inspire epistemic discourse.

Ethnic cleansing, racial bigotry, religious fanaticism, xenophobia, and cultural superiority are examples of rhetorical politics. The International Covenant on Civil and Political Rights captures the meaning of epistemic discourse when it proscribes any propaganda for war and prohibits any advocacy of national, racial or religious hatred that constitutes incitement to discrimination, hostility or violence. Although the Covenant prohibits every person from engaging in any speech of low moral order, its provisions are more relevant to the realm of political discourse. The speech of elected officials and candidates seeking political office often carries more weight than that of ordinary people. Therefore, they are under a special obligation to maintain political discourse at a higher level of moral intelligence. The people of Free State are themselves critical of rhetorical politics. They will not allow their leaders to engage in a political discourse that rakes raw and base sentiments.

To further strengthen its epistemic character, Free State places special responsibility on the media to reject rhetorical reporting. Freedom of the press is a fundamental value of Free State. Nonetheless, the press is not exempt from the epistemic constraints of moral intelligence. The evolution of Free State would itself establish a moral climate in which rhetorical reporting becomes morally and culturally unacceptable. In most cases, therefore, Free State would not be obligated to suppress rhetorical reporting through coercive laws.

The second objective of Free State is to establish a legal, moral and spiritual culture that protects the human dignity of each individual. Free State also accepts the general principle that each individual is entitled to the full development of his or her personality. Accordingly, Free State embraces the law of human rights. These rights satisfy the individual's basic needs. In the words of John Rawls, these rights also shape the background institutions of the community, enabling individuals to freely pursue their talents and life plans. As these rights emerge from the shared wisdom of the peoples of the world, no social theory or utilitarian calculus may be invoked to trump them.

Here one must note an important distinction between civil rights and human rights. Since classical international law obligates no state to implement individual rights and defines such matters as falling within the domestic jurisdiction of the state, civil rights are the creature of the nation-state. Even when codified in its domestic laws, the nation-state controls the scope and content of civil rights. Consequently, civil rights have been denied to specified target groups, such as women, racial or religious minorities. In contrast to civil rights, human rights flow from the inherent dignity of the human person. The nation-state may use its discretion to allocate civil rights to some groups, but not to others. Free State has no such discretion.

Under the impact of the law of human rights, which originated with the United Nations Charter, most nation-states have begun to accept the obligation of protecting these rights. Barbara Stark remarks that nation-states endorsed the radical notion of human rights in horrified response to the atrocities of the Second World War. Still, some nation-states resist even signing the human rights treaties while others are reluctant to embrace the full scope of these rights. Unlike the nation-state, the law of human rights is the integral part of each Free State's domestic legal order. So each person present within the territory of any Free State is entitled to human rights without discrimination on the basis of race, color, sex, religion, birth, caste or any other status.

In contrast to the nation-state, Free State discards from its internal laws and jurisprudence the concept of citizenship as a prerequisite for granting fundamental human rights. Accordingly, all persons present within the territory of Free State are entitled to equal enjoyment of fundamental rights. The distinction between permanent and temporary residents or between residents and tourists cannot be the basis for denying fundamental human rights. Even regional human rights treaties are universal in this regard. The European Convention on Human Rights, for example, extends its protection to all persons present within the territory of any member state.

Unlike the nation-state, moreover, Free State undertakes to promote the social and economic welfare of all residents. This is in direct opposition to the Grotian theory that places no such obligation on any government. Grotius recognizes that many governments in fact strive to improve the condition of their people. They are, however, under no international legal duty to do so. Consistent with the Grotian theory, even classical international law treats the questions of social justice as matters belonging to the domestic jurisdiction of the nation-state. Leaving the welfare of the people to the state's internal domestic order was in part prompted by the notion of nations' cultural and social diversity. Moreover, classical international law lacked the authority to regulate socioeconomic policies within the sovereign borders of the nation-state. Relying on these norms of classical international law, some states still assert that they have no legal obligation to protect individuals' social and economic rights.

The human rights law has transformed the international norm of indifference to national conceptions of social and economic justice. No longer may the state invoke its cultural norms or its conception of social justice as a lawful basis to keep its people hungry, illiterate or shelterless. Any socioeconomic system designed to create or preserve a permanent underclass of malnourished people living in inadequate housing is incongruent with the norms of human rights. Such a system has always been criticized in the realm of morality. Now it is illegal in the realm of contemporary international law. A minimum degree of social and economic protection for each individual is essential to preserve the dignity of the human person.

The preamble to the International Covenant on Economic, Social and Cultural Rights, a human rights treaty signed by an overwhelming majority of nation-states, sets the moral tone in the following words: The ideal of free human beings enjoying freedom from fear and want can only be achieved if conditions are created whereby everyone may enjoy economic, social and cultural rights, as well as civil and political rights. This pronouncement refutes the dichotomy between civil-political rights and social-economic rights, a dichotomy that for decades divided the world into two camps: the capitalist world that promised to protect only civil and political rights and the communist world that pledged to protect only social and economic rights. With the widespread collapse of oppressive communism and with the widespread softening of exploitative capitalism, the two sets of rights have merged in significance. This merger underscores the simple point that few human beings can fully develop their personalities or preserve their dignity unless they enjoy a decent standard of living available in a politically free society.

Paul Brest argues that minimum protections for the necessities of life are preconditions for civic republican citizenship. However, the realization of even minimum social and economic rights, such as adequate food, clothing, housing, physical and mental health, and just and favorable conditions of work, require both resources and commitment. If the state lacks the resources, even a constitutional protection of social and economic rights has no more than paper value. If the state has the resources but lacks the commitment, it may not do much to alleviate the condition of the underclass. The law of human rights obligates governments to undertake a legal commitment to provide social and economic rights to all. In order to marshall resources to materialize these rights, the state must seek ways, including international assistance and cooperation, progressively achieving the full realization of these rights.

Accordingly, Free State undertakes to create a legal order in which civil and political rights are not divorced from social and economic rights. It actively works toward raising the standard of living of all. With the support of the private sector, the government finds ways to solve basic socioeconomic problems such as hunger, inadequate housing, epidemics and unemployment. A free market economy may provide incentives to produce more food, build more houses, furnish good health care, and provide affordable insurance for the sick and the old. Yet Free State cannot leave the realization of social and economic rights to the dynamics of the free market. Barbara Stark points out that the regime of social and economic rights presupposes that the market-based opportunity alone cannot ensure survival, much less a decent standard of living for all. Accordingly, Free State plays an active role in correcting the failure of the free market to provide these rights.

To improve its food supplies and to reform inefficient agrarian systems, for example, Free State provides incentives, information and technical assistance to the private sector. If local expertise is inadequate or underdeveloped, Free State seeks international cooperation to improve the production, conservation and distribution of food. Sufficient food supplies do little good if the means of food conservation are inadequate to plan for a possible drought or if the means of food distribution are unable to alleviate famine in remote areas. Similarly, the government is actively involved in solving problems of inadequate housing, disease and unemployment. No Free State may ever relinquish its obligation to promote the material well-being of the people in a democratic society.

In addition to protecting the basic human rights of all, Free State takes affirmative moral steps to eradicate predacious racism, sexism, fanaticism, caste systems and other forms of social hatred, bigotry and prejudice. In this respect Free State is not morally neutral, nor does it accept the spurious distinction between state and society, dividing public and private action. Most important, Free State rejects the separation of law and morality. Racial or religious intolerance in society, for example, must be morally proscribed if the state is to legally prohibit racial or religious discrimination. If laws punish a behavior that morals fail to teach, a gulf is created between state and society. A legal regime without a corresponding moral regime is based on fear of sanctions rather than moral intelligence. In view of inseparable nexus between state and society, law and morality, Free State disseminates the awareness of human rights at all stages of individuals' moral development, especially childhood.

Consistent with the regime of human rights, Free State places special emphasis on individual and communal education. Individual education is directed to the full development of the human personality and its sense of dignity. It is oriented toward providing necessary skills that individuals need to find meaningful jobs. Communal education promotes understanding, tolerance and friendship among all Free States and all racial, ethnic or religious groups. Predacious theories such as racial or gender superiority are effectively exposed and countered, laying bare the intentions of those who champion them.

It is important not to confuse education with mere literacy. Just like oral and visual media, literacy is a medium that facilitates education. The mere ability to read or write does not assure education, just as the mere ability to see or hear does not assure education. The concept of education, obtained through any medium, must be closely tied to moral intelligence. Education trapped in the excesses of moral relativity, value skepticism, national, racial or religious superiority may not inculcate higher levels of moral reasoning. When education is shorn of moral intelligence, even literate people can perpetrate serious violations of human rights.

To sharpen people's moral intelligence, the teachers of the world shoulder a special responsibility to teach the history of slavery, genocide, colonialism, apartheid, religious persecution, ethnic cleansing, subjection of women and extermination of indigenous populations. The purpose of teaching the excesses of human prejudice must not be to denigrate any one particular racial, ethnic or religious group. It must warn students that human prejudice is a powerful destructive force and that they are morally and legally bound to help maintain a gracious world in which the human dignity of every individual is fully protected. This view of education is consistent with the Universal Declaration of Human Rights, which requires every organ of society to promote respect, recognition and observance of these rights. Free State establishes a firm bond between education and the law of human rights.

Free State, however, is no mere consumer community in which individuals are preoccupied with the accumulation and consumption of rights and resources without regard to their intellectual and spiritual development. No individual deprived of basic necessities can pursue the other more complex joys of life. However, if a socioeconomic framework encourages individuals to cultivate an unchecked enchantment with consumer goods, it may generate confusion and cynicism with respect to the intellectual and spiritual dimensions of human life without which a full development of human personality cannot occur. Individuals may conclude that pursuit of happiness is equated with the purchasing power in the market, a conclusion that may inculcate and legitimize selfishness, predation, disrespect for morals and even laws. More importantly, an intellectual and spiritual deficit in the lives of individuals distorts the cultural balance of the community, de-emphasizing the significance of compassion and moral intelligence.

To disseminate moral intelligence, Free State tempers the call for individual rights with a corresponding sense of civic duties. No regime of rights is sustainable if individuals fail to appreciate mutual obligations. This is consistent with the teachings of the Universal Declaration of Human Rights that states without ambiguity: "Everyone has duties to the community in which alone the free and full development of his (and her) personality is possible." When individuals understand the inseverable connection between rights and duties, they are more likely to treat each other with equal respect and dignity. They may respect each other even without the fear of sanctions. On the other hand, a community in which the fear of law is the prime motive for respecting the rights and freedoms of others suffers from a deficit of moral intelligence. Such a community may still protect basic rights and liberties; however, its lack of rooting in moral intelligence increases the cost of law enforcement since individuals without a fully developed sense of civic responsibility are likely to evade the law whenever they can.

Moral intelligence is not limited to a voluntary respect for others' legal rights and freedoms. It is also corrective in nature, because it fights the existing injustices built into law. For example, those who fought against legal slavery and against legal but unjust exclusion of women from the political process were driven by moral intelligence. Of course, not every legal dispute has such an underlying moral lucidity. Legal controversies often stem from moral controversies, and confusion in one domain may cause confusion in the other. Nonetheless, Free State encourages moral critique of law as well as legal critique of morality so that individuals may continue to exercise their moral judgments in matters of law. In this respect, Free State moderates legal positivism that separates the realms of law and morality, legal and moral intelligence, thereby creating schizophrenic individuals and communities.

Furthermore, Free State establishes a moral climate in which individuals may fulfil their spiritual needs. Simple virtues, such as compassion, generosity and sharing, are the elements of moral intelligence. Discovered centuries ago by almost all cultures and religions, these virtues are still meaningful for attaining spiritual satisfaction. Individuals draw happiness from giving and sharing, not simply from taking and keeping. Taking care of the sick, the disabled and the poor and doing volunteer work for the benefit of others have been part of every human culture.

In addition to providing for the individual's moral and spiritual needs, Free State highlights the significance of science, art and literature in individual and collective life. It encourages the media to disseminate scientific information that people may use to live safer and healthier lives. With due sensitivity to conventional beliefs, Free State favors scientific inquiry and rational attitudes toward solving social problems. As education spreads in the context of rational and scientific understanding, the people may wish to enrich their lives with aesthetic and literary knowledge. To fulfil these needs of the community, Free State supports artists, writers, poets and scholars engaged in creative pursuits. These undertakings are consistent with the Universal Declaration of Human Rights, which states: "Everyone has the right freely to participate in the cultural life of the community, to enjoy the arts and to share in scientific advancement and its benefits." Thus Free State promotes a wholesome culture in which all facets of human knowledge interact and inform the community. Such a wholesome culture provides plentiful opportunities for every individual to experience a more joyful life.

The third objective of Free State is to protect the unity of One Earth. Unlike the sovereign borders of the nation-state, the administrative borders of Free State maintain the physical unity of the earth. No barbed wire, man-made ditches or concrete walls are made to separate territories that nature meant to unite. The territory of each Free State is seen as an inseverable part of One Earth, thus bringing a fundamental shift in the way nation-states have conceptualized and resolved environmental questions in the past. No Free State may use its territory to inflict environmental harm on a neighboring Free State, a principle recognized even in the legal regime of nation-states. Furthermore, no Free State may abuse or neglect its own territorial environment. If a Free State lacks the resources to repair environmental damage caused in its territory, other Free States are obligated to offer technical and financial assistance. Edith Weiss argues that many bilateral and multilateral treaties contain these obligations. Moreover, the duty to provide emergency assistance arises from the simple principle that the territorial units of Free States constitute a single, indivisible whole, thereby imposing on all the peoples of the world the individual and collective responsibility to maintain the well-being of One Earth.

Although Free State is a human construct to organize the sociopolitical life of diverse human communities, its territory belongs to all forms of life. Therefore, Free State repudiates the predacious viewpoint under which human populations proclaim superiority and sovereignty over ecosystems, organisms, land, marine and atmospheric resources – engaging in indiscriminate extermination and exploitation of natural systems. Instead, it embraces the gracious principle codified in the World Charter for Nature: "Lasting benefits from nature depend upon the maintenance of essential ecological processes and life support systems, and upon the diversity of life forms, which are jeopardized through excessive exploitation and habitat destruction by man." Correspondingly, the territory of each Free State is a natural home for all forms of life, including humankind. In efforts to preserve diverse life forms, Free State is guided by a moral code of action developed by epistemic communities trained in relevant fields.

Contemporary international law grants each state a permanent sovereignty over natural wealth and resources found in its territory. This principle offers a counterpoint to colonialism which exploited resources of distant territories for the benefit of the few and often to the exclusion of the native population. Free State rejects the exploitation of natural resources for the sole benefit of any one population. Just as oceans and air belong to the peoples of the world, so should the solid surface of the earth. No Free State can morally afford to live in utter prosperity derived from natural resources when another Free State lacking such resources lives in abject poverty. Richard Falk argues that contemporary international law is aimed at promoting decency in the world, since poverty and mass misery anywhere in the world affects our identity as a single species.

Free State, in its higher stage of moral evolution, may reject the concept of exclusive sovereignty over natural resources found in its territory. Instead, it may be willing to share the benefits of natural resources on a regional or global basis. This norm is already a reality in the context of a federated nation-state in which constituent units exercise no such exclusive sovereignty over the natural resources found within their administrative borders. Once the concept of sovereign borders is changed, the peoples of the world would be willing to share the resources that, over millions of years, the natural forces created on and beneath the surface of the indivisible earth.

This principle of sharing, however, does not repudiate private ownership. The Grotian distinction between sovereignty and ownership may be modified to strike a new balance between private ownership and Free State's prerogative over its territory. Free State does not mandate but does allow private ownership of land and other resources. Private ownership, however, is subject to Free State's administrative authority. For example, Free State may lawfully enforce its criminal jurisdiction over private lands. It may also regulate uses of private land to promote public health and public morality. Regulatory restrictions on the uses of private land may or may not require compensation. If the public uses of private property are limited to protect fundamental interests of the community, Free State may decline to offer any compensation. But if imposed restrictions substantially affect the customary uses of land, private owners may seek appropriate compensation. No rigid formula is available to resolve the tension between legitimate expectations of private ownership of land and the communitarian interests for the regulation of territory. The sharing principle therefore remains flexible, allowing Free States to solve such problems within the contexts of their own circumstances.

In a vivid contrast to the nation-state, Free State exercises authority over the territory but does not derive from it. The authority that Free State exercises over its territory is not sovereign, but rather is exercised in a complex web of regional and global interdependence. Free State's authority over its territory is nonetheless substantial. Consistent with the principle of subsidiarity, Free State enjoys the prerogative to find local solutions to local problems. In the

European Union, for example, central political and epistemic institutions may propose to member states the ways and means to improve the quality of air and water. Yet an overly centralized system distorts the more intimate relationship between Free State and its permanent residents. Such a centralized system may even be detrimental to the very nature of Free State in which permanent residents are actively involved in the affairs of local government. Free State maintains a sensitive balance between local freedom and regional or global enmeshment. It claims no exclusive sovereignty over its territory, and yet it spurns any excessive external control that undermines its special relationship with its own land. The mutation process from the nation-state to Free State may itself strike a balance between competing interests of local government and regional or global enmeshment.

To further advance the unity of One Earth, Free State enables its people to relate to the rest of humanity. The nation-state forges its relationship with individuals through the concept of patriotism, a profound psychological attachment to the existence and objectives of the nation-state. Flags and national anthems are powerful patriotic symbols that the citizens of a nation-state hold in high respect. Patriotism may also deepen the bond of ethnicity, often reinforcing a shared sense of economic, religious or cultural superiority. It prepares individuals to sacrifice their lives if the nation-state goes to war. In addition to the forces of patriotism, the nation-state uses its coercive legal authority to punish sedition, treason or even mere criticism of the state and its ideology. If not enough people volunteer to fight a war, the nation-state may use its laws to draft reluctant individuals. Thus a combined mix of psychological volition and legal coercion establishes a complex bond between individuals and the nation-state.

Moderating the concept of patriotism, Free State introduces the alternative notion of morally intelligent respect. Based on the simple intuition that a shared sense of the community is essential for any meaningful coexistence, Free State encourages individuals to feel morally intelligent respect for who they are and where they live. Free State considers the individual a situated-self, a person located in and formed by the community. Individuals may freely pursue their ethnic, religious and cultural identities without fear or confusion. They may preserve and promote local culture, including folk songs, dance, sports, cuisine, manners, mores and humor – rejecting any and all forms of cultural imperialism that denigrate disparate cultures by derogatory terms of localism and provincialism. Morally intelligent respect for one's own culture, religion or community is a human need that connects similarly situated individuals.

Morally intelligent respect for one's community, however, should cause no alienation from the rest of the world. It protects local culture in so far as it is compatible with general principles of tolerance and friendship among the peoples of the region and the world. Herein lies the crucial difference between patriotism and morally intelligent respect. Patriotism prepares individuals to love their own nation-state, but its extreme versions may generate hostility, hatred, even genocidal inclinations toward other nations and peoples. Morally intelligent respect rejects such excesses of patriotism. Unlike patriotism that thrives on the people's unexamined commitment to the state, intelligent respect allows individuals to use their common sense, wisdom and virtue in accepting or rejecting the policies of Free State, taking care to reject the state's attempts to demonize other communities, cultures, religions and races. Free States may use flags and anthems to symbolize their separate identities. However, the psychological basis of these symbols changes from blind devotion to critical acceptance.

The notion of morally intelligent respect for one's community is consistent with the freedom of movement available in the era of Free States. Unlike patriotism that disables individuals from integrating into new communities, morally intelligent respect is a much more adaptive attitude. When people are free to move among Free States and live in communities of their choice, they develop a sense of attachment that is neither rigid nor belligerent. Just as individuals may relocate within a nation-state without any feelings of betrayal of the community where they were born, so they may relocate to different parts of the world without sacrificing their sense of belonging to their previous communities. Some may be proud of their ancestral communities in the same way as others are of their adoptive communities. The notion of morally intelligent respect for one's community provides cultural and spiritual stability to both the individual and the community. It, however, is a dynamic concept. It empowers individuals to choose and adopt new communities without fear or guilt.

If the purposes of contemporary international law can be successfully achieved, the promise of Free State will reorganize life on One Earth. Moral clarity in itself is a powerful force to guide human behavior, and therefore contemporary international law presents a powerful moral vision of what is within the human capacity to achieve. Presently, not all nation-states are committed to the ideals of human rights and moral intelligence. Widespread patriotism, the forces of ethnicity, religious fanaticism and the predacious logic of national interests reinforce the idea of the nation-state. To men and women willing to die for their country, the concept of Free State may seem merely fanciful. Free State, therefore, will remain no more than an ideal until the forces impeding its evolution are overcome.

Chapter Eight

The Evolution of Free State

The evolution of Free State is closely related to the purposes of contemporary international law. Global forces of economic integration, environmental unity, information flow and migration continue to weaken the geopsychological borders of the nation-state. But these forces by themselves are inadequate to cause the mutation of the nation-state into Free State. A more fundamental transformation in the conditions of global life, consistent with the purposes of contemporary international law, must also occur before nation-states would relinquish their traditional attributes.

The purposes of contemporary international law most pertinent to the evolution of Free State may be found in the United Nations Charter and other eminent international agreements. The first purpose is to outlaw war. Many agreements obligate nation-states to refrain from the threat or use of force in their international relations. They are also obligated to resolve all disputes by peaceful means. If nation-states comply with these norms, they cannot prevent their evolution toward Free State. But the absence of war alone is inadequate to establish Free State. The second purpose obligates nation-states to develop friendly relations and forge cooperation in solving international problems of an economic, social, cultural or humanitarian character. This shift from belligerence to cooperation promises to create conditions of stability and well-being under which the peoples of the world can strive for shared economic and social progress in pursuit of a decent standard of living. But even widespread global prosperity cannot construct a world free of sovereign borders if ethnic obsessions continue to assault the dignity of the human person. So the third purpose seeks to eliminate all social barriers based on race, sex, language or religion. Under the combined impact of these purposes, contemporary international law envisions a peaceful, prosperous and pluralist world.

Though laudable, the purposes of contemporary international law may pose the most difficult challenge ever faced by the human race. They wish to transform a world that for centuries has been marred by armed conflict, poverty and extreme forms of discrimination. To many these purposes seem so utopian that their possible implementation is no more than an optimistic dream. Yet these purposes must not be denigrated or, worse, discarded from the realm of law in favor of the contrary view that war, destitution and discrimination are immutable facts of human life. Such a pessimistic view of human intelligence cannot be a viable basis of international law, nor has it ever been. Constant effort toward enforcing the purposes of contemporary international law is and ought to be the commitment of law. The path toward the gracious world that contemporary international law proposes to establish is neither straight nor without hazards. The challenge of the path, however, does not diminish the value of the destination.

Although tied to the purposes of contemporary international law, Free State is not waiting for the gracious world to bloom. As a dynamic entity, it wishes to create such a world. But Free State is a legal and moral construct that evolves only when a suitable legal and moral environment is established. Thus a reciprocal relationship exists between Free State and the legal environment. Due to this reciprocity, a change in the legal environment shapes the characteristics of Free State just as the characteristics of Free State alter the legal environment. Seeking equilibrium, one adapts to the other. Thus, Free State is neither independent nor sovereign, nor is it formed solely by the external environment. In many ways Free State is an interactive organism, just like a plant that absorbs water from the environment and delivers oxygen through its leaves. But this process of interactive evolution becomes unstable when warfare, destitution and ethnonationalism oppose the emergence of Free State.

In order to understand the evolution of Free State, one must not underestimate the difference between egregious violations and minor infringements of contemporary international law. Free State cannot emerge if egregious violations of contemporary international law continue to occur. For example, if standards of living across the globe remain dramatically uneven, thus maintaining the current division of the world into rich and poor states, the nation-state will continue to be the best mode for preserving such inequities. Rich nation-states will police their sovereign borders, as they do now, to exclude the poor and the wretched from entering their territory. Likewise, egregious armed conflicts may also reinforce the importance of sovereign borders.

In contrast to egregious violations, minor infringements of international law may not impede the evolution of Free State. The example of the European Union demonstrates that minor disparities in national standards of living in the region do not automatically motivate affluent nation-states to close their borders. Therefore, absolute parity in standards of living is no prerequisite for the establishment of Free State. Nor need absolute peace be achieved in all parts of the world before Free State can be established. Free State may be an ideal difficult to achieve, but it is not a utopia seeking a perfect world.

Thus the legal and moral environment supportive of nation-states and rooted in the dying concepts of classical international law must undergo a transformation for Free State to emerge. If egregious violations of contemporary international law cease, the sovereign borders of the nation-state will likely evolve into the open borders of Free State. But an egregious violation against any one purpose of international law inevitably leads to weaknesses in other purposes as well. For example, states in a region will fail to devote their resources to economic development if they refuse to establish peaceful conditions. With this caveat in mind, it may now be examined how a good faith pursuit of the three major purposes of international law – the establishment of peaceful conditions, equitable development and pluralist association – may shape an environment most favorable to the mutation of the nation-state into Free State.

1. PEACEFUL CONDITIONS

A world without sovereign borders cannot evolve unless peaceful conditions are established. If states rely on the use of force to conduct international relations, a general threat of armed conflict will loom over the world and the maintenance of sovereign borders will be inevitable. Nation-states engaged in hostilities protect their borders more stringently against each other than those at peace. Even regional Free State cannot come into existence unless the region is peaceful and the likelihood of regional aggression is minimal. The European Union, for example, is able to successfully open its internal borders because no member state is at war with any other. On the other hand, the South Asian Association for Regional Cooperation, a regional economic community comprised of India, Pakistan and five other regional states, has failed to open its internal borders even for the exchange of goods, primarily because India and Pakistan are engaged in a protracted armed conflict over Kashmir. These examples demonstrate that while the nation-state is more suited to a world of hostilities, Free State flourishes under peaceful conditions.

Since armed aggression has been a human condition for centuries and will most likely continue to remain so, the idea of Free State might be regarded as nothing more than a fantasy. And even if the world becomes peaceful, there is no guarantee that war would never erupt in the future. Since Free State depends on peaceful conditions, any future war may compel states to resurrect their sovereign borders – a scenario under which Free State will regress into the nation-state. The European Union, a region currently conducive to the emergence of regional Free State, may relapse into dissension if Germany and France turn against each other, as they frequently have in the past, or if either strives to dominate the Union against the wishes of other member states, many of which already fear such a domination.

Few would deny that over the centuries armed conflict has defined mutual relations between communities throughout the world. Thus the view that armed conflict would continue to define interstate relations in the future cannot be dismissed as unwarranted pessimism. Unlike the Marxist state that inevitably rises from the ashes of historical determinism, Free State is a creature of human will and intelligence. Free State may shape historical forces but it cannot determine them. It may help establish peaceful conditions but it cannot prevent all moral breakdowns or violent eruptions. Free State will be relegated to the archives of utopias if armed conflicts continue to determine international affairs.

Despite the unpredictability of the future human course, the development of international law over the centuries points toward the evolution of peaceful conditions. A brief overview of the normative history of war intimates that law has progressively limited the uses of force in interstate relations, thus revealing a profound human longing to eradicate militarized aggression. If this trend continues, peaceful conditions supporting the rise of Free State may finally be instituted.

In pursuit of the ideal of a gracious world without militarized violence, contemporary international law has outlawed many of the traditional bases of aggressive war. The General Treaty for the Renunciation of War (1928), commonly known as the Kellogg-Briand Pact, is a solemn declaration that the high contracting parties condemn recourse to war for the solution of international controversies and renounce it as an instrument of national policy in their relations with one another. The Vienna Convention on the Law of Treaties (1969) makes it unlawful to procure a treaty by the threat or use of force in violation of the principles of international law embodied in the United Nations Charter. Article 2(4) of the United Nations Charter repudiates the threat or use of force in international relations in any manner inconsistent with the purposes of the United Nations. It specifically prohibits the use of force against the territorial integrity or political independence of any state. A plain reading of the Article precludes the use of force to acquire territory or to forcibly change any state's political or legal system.

A strict reading of Article 2(4) also outlaws the self-righteous and potentially abusive doctrine of humanitarian intervention favored by scholars like Anthony D'Amato, Richard Lillich, Myers McDougal and Michael Reisman. Challenging what Reisman calls "the paper world of the Charter," the advocates of humanitarian intervention, whether motivated by national interests, realpolitik or human rights idealism, are not prepared to eradicate the use of force in all circumstances. Some states, such as the United States and India, have invoked the doctrine to violate the territorial integrity and political independence of other states for the sake of preventing human rights violations both real and alleged. In the cold war years, humanitarian intervention derived further legitimacy from the inability of the United Nations to act decisively even in cases of egregious human rights abuses. In this period of normative confusion and superpower rivalry, armed force was defended on many other legally dubious bases on the fringes of humanitarian intervention. The Soviet occupation of Afghanistan and the United States conquest of Grenada stand out as lucid departures from the binding norms of the Charter.

Humanitarian intervention is defensible to the extent that the world should not bury its head in pacifism when a state commits genocide. Even in less extreme cases of human rights abuses, the world must show its disapproval and may have to use force to alleviate the situation. Nonetheless, collective humanitarian intervention should not be confused with unilateral state action. The United Nations Charter authorizes the Security Council to impose economic sanctions and use armed force if necessary to maintain or restore international peace and security. Peacekeeping in Somalia and peacemaking in Bosnia are recent examples of such collective humanitarian intervention. But unilateral state action, such as the "Afghanistan's invitation" to the Soviet forces, carries far less legitimacy. If the United Nations continues to act in a timely and effective manner, it will become increasingly difficult for states to claim unilateral authority to prosecute humanitarian causes. Most important, the rehabilitation of the United Nations as a collective moral entity and the final arbiter of the just use of armed force may prove to be one more step toward the era of Free State.

In addition to proscribing any predacious use of armed aggression, the Charter requires states to resolve their disputes through peaceful means such as negotiation, conciliation, mediation, arbitration or judicial settlement. This approach is fully consistent with the establishment of Free State, which repudiates the use of force not only to appropriate illegal advantages but also to resolve disputes. A perfect world in which no dispute arises at all is inconceivable. But even if a living world cannot be unfettered by disputes, it can nonetheless change the way disputes are resolved. If states are willing to settle their disputes through peaceful methods, they become better able to open their borders to each other's goods and nationals. If borders are already open and states are already economically and socially enmeshed, they are more likely to resolve their disputes without violence. Thus Free State and peaceful resolution of disputes reinforce each other.

To further reorient states' behavior from armed conflict to active cooperation, the Charter reminds the international community that peaceful conditions are necessary for solving basic human problems such as poverty and disease. Free State as an entity fully enmeshed at regional and global levels seeks and lends cooperation to raise the standard of living and find the cures for diseases. It therefore actively helps regional and global organizations, as well as their epistemic institutions, to find efficient and durable solutions to common problems. Again, a perfect world without famine or disease may not always be possible, since uncontrollable forces of nature may compel food shortages and interject new diseases. Nonetheless, peaceful conditions must be maintained if resources are to be rationally allocated to eradicate present and future causes of famine and disease.

Even the traditional right of self-defense has been brought under legal constraints. The Charter recognizes the inherent right of individual or collective self-defense if an armed attack occurs. However, a state exercising the right of self-defense is obligated to immediately report its counter-measures to the Security Council, the United Nations organ responsible for maintaining international peace and security. Moreover, the right of self-defense in no way affects the authority of the Security Council to take at any time such action as it deems necessary in order to maintain or restore international peace and security. This regulatory authority of the Security Council assures that the right of self-defense is not abused. Moreover, the involvement of the Security Council internationalizes the conflict placing responsibility on the entire international community to contain the spread of war and deter the aggressor. In the case of Bosnia, the Security Council established a new precedent in limiting the right of self-defense. By refusing to lift the arms embargo on the Bosnian government, the Council weakened Bosnia's capacity to defend against Serb attacks. Even though the Security Council's decision has been widely criticized, one reason for maintaining the arms embargo was to contain the possible spread of war and associated brutality. However, this limitation on the right to self-defense may be acceptable only if the United Nations is willing to provide humanitarian intervention in a timely fashion to the aggrieved state.

Thus the Charter aims to regulate what had been left unregulated for centuries. These more restrictive legal norms governing the use of force surfaced after the intolerable devastation of the two world wars of the twentieth century. L. Oppenhiem points out that prior to the General Treaty for the Renunciation of War states used force for several legally permissible reasons. Force was used as a means of self-help to enforce claims against an otherwise reluctant state. War was also recognized as a lawful means to modify existing rights and obligations, even when the modification sought was without merit. In addition, the use of force was considered lawful to gain political and other advantages over another state. Ian Brownline recounts that "the right of states to go to war and to obtain territory by right of conquest was unlimited although some qualifications to this position had appeared by 1914." Had these predacious norms, which sustained the era of empires, continued to exist, the evolution of the nation-state into Free State would have been retarded.

The United Nations Charter was not the first legal attempt to make a dramatic departure from the predacious past. In fact, the law of peace was in the making centuries before the Charter was enacted. The distinction between just and unjust war favored by Grotius and others played a critical role in weakening the broad-based lawfulness of war: a war must be just in order to be lawful. This superimposition of justice upon war changed the meaning of armed conflict. Raw force in itself was no longer a sufficient legal basis to shape interstate relations and draw advantages from weak states. Even though first empires and then nation-states manipulated the distinction to label their wars as just, they nonetheless lost the absolute moral freedom to engage in war at will. Under the impact of moral teachings, many customary rules of international law began to develop. The new rules declared the unlawfulness of many traditional causes of war, including the imperial wish to conquer land, the self-righteous faith to subdue those who practiced a different religion, and the predacious practice to capture slaves. In 1907, recourse to armed force even for the recovery of contract debts was declared unjust and thus illegal.

To further restrain the use of force, even the potentially abusive concept of just war has been discarded. Classical international law held that, since states enjoy equal sovereignty, no state can lawfully impose its conception of justice on others. This formal logic strived to suppress the self-righteousness embodied in the concept of just war. Peaceful conditions will end if each nation-state is vested with the legal authority to define "just war" for itself. But even if a universal definition of just war could be agreed upon, an aggrieved state might not be able to assert rights against a more powerful state. Thus the notion of just war primarily serves the interests of powerful states. Even when an aggrieved state seeks its remedy through war, it may or may not employ a reasonable and proportionate use of force. Thus the concept of just war required further regulation with respect to the amount of force used. But even when reasonable force is used in a just war, the destruction caused often outweighs its benefits. Collateral damage in any war, such as the destruction of the environment, life and property, is almost always beyond the best intentions of the generals.

Accordingly, contemporary international law mandates that all interstate claims and conflicts, just and unjust, be settled through peaceful means. Conversely, it also asserts that no interstate conflict, including one that has festered over a long period, may justify unilateral armed aggression. Peaceful resolution of disputes, however, cannot become a reality unless an effective international machinery persuades and pressures states not to use force. When a culture of peaceful resolution of disputes is established, nation-states will be able to renounce war as a method to resolve their conflicts and take an evolutionary step toward Free State.

This raises a question about whether armed resistance to oppression is permissible in the evolution toward Free State. Peaceful conditions cannot flourish when egregious oppression exists. Thus the paradigm of absolute non-violence becomes an elusive ideal. If the oppressor, whether an irremovable government or a foreign occupier, receives no threat from its victims, no change will occur unless the oppressor morally develops, a development that may not occur for decades. Oppressors, themselves at a lower level of moral intelligence, want and even force their victims to adopt the morally virtuous philosophy of non-violence. They do so to assure that their own lives and property are safe from revolutionary violence. To resist manifest injustice, however, the oppressed often refuse to embrace such non-violence. Consequently, a cycle of violence continues to impede the moral evolution of oppressive nation-states. Due to actual or perceived threat from internal or external "enemies," oppressive nation-states often tend to isolate themselves. The world may also shun them, thus further aggravating their isolation. South Africa under apartheid was such a state before it decided to peacefully change its oppressive system.

Notwithstanding its broad peaceful objectives, contemporary international law authorizes peoples forcibly deprived of the right of self-determination or under racist or alien domination to seek independence by force if necessary. But this exception is available to oppressed "peoples," not states. Moreover, the exception allows armed resistance only to remove oppression, not to resolve conflicts. Oppression should therefore not be confused with a mere presence of conflict. A conflict arises when states assert competing claims with respect to a disputed matter. The competing claims may be asserted with respect to the facts of the controversy, the issues involved, the applicable law or the remedies sought. Distinguished from conflict, oppression occurs under a set of exceptional circumstances in which the injury suffered by a people is so manifest that the acts of the aggressor lose all lawful basis. Unlawful occupation and ethnic cleansing are illustrations of oppression. Some situations may involve both conflict and oppression, weakening the distinction. Nonetheless, the degree of injustice involved in an oppressive situation is so offensive to the collective conscience of the international community that few states would characterize such a situation as a conflict.

While oppression impedes the rise of Free State, armed resistance is not the only method to remove oppression. To prevent oppression, contemporary international law offers solutions other than violence. First, the law of human rights and obligations proposes a structural change in the concept of the state: it subjects the government to the will of its people and binds all legal systems to respect the inherent dignity of every man and women without any unlawful discrimination. If the law of human rights and obligations is seriously implemented, domestic oppression and associated violence can be substantially reduced. In its evolution toward Free State, therefore, each nation-state must institute a morally intelligent legal system in which the grievances of any segment of the population do not reach the point of oppression.

Second, the concept of self-determination offers to resolve intricate demands for secession, another major source of contemporary violence. If nation-states relinquish the practice of suppressing secessionist movements by force and allow peaceful dialogue, leaving open the option for separate statehood, the amount of violence will dramatically decrease. The peaceful movement for an independent Quebec, the French province of an otherwise predominantly English-speaking Canada, offers hope that violence can be substantially reduced if both the state and secessionists adopt a peaceful attitude to resolve the conflict arising from the competing norms of territorial integrity and self-determination. Nothing in international law prohibits a nation-state from voluntarily allowing secession. The mutual, peaceful partition of Czechoslovakia into two separate states is a case in point.

Excepting such peaceful partitions, contemporary international law is unclear about the right to secession. In opposition to such a right, most nation-states invoke the principle of territorial integrity embodied in the United nations Charter. On the basis of this principle, nation-states justify the use of force to suppress secessionist movements. Russia's massive use of force to silence Chechnya's demand for separate statehood is the most recent example. Underlying the legal issue is the additional concern that a freely available right to secession might break up many nation-states into small, dysfunctional units.

When critically examined, this fear of fragmentation is without substance. Most communities benefit from consolidating their resources into a bigger sociopolitical organization, such as a large state. Most important, ethnic and cultural ties bind many peoples together, encouraging them to live in the same state. Most constituent units in India, for example, would refuse to secede even if they had the right to do so. Similarly, few states in the United States would opt for an outright secession if such a right became available. They may demand devolution of central authority, but their commitment to the existence of the United States as a single entity is presently unshakable.

But even if the availability of the right to secession downsizes some nation-states, the benefits of such a right are greater than the cost of maintaining territorial integrity by brutal suppression and violence. If the establishment of peaceful conditions is indeed a preferred value, as it ought to be, the right to secession should override the norm of territorial integrity. This view is also consistent with the right of self-determination, a liberal interpretation of which would include the right to secession. International law is unclear about why the right of self-determination is unavailable against nation-states when it is available against colonial empires and all forms of alien domination. If forced cohabitation causes violence, people ought to have a right to separation. The right to secession, exercised through a peaceful dialogue between the parties or through a fair and transparent procedure such as a globally-monitored referendum, is thus a more sensible course of action.

If the right to secession is provided by international law, the progression of the nation-state toward Free State will accelerate, since nation-states will have no excuse to use force to suppress secessionist movements. Even secessionists might exercise caution before severing their relationship with existing states. The right to secession within the framework of nation-states is seen as a means for territorial loss. However, if borders are open for the free flow of goods, services, capital, labor, tourists and migrants, the right to secession assumes a new meaning. Then, the right may simply bind the central government to repatriate authority to a seceding unit, an imperative without much consequence if the unit is tied to the regional economy. In this sense, therefore, the right to secession advances progression of the nation-state toward Free State, just as the evolution of Free State imparts new meaning to territorial secession.

On the basis of this logic, the borders between India and Pakistan will probably relax if the Kashmir dispute is resolved. Presently, however, the Kashmir dispute is viewed in terms of territorial loss and gain. If the people of Kashmir are allowed the right of self-determination, Indian policymakers fear the Kashmiris will choose to secede from India or, worse, join with Pakistan. As a result, India is willing to suppress an entire population but unwilling to compromise its territorial integrity, perpetuating a cycle of violence between its security forces and secessionists. If India concedes the right of self-determination to Kashmiris, India and Pakistan become better able to move toward Free State with open borders. The resolution of the Kashmir dispute would decrease a major source of violence. Moreover, the war-like situation between India and Pakistan, both of which have nuclear weapons, will subside. The South Asian Association of Regional Cooperation, a regional community that has thus far failed to bring promised prosperity primarily due to the India-Pakistan conflict, may begin to bear fruit. The nations of the subcontinent, containing close to fifth of the world's population, with most people living in wretched social conditions, will greatly benefit if the region is peaceful, borders are open for free trade and resources are devoted to solving basic problems rather than perpetuating a state of war. Thus the right to self-determination, if freely granted, may downsize some nation-states. Yet this approach seems more sensible than forced retention of a population that causes violence and impedes the evolution of Free State.

Related to the question of interstate violence is the presence of weapons. Does the very existence of weapons of war retard the development of Free State? Underlying the answer to this question is the observation that repudiation of violence occurs at two successive developmental stages of moral intelligence. Initially, the use of force is renounced but weapons of war are retained; in the second stage, the weapons themselves are substantially reduced or totally eliminated. At the first stage, even though war is legally impermissible, the potential for war continues to exist. The presence of weapons sustains a climate of fear while mutual distrust among states justifies the need for weapons. Nation-states may further defend the retention of weapons on the theory of future self-defense: that is, a nation must keep weapons to defend itself against a future enemy even if no such enemy presently exists.

Thus a universal culture of fear rooted in the deepest layers of historical memory still persists. The peoples of the world do not yet trust each other. Although contemporary international law is still preoccupied with the first stage of non-violence, it has made some progress toward the second. The legal regime of disarmament is currently confined to weapons of mass destruction, such as nuclear, biological and chemical weapons. The recent renewal of the nuclear non-proliferation treaty for an indefinite period is a hopeful sign. Though weapons of mass destruction are still plentiful, it appears that the international community has at least begun to move toward the second stage of non-violence at which both war and the weapons of war are renounced.

Even though Free State seeks the second stage of non-violence as its permanent companion, it may initially develop without disarmament. The example of the European Union demonstrates that the presence of weapons of mass destruction does not automatically hinder the emergence of regional Free State, provided the member states are at peace with each other. However, when a region, such as the Indian subcontinent, is permeated with unresolved conflicts, the presence of weapons further aggravates mutual doubts and regional tensions. In such cases, the development of Free State can best be accelerated by focussing on resolving outstanding conflicts rather than dismantling weapons, because the presence of conflict is a far more serious impediment to friendly relations and a far more serious inducement to the use of weapons.

The same logic can be extended to the legal environment in which global Free State would emerge. The presence of interstate conflicts rather than the mere presence of weapons is a more serious impediment to the emergence of global Free State. No one disputes that weapons of mass destruction are dangerous *per se*. For example, any accidental use of nuclear or biological weapons can inflict serious injury. Advocates of the destruction of weapons of mass destruction thus offer a sensible goal that ought to be pursued. No weapons, however, will be dismantled if outstanding conflicts remain unresolved. States that have no outstanding disputes rarely go to war. Weapons are dangerous primarily because they can be used in the heat of conflicts. Therefore the resolution of current conflicts ought to be the first serious undertaking.

One need not embrace the utopian belief that once outstanding global disputes are resolved, Free States will come into existence and the world will no longer be threatened by the weapons of war. No future world, not even one comprised of Free States, will be without conflicts. Therefore, the key norm of the law of peace is the commitment to resolve all interstate disputes, present and future, through peaceful means rather than by recourse to force. When this commitment is weakened, weapons become ominous in interstate controversies. If a moral regression occurs in the future and the commitment to peaceful resolution of disputes evaporates, weapons of mass destruction will pose a serious threat to the survival of human civilization. To avoid such a catastrophe, Free State makes an unwavering commitment to a complete disarmament of weapons of mass destruction.

Right now, many nation-states are engaged in armed conflicts; many also have weapons of mass destruction. States devote their human and natural resources to building armies, buying weapons and fighting bloody wars of mutual attrition rather than spending on socioeconomic development. In the words of G. Sarpellon, many of the problems of development could be solved if the "expenditure on death" is turned into an "expenditure on life."[1] This important observation shows the inherent relationship between peace and development, another essential condition for the evolution of Free State.

2. EQUITABLE DEVELOPMENT

Related to the law of peace is the right to development, an emerging aspect of contemporary international law without which not even peaceful conditions can assure the evolution of Free State. Nation-states at peace with each other, such as the United States and Mexico, will continue to retain closed borders if a serious gap exists in their respective standards of living. In most cases, however, rich nation-states insist on closing their borders to their poor neighbors. They fear that open borders will encourage massive migration. Rich nation-states may relax their borders to allow free trade with poor states. They may even allow free flow of investment capital. But their borders remain closed to the free circulation of workers and persons, walled off by strict immigration policies which preserve their higher standards of living. Thus closed borders and a higher standard of living develop a symbiotic correlation, one sustaining the other.

On the other hand, nation-states enjoying a more or less equal standard of living seem more inclined to open their borders to each other's nationals, at least for tourism if not for permanent residence. The United States' borders are much more open with Canada than with Mexico, even though all three states are parties to the same North American Free Trade Agreement. Similarly, the European Union has been successful in dismantling its internal borders in part because member states enjoy parallel standards of living, though Greece and Portugal are presently lower on the scale. These examples demonstrate that comparable, though not necessarily equal, standards of living among nations facilitate the rise of Free State, whereas seriously disproportionate standards of living are more conducive to the retention of the nation-state.

---

1. In 1986, the Council of Europe organized a consultation on poverty in Europe. In presenting his conclusions, G. Sarpellon, the Special Rapporteur, pointed out that the poor must take charge of their own destinies. He further pointed out that the drive to eradicate poverty is largely a matter for those who are <u>not</u> poor.

If a decent standard of living among all the peoples of the world constitutes a condition for the rise of Free State, we are faced with a formidable goal. Contemporary international law proposes to eradicate poverty, disease and illiteracy throughout the world. The United Nations Charter promises higher standards of living, asserting that the creation of conditions of stability and well-being are necessary for peaceful and friendly relations among nations. It has established the Economic and Social Council to promote international cooperation in economic, social, cultural, educational, health and related matters. This commitment to world-wide social justice developed into a more serious moral and legal obligation in subsequent documents. The Universal Declaration of Human Rights asserts in unambiguous terms that everyone has the right to an adequate standard of living. The International Covenant on Economic, Social and Cultural Rights reaffirms the need for continuous improvement of living conditions. It adds, however, that states are obligated to seek and lend international cooperation in raising their peoples' standard of living. To renounce any bifurcation of human rights and obligations, the International Covenant on Civil and Political Rights recognizes that civil-political rights cannot flourish in states that lack the means to provide economic-social rights. In more recent years, international environmental law has emphasized the indivisibility of One Earth, highlighting the interdependence of all states, rich and poor, and appealing to the international community to create conditions necessary to improve the quality of life. These and other international norms that promote adequate standards of living across the world may collectively be called the law of development.

The law of development is consistent with the normative framework of Free State. It proposes several specific policies to bring about a gracious world in which the entire globe enjoys the standard of living needed to preserve the inherent dignity of the human person. First, the law of development binds each government to take steps to the maximum of available resources to improve the people's standard of living, thus departing from the Grotian theory under which government had no such international obligation. This international duty imposed on governments seeks to establish social justice so that economic benefits are no longer confined to select elites within the state.

Second, the law broadens the scope of economic cooperation by obligating states to assist each other in providing the means and technology to improve living conditions. For example, states that have developed methods or machines for more efficient production or conservation of food are under an emerging legal obligation to share their know-how to improve inefficient agrarian systems in developing states.

Third, the law of development clarifies the rights and obligations of multinational enterprises that play an important role in forging international economic relations. It replaces the old idea that such enterprises function for the exclusive benefit of their home states, an approach that resulted in an unfair drain of natural resources and other benefits from host states to home states. Multinational enterprises, mostly headquartered in developed states, continue to prefer particular nation-states or regions, even though the scope of their economic power and production is often global. The old corporate loyalty to a single nation-state, however, is waning because such corporate patriotism is unprofitable. So now most developing nation-states entice multinational enterprises, by relaxing previously strict laws on foreign investment, repatriation of profits and currency convertibility. These states further undertake to institute more acceptable standards of compensation should foreign assets be nationalized.

In accordance with changing global realities, even powerful multinational enterprises have become more willing to carry out their activities in conformity with the development and environmental policies of host states. Multinational enterprises are prepared to distribute decisional authority among their dispersed entities so that each local entity may contribute in an informed manner to the economic and social development of its host state. They also promise to employ nationals of the host state at all levels of labor and management, reinvest profits in the host state, and provide reasonable wages and decent working conditions. They undertake to respect the social and cultural objectives, values and traditions of host states. If multinational enterprises fulfill their obligations in good faith, as some already do, they can build a beneficial framework for universal economic development. If, however, they use developing nation-states as exploitable habitats for natural resources and low wages, lesser environmental restrictions and more profits, the rise of Free State will be seriously impeded.

Even if multinational enterprises respect equitable development, other serious obstacles remain. Vast disparities between rich and poor states sometimes seem unbridgeable. The attitude of rich states toward universal development is mercurial. Many rich states offer assistance to developing states, but the pressure to devote more resources to domestic problems weakens the ethic of sharing. Some states consider the ethic of sharing idealistic, even against human nature, which is presumably selfish. Some view economic prosperity in terms of racial, religious and national superiority, an explanation that suggests in subtext that some nations are justly impoverished because of their genes, faith or culture. Some view the existing disparity as a permanent human condition, an ongoing socioeconomic battle between rich and poor, in which the latter must always lose. The collapse of egalitarian models, including the recent setbacks suffered by socialism, further confirms that the psychology of predation produces more efficient and vigorous markets. Consequently, commitment to international cooperation inspired by the egalitarian ethic of sharing remains half-hearted at best.

The principle of self-help, on the other end of sociopolitical organization, generates national pride but produces less than spectacular results in part because no amount of self-help can free a national economy from the web of global enmeshment. Even though some developing states have shown encouraging economic growth in the past few decades, many others lag behind. And those lagging behind experience shared helplessness as their social, economic and political institutions fail, year after year, to produce beneficial results. Some ruling elites, consistent with the Grotian theory, remain indifferent to the plight of their people. Some lack the skill to manage the human and natural resources of their states. Widespread corruption among public officials and widespread illiteracy among the people are additional impediments to sustained economic progress. To make matters worse, the educated and skilled individuals who might contribute to a nation's economic and social development often leave their home states because of political oppression or the desire for self-improvement. Just like the depletion of natural resources, this brain drain from developing states is detrimental to socioeconomic progress.

Thus the law of development provides a normative framework for achieving equitable prosperity among the peoples of the world. But the lingering forces of political and economic nationalism are yet unprepared to relinquish their hold on the markets. The predacious urge to hunt for exploitable opportunities continues to shape the behavior of many multinational enterprises. The ethic of sharing, despite its noble aspiration, fails to persuade rich nations to share their affluence and methods of production with the rest of the world. As always, the forces of self-interest and moral intelligence pull toward two different worlds, one of nation-states and the other of Free States.

Free State, however, need not defer its emergence until universal prosperity is obtained. Equitable development is a process that begins with small steps. It may begin at the regional level, with the initial participation of few nation-states. It may also begin with a mere exchange of goods. For example, despite disparity in the standards of living between the United States and Mexico, the North American Free Trade Agreement has begun a process that may gradually evolve into a further relaxation of borders. The example of the European Union demonstrates that once the process of regional free trade is commenced, it swiftly gathers momentum. Currently, borders within North America are being dismantled to allow the free exchange of goods, services and capital. But as regional markets are further enmeshed, managers and technicians in trade, commerce and technology will come under increased pressure to think and act in regional terms. Regional markets necessarily institute regional legal systems to clarify rules of competition, rules for the protection of the regional environment, rules for solving disputes between regional labor and management, and even rules for social justice. If the region is economically asymmetric, companies may move across borders to gain comparative advantage. When companies can freely move across national borders, wages begin to equalize – just as water seeks its own level when allowed to flow unimpeded. So step by step regional Free State begins to take shape.

One must not conclude, however, that regional Free State is necessarily a creature of prosperity or that poor states must raise their standards of living comparable to rich states before they can evolve into Free States. Free State begins to evolve as soon as sovereign borders are relaxed. If nation-states with higher standards of living can open their borders to each other, nothing prohibits poor states from commencing a similar process of integration. Rich states may continue to retain closed borders with poor states. But poor states have little reason to do the same to each other. In fact, the need for border-free cooperation is more manifest among poor states. Developing states can greatly benefit from pooling their resources, talents and strategies. This beneficial process of merger employs regional resources in a more efficient and productive manner. Moreover, a united region can more effectively resist possible exploitation by multinational enterprises. Thus, shared economic difficulty among nations is not a hindrance to the rise of regional Free State.

Consider Africa. The African Charter on Human and Peoples' Rights (1981) summons member states "to pay a particular attention to the right to development." African nation-states, after decades of alien exploitation and domination, had an understandable need to emphasize territorial sovereignty in the constitution of the Organization of African Unity. The African Charter emphasizes the equality of all peoples, asserting that nothing shall justify the domination of one people by another. African states may choose to develop individually, or they may pool their resources at regional or subregional level. But now that Africa is predominantly free from colonial rule, the norm of regional cooperation should take precedence over maintenance of sovereign borders, a concept alien to African tradition.

The Charter emphasizes African cultural values of tolerance, dialogue and consultation rather than predation and litigation. Although the African continent encompasses great cultural variety, the peoples of Africa are rightfully proud of their common commitment to the ethic of sharing and the peoples' collective rights in line with individual rights and duties. The values of consultation and sharing are particularly relevant to regional solidarity. Based on these values, the states of Africa may open their borders and unleash the creative energy of their peoples. United and speaking in one voice, they can effectively protect their freedom and development from external exploitation. More important, they can coordinate their talents and efforts for the creation of a continent of Free States.

International economic organizations can play a supportive role in the social and economic development of nation-states. Epistemic bodies within these organizations possess the technical knowledge and experience that the ruling elites of some developing nation-states lack. These bodies can offer their help in proposing solutions to economic problems of developing states, enabling these states to effectively compete in regional and global markets. They can further assure that the enmeshment of national economies does not function for the benefit of a few states. Right now, the orientation of these epistemic bodies is still tied to the developed world, since most professionals and experts are the nationals of a few prosperous countries. If epistemic bodies are diverse in composition and their first commitment is to raising the standard of living of all the peoples of the world, they can play a critical role in the evolution of Free State. On the other hand, if international economic organizations fail to support equitable development across the globe or impose a caste system under which some states rule supreme while others are relegated to the status of the untouchable, the global economic order will remain unstable. Moreover, such a system will continue to offend the principles of moral intelligence that must always inform the enterprise of human civilization.

3. PLURALIST ASSOCIATION

Pluralism is the third condition essential for the evolution of Free State. Even if states enjoy peaceful conditions and comparable standards of living, ethnic differences may still motivate them to retain closed borders. For example, the Islamic background of Turkey has been used to exclude the nation from the European Union. Even though the current member states of the European Union have for centuries fought religious wars among themselves, they nonetheless believe they possess a common heritage that Turkey does not share. And though Turkey is a secular state by virtue of its constitution, few would deny the Islamic character of its people. Similarly, if Mexico is able to achieve a standard of living comparable to those of the United States and Canada, racial, linguistic and cultural difference may still limit the ability of Mexican nationals to freely enter and reside in Canada and the United States, as freely as citizens of the European Union can enter and reside anywhere in any member state. Thus it appears that the Aristotelian concept of perfect association will continue to compete with the emerging notion of pluralist association.

But as regional identities sprout in different parts of the world and sovereign borders are relaxed, the Aristotelian ideal of perfect association as the basis of territorial states will become unsustainable. Instead, the concept of pluralist association is likely to emerge as the new basis to organize Free State. In contrast to perfect association, pluralist association is an all-inclusive concept that allows peoples of diverse backgrounds to live together under a single government in accordance with the rule of law informed by human rights and obligations. Pluralist association does not repudiate but de-emphasizes homogeneity as the exclusive basis of Free State. As borders are relaxed, some poor, remote or otherwise unappealing areas may fail to attract diverse ethnic, religious or linguistic groups. Such areas may retain their prevailing homogeneity. No basis exists to insist that such homogeneous communities cannot found Free State. Nonetheless, as a general principle, pluralist association de-emphasizes homogeneity as the *sine qua non* of Free State. It accommodates the new realities of regional and global migration, a rising trend that would reshuffle the demographics of many traditional communities. Hence Free State as a pluralist association seems most suitable to a world in which mobility rather than inertia determines the ethnic contours of communities.

A greater understanding of the ethnic barrier comes from the examination of the concept of self-containment, an idea related to the Aristotelian notion of perfect association. Despite the difficulty inherent in defining the precise contours of a perfect association, broad categories are available to classify people by race, religion, language or a combination of these and other attributes. Perfect association builds a state by focussing upon the shared characteristics of a people, however defined. Self-containment preserves existing classifications, real or perceived; therefore, it rejects all intrusive foreign elements. If perfect association is defined in terms of race or religion, for example, self-containment mandates that people associate only with those who share their race or faith. Racial self-containment may require *de jure* or *de facto* racial segregation to sever social contact between races, and it may enact miscegenation statutes to prohibit conjugal connection between races. Religious self-containment dictates that people of a given religion not associate, marry or have children with people of another religion.[2]

Sovereign borders of the nation-state furnish a powerful mechanism for forging a perfect association by excluding or suppressing difference. They provide a geopsychological box for ethnic self-containment. Even though few nation-states can truly claim to have a perfect association among their people, most at one time or another have used their sovereign borders to exclude those considered different. Some still do. The example of the United States provides useful insights into the process of self-containment. The American Civil War was in a sense a war between the proponents and opponents of ethnic self-containment. The South championed the notion of white self-containment, while the North wished to dismantle it by abolishing slavery and expanding the definition of citizenship to include African-Americans. The war abolished slavery, but the idea of white self-containment re-surfaced in the guise of *de jure* racial segregation. The idea of white self-containment was not confined to racial relations within the nation. Until the 1960s, legal immigration in the United States was primarily confined to Europeans. This policy was designed to exclude people of African and Asian descent, even though sizable populations of Africans and Asians were already present – Africans who had been brought as slaves and Asians who had been brought as railroad coolies. Gradually, however, the United States not only disavowed *de jure* racial segregation but also changed its immigration policy to allow non-European immigrants, thus finally rejecting the overt forms of white self-containment.

Even though most states continue to practice one form of self-containment or another, Saudi Arabia offers a unique example. Containing ancient Muslim shrines in the holy cities of Mecca and Medina, Saudi Arabia exercises strict controls over who can enter the state. While Muslims from all over the world may visit the shrines by obtaining a visa, non-Muslims are rarely allowed into the holy cities. Even with respect to Muslims, a distinction is made between Arabs and non-Arabs because Saudi Arabia sees itself as an Arab state. In its immigration policy, however, Saudi Arabia is equally strict toward all Muslims. Due to its small native population but impressive oil-based economy, Saudi Arabia imports "guest workers" from all over the world. But the guest workers, even if they have lived most of their lives in Saudi Arabia, are not entitled to citizenship and must leave on the expiration of their employment contracts. Thus, Saudi policies advance a rigid form of self-containment, leaving little room for the Saudi nation-state to evolve into Free State with borders open to all the peoples of the world.

---

2. A recent papal instruction prohibits Christians from marrying Muslims. In Islam, Muslim men may marry Christians and Jews but Muslim women cannot marry outside their faith.

Many people desire to live among their own kind; this desire might reveal the inherent flaw in the vision of Free State. Thus even if the nations of the world enjoy decent standards of living and forever renounce the use or threat of force, they may still close their borders to the people of a different race, religion or culture.

This observation, despite its apparent accuracy, nonetheless cannot be totally accepted because common identities themselves undergo constant revisions and transformations. Few would deny that common identities are human constructs. They can be both made and unmade. In former Yugoslavia, the old ethnic identities of the Serbs, Croats and Muslims failed to merge in the single Slavic identity that Marshall Tito wished to create. In the United States and the European Union, old identities are welded together to make new ones. The example of the European Union demonstrates how a common identity may evolve to become more inclusive. After fighting bloody wars for centuries, Germans, French, Italians, Spaniards and others have opened their borders to each other for the sake of a new common identity as Europeans. Similarly, many European groups who migrated to the United States have adopted a new common identity as Americans. Legally even people of African and Asian descent living in the United States are Americans, though the label "American" still evokes the images of white men only. The founding of Israel demonstrates how Jews of diverse linguistic and ethnic backgrounds, ranging from Russians to Ethiopians, can come together to assert a common identity. Similarly, the Arabs have forged a common identity among historically distinct peoples such as Syrians, Egyptians and Mesopotamians (Iraqis). Many nations of South America share much in common and could easily assert a new common identity. In fact, nations in any region can usually find several bonds among themselves to invent a credible common identity.

The evolution of regional Free State is thus tied to the maturation of common identities. Once again, a region need not first develop a common identity before Free States may evolve. Free State as an interactive organism shapes regional and global forces as much as it is itself shaped by these forces. A regional process of integration, even if first confined to something as simple and limited as duty-free goods, begins to weld a regional identity. As regional enmeshment deepens in diverse spheres, the common identity is reinforced. Not even political developments in any regional state remain strictly a domestic matter, since they are perceived to affect the whole region.[3] The institution of a regional economy unites labor unions, thus establishing regional ties among workers and managers. If regional economy results into economic disparity, questions of social justice assume a regional character. Most important, the exchange of information, news, music, folk songs, cartoon comedies, movies and bedtime stories lay the foundation for cultural diffusion and a

3. The 1967 overthrow of democratic government in Greece, for example, invited a strong response, and Greece's membership in the Council of Europe was temporarily suspended.

more involved common identity. In this gradual process of integration, sovereign borders begin to melt as ordinary people establish cultural and social bonds across artificial territorial barricades.

The construction of a common regional identity may or may not demolish the micro-identities of ethnic, linguistic or religious communities. Micro-identities will probably survive, since the human inclination to differentiate one group from another is deeply rooted in historical and existential experiences. But this urge to retain micro-identities poses no serious threat to a common regional identity or Free State. Human beings have the intelligence to simultaneously accommodate several identities. Despite demolishing national borders, states are likely to retain their separate linguistic and cultural identities for many years to come. Even within a single state, micro-identities derived from local dialects and cultural variations may persist and even flourish. Recall that one goal of the European Union is to facilitate the blossoming of diverse cultures. Therefore the construction of a common regional identity should not be seen as a displacement of local identities. Just as an extended family does not replace the identity of a nuclear family, so a regional identity is not meant to replace micro-identities. The two can coexist and may even reinforce each other. Thus the fear that open borders among diverse communities will subsume micro-identities is exaggerated.

The dynamics of building a common regional identity, however, forewarn against the imperial imposition of any one national identity over the entire region, a course of action that not only impedes the advent of Free State but may in fact propel the region toward conflict and instability. Such a fear haunts the European Union. Even though the Community law and legal institutions of the Union are designed to prevent domination by any one national group, apprehension lingers that Germany, the most powerful economy and historical successor to the Holy Roman Empire, may impose its will on the Union, resurrecting old rivalries with its neighbors, particularly France. The concern for regional imperialism is even more pronounced in North America where the United States, a state mighty in wealth and armed force, outshines the region without a rival. To aggravate the fright of an already subordinated region, the United States often engages in rhetoric about leading the world as a sole superpower, a discourse that may be derided in Europe and Asia, but sends a threatening message to the region, as did the conquest of Grenada and the invasion of Panama. In addition, many regional states already accuse the United States of narcissistic hegemony. It remains to be seen whether the Americas cultivate a healthy common regional identity, one that most communities will freely embrace to advance the evolution of regional Free State.

Consistent with Article 27 of the International Covenant on Civil and Political Rights, Free State promotes and preserves pluralist association of diverse groups. Free State allows ethnic, religious and linguistic groups the right to enjoy, in community with the other members of their group, their own cultures, to profess and practice their own religions, and to speak their own languages. This protection of micro-identities, however, does not require or even encourage any group to embrace a quarantined ethnic, religious or linguistic identity or adopt a sense of community that breeds suspicion, stereotypes, hostility and hatred against other groups. Pluralist association is not simply a conglomeration of atomistic neighborhoods segregated by race, religion or language. Therefore, Free State is within its rights and obligations to promote contact and communication among diverse groups in order to make pluralist association a more humane and morally intelligent social organization.

In multilingual states, such as India where people speak almost twenty different languages and many more dialects, each group is entitled to preserve its language so that it may enjoy its written or oral literature, folk songs, jokes, proverbs and other social and cultural aspects tied to the structure and diction of the language. To force linguistic groups to give up their languages is tantamount to cultural genocide, a policy forbidden by contemporary international law. However, if each separate group makes no effort to speak other languages, in addition to its own, linguistic borders can breed the same ills as sovereign borders of the nation-state do. To maximize social and cultural contact among diverse linguistic groups and to facilitate trade and commerce among them, the development of a common language is inevitable.

The common language might develop by a free and creative mixing of local and regional languages. In India for example, Hindi and Urdu evolved as common languages by mixing a thousand dialects over the centuries. Consequently, most linguistic groups in India speak not only their local or provincial languages but also speak a common language. This bilingualism preserves both inter-group communications and local identities. In the United States, those who argue that all linguistic groups must speak English wish to maximize contact among diverse linguistic groups, a goal with which few would disagree. But thee advocates of "English only" fail to appreciate that a common language need not be imposed since one will emerge from an evolutionary process of simultaneous integration and differentiation. English as a common language can thus be preserved and enriched without suppressing other languages in the United States or the region.

Even in regard to religion and ethnicity, pluralist association strives to achieve the same two purposes: inter-ethnic contact and the preservation of difference. In a pluralist association, each religious group is free to practice and profess its faith. But inter-faith contact and communication brings diverse groups together in a spiritual union, promoting respect for each other and enabling the people to experience a more profound sense of religion underlying all sects. The purpose of inter-faith communication is not to diminish the significance of any sect, but to provide a basis for diverse religious groups to develop a common language of moral intelligence rooted in compassion, virtue and the ethic of sharing.

In matters of ethnicity, each ethnic group is free to enjoy its racial and cultural uniqueness. Affinity for one's own ethnic group is natural and ought not to be suppressed. However, in order to promote contact and communication among ethnic groups, pluralist association develops a united community that repudiates the false notions of racial superiority, miscegenation and ethnic purity. The purpose of inter-ethnic contact is not to dominate or subordinate any ethnic group, but to humanize racial differences and accentuate the beauty and delectable complexity each ethnic group contributes to the human race.

Free State is thus distinguishable from the ethnic, civic and authoritarian models of social organization. As a pluralist entity, Free State is unquestionably distinguishable from the ethnic state that asserts homogeneity as the exclusive basis of social organization. Free State resembles the civic state to the extent that both models support pluralist association as a preferred basis for social organization. Nonetheless, Free State repudiates the civic state's notions of forced assimilation, the cult of new nationalism, war-prone patriotism, constitutionalism divorced from universal human rights and obligations, and *de jure* or *de facto* domination of one group over another. Most important, Free State rejects all forms of the authoritarian state, which impose a coercive order to suppress diversity of opinion, religion, culture or language. Free State is distinguishable from all three models to the extent that Free State exists without sovereign borders, liberating the peoples of the world from artificial, dysfunctional and ominous geographical imprisonments. In the era of Free States, the peoples of the world can freely travel anywhere they choose and live wherever they please, as they already do within federated states or free regions such as the European union. Thus Free State promotes maximum freedom on One Earth so that the peoples of the world can establish pluralist associations.

Furthermore, Free State envisions a dynamic world in which ethnicities, religions and languages may change. People of diverse races may intermarry, producing genetically multifarious communities as has already happened in many parts of the world including the Middle East, India, Brazil and to lesser extent in South Africa and the United States. Likewise, a section of population belonging to an otherwise homogeneous ethnic and linguistic community may change religion. The rise of Lutheranism provides a dramatic example of such a change. The evolution of languages reveals that linguistic communities borrow words, alphabets and grammar from other languages, sometimes on a wholesale basis. The borrowing of the Latin script transformed not only the oral culture of Western Europe but the constitution of its many languages. The rise of English, a relatively minor language for centuries, to the pinnacle of international communication, further reveals how no linguistic community can be etched in stone. In view of these changes, the idea of perfect association – under which the people share the same racial characteristics, profess the same religion and speak the same language – cannot be the basis of a vigorous, ever-changing, dynamic world. In fact, forces of evolution are such that even a community of rocks must evolve to adjust its habitat.

Recognizing the dynamism of human civilization, Free State embraces the right of freedom of movement codified in the International Bill of Rights. The Universal Declaration of Human Rights states that everyone has the right to freedom of movement and residence within the borders of each state; and everyone has the right to leave any country, including his own, and return to his country. The International Covenant on Civil and Political Rights reaffirms the right to liberty of movement and freedom to choose one's residence. These provisions protect individuals' liberty to move within their state of residence without undue legal restrictions. They also prohibit states from arbitrarily hindering the movement of foreign nationals who are lawfully admitted into the territory. They also establish a right for individuals to leave their country, prohibiting their home states from imposing undue restrictions on the right to travel. Nonetheless, the International Bill of Rights imposes no obligation on any state to open its borders to all persons who wish to reside there. Accordingly, nation-states possess a substantial discretion to choose for themselves the conditions under which they will allow foreign nationals to enter their territories. This power to control immigration has been one of the most defining characteristics of the nation-state.

Many changes, however, have occurred that diminish the formal and functional authority of the nation-state to control the movement of foreign nationals. Most states are under a legal obligation not to expel or return refugees to a state where their lives and freedom are threatened because of race, religion, nationality or political beliefs. Even though some states find legal loopholes in this obligation, many others implement both the letter and spirit of treaties dealing with refugees. The law of human rights and obligations has further diminished the authority of nation-states to formulate an arbitrary immigration policy. For example, both Canada and the United States at one time restricted immigration to European applicants. Now, no state may openly practice any such unlawful discrimination.

Even though states theoretically continue to have substantial authority to restrict the immigration of foreign nationals, many functional imperatives prohibit them from doing so. Most states encourage tourism in order to raise revenues; some need foreign students to fund their universities. Others grant immigration status to rich individuals who are prepared to invest capital in the host state. still others need foreign labor, technicians and professionals to assist their economies. Thus as a practical matter, the sovereign borders are closed only to the poor of the world, a class for whom the right to freedom of movement has been elusive.

The idea of a border-free world worries many people who fear that criminals, drug traffickers and terrorists would have much more freedom and space to operate with impunity. The fear is real to the extent that criminals confined to a territory might be limited in the scope of their activity. And some criminal cartels would welcome the day when they can cross borders without submitting to check-points. This fear, however, is an insufficient basis to impede the freedom of movement across nations and regions. An integrated region or world with mutual obligations to fight crime provides more reliable deterrence to international crime. Ironically, the era of nation-states itself is most conducive to international crime, because many nation-states furnish safe havens for international criminals. Sovereign borders of these supportive states, which encourage international crime and offer protection to perpetrators, impede rather than promote a world criminal justice system that would assure the arrest and prosecution of criminals. A world of Free States, in which enforcement agencies use a global network to coordinate their efforts, can more effectively fight international crime. In the years to come, the European Union's efforts to fight international crime within its borders will be helpful.

As peaceful conditions, equitable development and pluralist association institute a gracious world, the freedom of movement across the globe will become increasingly more meaningful. Even if states enjoy peaceful conditions and comparable standards of living, some may nonetheless close their borders to preserve their ethnic, religious or linguistic purity. These fantasies of purity will be difficult to maintain, however, as human civilization enters the dynamic stage of more vigorous contact and communication among communities. To accommodate the realties of the dynamic world, the idea of pluralist association provides a more realistic basis for sociopolitical organization. Ethnic, religious and linguistic groups may continue to enjoy their unique associations. However, the changing norms of human civilization allow no state or region to build an iron curtain around itself.

This leaves one final but important question: will Free State ever evolve in the real world? The example of the European Union intimates that regional Free State may indeed come into existence even if global Free State does not. In fact, regional Free States can blossom in any region that follows a process of integration informed by the principles of peaceful conditions, equitable development and pluralist association. Most regions may ultimately have no choice but to integrate when regional economies compel states to open their borders to the free flow of goods, services and capital. Likewise shared environmental problems will obligate states to coordinate their economic development so that actual and potential damage to a region's water, air and ecology can be rationally assessed, repaired and prevented. The information revolution will further deepen regional enmeshment.

If regions in fact dismantle their internal borders and nation-states indeed transform into regional Free States, the question remains whether the world is then destined to move to the next stage of dismantling even the regional borders. Will the peoples of the world ever live free of borders? Even though Free State promises to establish a gracious world, the course of human history cannot be predicted. The global Free State may never come into existence. Instead, the world may become divided into regions, thus replacing the sovereign borders of nation-states with the sovereign borders of regional communities. Even regional communities may practice exclusion, as do nation-states. For example, the European Union may continue to exclude Turkey from its membership, forcing the Islamic nation to look eastward for a community. Even Asian and African minorities residing in the Union may be forced to leave Europe. The European Union may then become a culturally coherent region, but its internal coherence would fortify its existential borders against the rest of the world, the other. Across the Atlantic, the American community may establish open borders between Canada and the United States but not with Mexico. The Arab League may continue to exclude Israel from the region, and China may never open its borders to non-Chinese, thus remaining a region in and of itself.

Beyond the confines of nation-states and beyond the shadows of ethnic self-containment, however, international markets and human rights, like determined artists, are interweaving the peoples of the world into one civilization free from barbed wire and concrete walls, which scar the earth's unity and fragility. Contemporary international law seems determined to end armed conflict that destroys life, property and liberty. The norms of moral intelligence rooted in compassion and goodwill seem determined to uproot the predacious world divided by the extremes of opulence and poverty, and ethnic obsessions that place immovable barriers in the way of mutual understanding and pluralist association. If moral intelligence succeeds in guiding the nation-states toward Free State, the peoples of the world may someday celebrate the unity of One Earth.

INDEX

Developments in International Law

1. C.R. Symmons: *The Maritime Zones of Islands in International Law*. 1979
ISBN 90-247-2171-7
2. B.H. Dubner: *The Law of International Sea Piracy*. 1980 ISBN 90-247-2191-1
3. R.P. Anand (ed.): *Law of the Sea*. Caracas and Beyond. 1980 ISBN 90-247-2366-3
4. V.S. Mani: *International Adjudication*. Procedural Aspects. 1980
ISBN 90-247-2367-1
5. G.M. Badr: *State Immunity*. An Analytical and Prognostic View. 1984
ISBN 90-247-2880-0
6. R.St.J. Macdonald and D.M. Johnston: *The Structure and Process of International Law*. Essays in Legal Philosophy, Doctrine and Theory. 1986
ISBN 90-247-2882-7; Pb: 90-247-3273-5
7. M.E. Villiger: *Customary International Law and Treaties*. A Study of Their Interactions and Interrelations with Special Consideration of the 1969 Vienna Convention on the Law of Treaties. 1985 ISBN 90-247-2980-7
8. M. Sornarajah: *The Pursuit of Nationalized Property*. 1985 ISBN 90-247-3130-5
9. C.F. Murphy, Jr.: *The Search for World Order*. A Study of Thought and Action. 1986
ISBN 90-247-3188-7
10. A. Cassese (ed.): *The Current Legal Regulation of the Use of Force*. 1986
ISBN 90-247-3247-6
11. N. Singh and E. McWhinney: *Nuclear Weapons and Contemporary International Law*. 2nd revised edition, 1989 ISBN 90-247-3637-4
12. J. Makarczyk: *Principles of a New International Economic Order*. A Study of International Law in the Making. 1988 ISBN 90-247-3746-X
13. O. Schachter: *International Law in Theory and Practice*. 1991 ISBN 0-7923-1024-1
14. K. Wolfke: *Custom in Present International Law*. 2nd revised edition, 1993
ISBN 0-7923-2009-3
15. G.M. Danilenko: *Law-making in the International Community*. 1993
ISBN 0-7923-2039-5
16. C. Tomuschat (ed.): *Modern Law of Self-Determination*. 1993 ISBN 0-7923-2351-3
17. A. Mouri: *The International Law of Expropriation as Reflected in the Work of the Iran-U.S. Claims Tribunal*. 1994 ISBN 0-7923-2654-7
18. L. Henkin: *International Law: Politics and Values*. 1995 ISBN 0-7923-2908-2
19. M.M.T.A. Brus: *Third Party Dispute Settlement in an Interdependent World*. Developing a Theoretical Framework. 1995 ISBN 0-7923-3423-X
20. L.A.N.M. Barnhoorn and K.C. Wellens (eds.): *Diversity in Secondary Rules and the Unity of International Law*. 1995 ISBN 90-411-0092-X
21. L.A. Khan: *The Extinction of Nation-States*. A World without Borders. 1996
ISBN 90-411-0198-5

KLUWER LAW INTERNATIONAL - THE HAGUE / LONDON / BOSTON